Identity\Difference

Identity\Difference

DEMOCRATIC NEGOTIATIONS OF POLITICAL PARADOX

Expanded Edition

William E. Connolly

University of Minnesota Press
Minneapolis / London

Published by the University of Minnesota Press
111 Third Avenue South, Suite 290
Minneapolis, MN 55401-2520
http://www.upress.umn.edu

Library of Congress Cataloging-in-Publication Data

Connolly, William E.
   Identity\Difference ; democratic negotiations of political paradox / William E. Connolly.— Expanded ed.
      p. cm.
   Originally published: Ithaca : Cornell University Press, 1991.
   Includes bibliographical references and index.
   ISBN 978-0-8166-4086-7 (pbk. : alk. paper)
      1. Political science—Philosophy. 2. Democracy. 3. Difference (Philosophy) 4. Identity. 5. Good and evil. I. Title.

JA 74.C659 2002
320'.01—dc21   2002026797

The University of Minnesota is an equal-opportunity educator and employer.

The more one is absorbed in fighting Evil, the less one is tempted to place the Good in question.

—Jean-Paul Sartre, *Anti-Semite and Jew*

However, I like the word [curiosity]. It evokes "care"; it evokes the care one takes of what exists and what might exist; a sharpened sense of reality, but one that is never immobilized before it; a readiness to find what surrounds us strange and odd; a certain determination to throw off familiar ways of thought and to look at the same things in a different way . . .; a lack of respect for the traditional hierarchies of what is important and fundamental.

—Michel Foucault, "The Masked Philosopher"

And not only Aristotle but the whole of Greek antiquity thinks differently from us about hatred and envy, and judges with Hesiod; who in one place calls one discord evil—namely the one that leads men into hostile fights of annihilation against one another—while praising another discord as good—the one that, as jealousy, hatred and envy, spurs men to activity; not to the activity of fights of annihilation but to the activity of fights which are *contests*.

—Friedrich Nietzsche, "Homer's Contest"

I don't want to become an identity junkie.

—Jan Clausen, "My Interesting Condition"

Contents

Preface

This book explores the politics of identity. Hence it also probes the politics of difference. If difference requires identity and identity requires difference, then politics, in some sense of that protean word, pervades social life. But does this mean that politics is (and therefore must be) always the same? Must the element of power in the relation of identity to difference perpetually reinstate itself in the same way? This work pursues the conviction that politics pervades the relation of identity to difference and that affirmation of the relational and constructed character of identity can nevertheless make a difference to the ethical quality of political life.

Let me call the relation of identity to difference the site of two problems of evil. The first problem of evil, residing in the theological determination of divine identity, turns upon human efforts to save the benevolence of an omnipotent god by exempting that god from responsibility for evil. Human definitions of the theological problem provide blowups, as it were, of issues woven into the solidification of human identities. On the political level, the first problem of evil issues in a series of attempts to protect the purity and certainty of a hegemonic identity by defining as independent sites of evil (or one of its many surrogates) those differences that pose the greatest threat to the integrity and certainty of that identity. The second problem of evil emerges out of solutions to the first one. It flows from diverse political tactics through which doubts about self-identity are posed and resolved by the constitution of an other against which that identity may define itself. To explore this territory is to struggle against the evil done by attempts to secure the surety of self-identity. Responding to the second problem of evil involves challenging those political tactics of self-reassurance; problematizing conceptions of identity, ethics, responsibility, politics, order, democracy, sovereignty, community, and discourse through which solutions to the first problem are sustained; and exposing rituals of sacrifice concealed by established presentations of these themes. As I see it, however, these counter-tactics of exposure and modification do not themselves escape implication in paradox. In fact, the urge to transcend paradox may be one of the drives concealing the second problem of evil.

This reflection on the politics of identity and difference eventually points to a rethinking of democratic theory. For if democracy is a medium through which difference can establish space for itself as alter-identity, it is also a means by which the dogmatization of identity can be politically legitimized. The point of critical reflection here is to introduce another competitor onto the field of contestation covered by the names "democracy" and "democratic theory," to modify the established terms of debate so that certain virtues of democracy underappreciated in alternative conceptions can be brought to the foreground.

Is there, then, a practice of democracy—or a strain of politics within democracy broadly defined—that responds to the problematic relation between identity and difference? I suspect there is, even though this theme only begins to find expression in the present book. Let me call this political imaginary "agonistic democracy," a practice that affirms the indispensability of identity to life, disturbs the dogmatization of identity, and folds care for the protean diversity of human life into the strife and interdependence of identity\ difference.

Agonistic democracy breaks with the democratic idealism of communitarianism through its refusal to equate concern for human dignity with a quest for rational consensus. It opens political spaces for agonistic relations of adversarial respect. Democratic agonism does not exhaust social space; it leaves room for other modalities of attachment and detachment. But it does disrupt consensual ideals of political engagement and aspiration. It insists that one significant way to support human dignity is to cultivate agonistic respect between interlocking and contending constituencies.

Agonistic democracy also departs from the political minimalism of democratic individualism. In contrast to the conventional view that the sanctity of the individual in a constitutional regime is best protected by restricting politics to its bare essentials, democratic agonism contends that spaces in which differences may constitute themselves as contending identities are today most effectively established by political means. In a world of closely woven interdependencies, distance must be generated by political means if it is to be at all.

Finally, agonistic democracy challenges the confinement of democracy to the governmental institutions of the territorial state. The politics of identity\difference flows beneath, through, and over the boundaries of the state. It overflows state boundaries when the state constitutes a set of differences to protect the certainty of its collective identity and whenever the established identity of a sovereign state itself becomes an object of politicization. "Nonterritorial democratization" provides one way to ventilate and supplement the institutional politics of territorial democracy under contemporary conditions of global life. Nonterritorial democratization, I suspect, has become a precondition for the health of contemporary territorial democracy.

The styles of presentation in this book embody, I hope, a philosophy of interpretation. If being exceeds every interpretation, perhaps each interpretation should find ways to build appreciation of this condition into its modes of presentation. Scratch the cultural ground with a sharp stick here and there, and drop a few seeds. Take a look at promising sprouts later in the season, watering some and pulling weeds crowding out others. (Ahh, the weeding . . . that is a delightful part!) Perhaps if others find anything worthy of cultivation a plant or two will grow, modifying the landscape of political discourse in this way or that. More likely, others will find new weeds to pull in their turn.

The will to system is a lack of experience, to say the least. To say more: within the academy it is a consummate form assumed by the will to dominate. A better alternative is to affirm simultaneously the indispensability of interpretation and the limited, porous, and problematic character of any particular effort.

I thank the publishers of the following essays for permission to reprint materials in Chapters 1, 2, and 3: "Freedom and Contingency," in *Life-World and Politics: Between Modernity and Post-Modernity*, ed. Stephen White (Notre Dame: University of Notre

Dame Press, 1990); "Identity and Difference in Global Politics," in *International/Intertextual Relations*, ed. James Der Derian and Michael Shapiro (Lexington, Mass.: Heath, 1989); "Identity and Difference in Liberalism," in *Liberalism and the Good*, ed. B. Douglass, G. Mara, and H. Richardson (New York: Routledge, 1990), 155–91. The corresponding chapters have been significantly revised for this volume.

The themes in this book were developed in two graduate seminars at The Johns Hopkins University in the fall of 1987 and the spring of 1989. I express my appreciation to the students in "Identity and Difference in Politics" and "The Problem of Evil" for the stimulating discussions and debates that marked those events. I hope they recognize traces of those discussions in these pages.

A larger group helped me to think through these issues when early versions of selected chapters were presented at Georgetown University, the University of Massachusetts, Princeton University, the Catholic University of America, SUNY–Albany, the University of Victoria, the University of Maryland, and the European University Institute, Florence. In addition, several individuals have read selected chapters in earlier incarnations. Judith Butler, David Campbell, Roman Coles, James Der Derian, Thomas Dumm, Jean Elshtain, Bonnie Honig, George Kateb, Alan Keenan, Thomas Kuehls, Mort Schoolman, Joan Scott, Michael Shapiro, Paul Shepard, and Sheldon Wolin have all offered comments and criticisms extremely helpful to me in completing the "final" version. I am also grateful to the two anonymous readers and John G. Ackerman at Cornell University Press and to Frank Hunt for their compelling suggestions concerning revisions. My most pervasive debts, perhaps, are to Jane Bennett and Dick Flathman, fellow theorists in Baltimore with whom I have discussed these issues extensively; each was willing, when pressed hard enough, to read and criticize these chapters in their earliest and roughest stages. I trust this version will enable each to discern more clearly where s/he has gone wrong.

Perhaps a book imprints the subjective effects of a series of lovers' quarrels; I am fortunate to be engaged with a quarrelsome bunch.

WILLIAM E. CONNOLLY

Baltimore, Maryland

Confessing Identity\Belonging to Difference

> The polemicist . . . proceeds encased in privileges that he possesses in advance and will never agree to question. . . . As in heresiology polemics sets itself the task of determining the intangible point of dogma, the fundamental and necessary principle the adversary has neglected, ignored, or transgressed; and it denounces this transgression as a moral failing; at the root of the error it finds passion, desire, interest, a whole series of weaknesses and inadmissible attachments that establish it as culpable.
>
> —Michel Foucault, "Polemics, Politics, and Problematizations: An Interview," in *The Foucault Reader*

"The politics of identity." It is often named today, sometimes to bestow dignity or authority on a minority, more often to subtract authority from minorities who neglect something said to be necessary to the larger society. "We are Muslim, African American, Gay, Feminist, Amerindian, Hispanic . . . , and you must not dictate to us in the name of a majority culture from which we differ." Or, "You give everything to your identity and not enough to the general principles of America, Christianity, the Enlightenment, Morality, Human Nature, or God." When the first mode of identity is invoked, the minority status of those who speak is rendered visible. When "identity politics" is attacked as impervious to the larger whole upon which it depends, a majority identity is implicitly invoked to characterize the whole. Even critics of identity politics participate, it seems, in the politics of identity.

Identity\Difference treats identity as ubiquitous to modern life. But

[xiii]

it neither endorses an enclave model of identity nor devalues minor identities in favor of a universal unsusceptible to further questioning. Does it, then, forfeit a place from which to speak? A few levelers and simplifiers say so. But such assertions fail to address the constitutive role of difference in identity itself. They simplify the paradoxical logic of identity to relieve themselves of the need to acknowledge connections and debts to the differences in which they are implicated.

Here in a nutshell is the thesis of this study: to confess a particular identity is also to belong to difference. To come to terms *affirmatively* with the complexity of that connection is to support an ethos of identity and difference suitable to a democratic culture of deep pluralism. A few more things can be said to unpack that thesis, and I proceed by reviewing, refining, and augmenting a few formulations.

> **An identity is established in relation to a series of differences that have become socially recognized. These differences are essential to its being. If they did not coexist as differences, it would not exist in its distinctness and solidity. Entrenched in this indispensable relation is a second set of tendencies . . . to congeal established identities into fixed forms, thought and lived as if their structure expressed the true order of things. . . . Identity requires difference in order to be, and it converts difference into otherness in order to secure its own self-certainty. (*Identity\Difference*, 64)**

Identity is *relational and collective.* My personal identity is defined through the collective constituencies with which I identify or am identified by others (as white, male, American, a sports fan, and so on); it is further specified by comparison to a variety of things I am not. Identity, then, is always connected to a series of differences that help it be what it is. The initial tendency is to describe the differences on which you depend in a way that gives privilege or priority to you. Jews, said Kant, are legalistic; that definition allowed him to define Kantian-Christian morality as a more spiritual orientation to duties and rights. Atheists, said Tocqueville, are restless, egoistic, and amoral, lacking the spiritual source of morality upon which stability, trustworthiness, and care for others are anchored. That definition allowed him to honor the American passion to exclude professed atheists from public office. Built into the dynamic of identity is a polemical temptation to translate differences through which it is specified into moral failings or abnormalities. The pursuit of identity feeds the polemicism Foucault describes in the epigraph at the beginning of this essay.

You need identity to act and to be ethical, but there is a drive to diminish difference to complete itself inside the pursuit of identity. There is thus a paradoxical element in the politics of identity. It is not an airtight paradox conforming to a textbook example in logic, but a social paradox that might be negotiated. It operates as pressure to make space for the fullness of self-identity for one constituency by marginalizing, demeaning, or excluding the differences on which it depends to specify itself. The depth grammar of a political theory is shaped, first, by the way in which it either acknowledges or suppresses this paradox, and, second, by whether it negotiates it pluralistically or translates it into an aggressive politics of exclusive universality.

Traditionally, the first problem of evil is the question of how a benevolent, omnipotent God could allow intense suffering in the world. Typically, the answer involves attribution of free will to humans to engender a gap between the creative power of the God and the behavior of humanity. What I call in this book "the second problem of evil" flows from the social logic of identity\difference relations. It is the proclivity to marginalize or demonize difference to sanctify the identity you confess. Intensifying the second problem of evil is the fact that we also experience the source of morality through our most heartfelt experiences of identity. How could someone be moral, many believers say, without belief in free will and God? How could a morally responsible agent, others say, criticize the Enlightenment, the very achievement that grounds the moral disposition they profess? Don't they presuppose the very basis they criticize?

A favorite practice in the academy is to convict others of the "performative contradiction," whereby they are said to affirm in practice what they deny in theory. When everything proceeds smoothly the critic eventually pulls the opponent to a place where the latter must accept the positive thesis of the critic. This move in philosophical discourse parallels a familiar one in religious disputes where those who deviate from your faith are convicted of a definitive fault to de-moralize it and bolster the necessity of your own. One can hardly avoid light use of the performative contradiction, to pose questions to others even as you identify sore spots and paradoxes in your own existential faith. But its use as the master tool of critique reflects the tacit assumption that the world conforms to a logic to be grasped through precise concepts. Theorists who play such an earnest game forget to ask whether those so convicted may find something positive in the very experience of paradox, as Augustine, Nietzsche, Kierkegaard, and Deleuze do when they treat paradox as a sign of something efficacious in the world that exceeds conceptual reach. At other times, as we shall see, heavy dependence on this tool reflects an implicit narrowing of options available to the adversary to those the critics already recognize as possibilities. Thus, those who do not embrace a transcendental basis of moral authority are often said by critics to reduce morality to desire or preference; for that is what morality would become to the critic if its transcendental basis were subtracted. Once that fateful representation is installed, conviction of a performative self-contradiction is only a step away. In Foucault's terms, polemicists proceed "encased in privileges [they possess] in advance and will never agree to question."

> Some of the contingent elements that enter into your identity are susceptible to reconstitution, and others remain highly resistant to it, even if you desire to transform them and even if there is cultural support for doing so. Let us call the latter branded or entrenched contingencies, to emphasize how they are both contingent formations and resistant to modification once consolidated. A branded contingency is a formation that has become instinctive, even though it may not be reducible to instinct as a biological drive. Indeed, the term "contingency" as used here in no way implies that a contingency is always something that can be changed through will or decision. There are obdurate contingencies . . . (*Identity\Difference,* 176)

A few readers who attended to the horizontal relation between identity and difference either ignored this exploration of the depth of identity or disparaged it. The first set acted as if I thought identity was something like clothing you put on and take off at will. Why make that assumption in the face of textual evidence to the contrary? It may be due to a presupposition on the part of the accuser that a deep identity must make contact with the essence of the soul or a transcendental principle infusing it. To link depth to contingency, as I do, is to upset that applecart.

To speak of deep contingency is to play up the role of culture in the formation of identity while appreciating the weight of identity as it becomes entrenched in corporeal habits, feelings, and dispositions. It is also to set up the possibility that some of those entrenchments might be recomposed modestly through artfully devised tactics of the self and its collective sibling, micropolitics. It is, of course, impossible to question or refashion all the hinges on which our thinking and judgment depend. And the most entrenched dispositions do feel like deep truths. Anyone who has lived, or imbibed Wittgenstein while doing so, appreciates the force of these pressures. That upon which one draws to express desire and to make judgments is not called up for examination during the activity of desiring and judging. Nonetheless, sometimes you encounter pressure before or after the action in question, to work actively on selective aspects of your identity that have become entrenched. That pressure might come from discordant dispositions already circulating in you, from unexpected interventions by others, from surprising consequences attendant on your action, or from a combination of these.

That is what happened to Bartolomé de Las Casas, whose work is reviewed in the second chapter of this book. This sixteenth-century Christian priest eventually drew on Christian love to recompose prized aspects of the Christian doctrine he brought with him to the "New World." He did so after agonizing over the destruction and suffering engendered by the massive Spanish effort to convert Aztecs to the true faith. Sometimes aspects of the unreflective background of experience are challenged by others in a way that dislodges them and renders them possible objects of tactical modification. The challenge may tap into an obscure strain previously suppressed by the drive to secure your identity as complete or universal. Relational arts of the self are applied to affective dispositions below the reach of direct intellectual self-regulation. So is their collective partner, micropolitics.

Others object to the idea of deep contingency on the grounds that it does not make identity fluid *enough*. It biologizes identity too much, they think. What conception of biology is invoked by such a response? I have recently reconsidered common assumptions in cultural theory about biological-cultural relays in my book *Neuropolitics: Thinking, Culture, Speed*. It seems to me that cultural theorists often reduce the biological to that which is fixed, genetic, or determinative. In doing so they either sink into the black hole of sociobiology, or more often levitate toward arid, disembodied conceptions of thinking, culture, identity, language, politics, and ethics to escape the curse of biology. To me, identity is biocultural. It mixes nature and culture into corporeal sensibilities. Moreover, nature and biology themselves have elements of artifice in them. Cultural practices are folded into different layers of the body/brain network according to the relative capacities and speeds of each layer. These layers both contain resistances to those inculcations and interact with each in the composition of identity. Identity is relational, biocultural, and replete with resistances.

To enunciate a biocultural reading of identity is to find an ethic anchored in the higher intellect or the will alone to be inadequate to life. Hence my objection to neo-Kantian theories of ethics. Sometimes it is wise to work tactically on the visceral register of identity, on thought-imbued feelings of attachment, faith, disgust, shame, ambivalence, love, or disdain that influence action and judgment but fall below direct intellectual regulation. In this book I begin to explore an ethic of cultivation, an orientation in which relational arts of the self are crafted to work on particular aspects of one's biocultural identity. This theme has been developed further in my recent work.

An ethic of cultivation exists in torsion—that is, in a relation of interdependence and tension—with the quest to affirm contingencies that have become entrenched. It is important to a generous ethical sensibility to come to terms in an affirmative way with much of what you have become through the checkered history of luck, circumstance, decision, habit, and fateful events. Strive to overcome deep resentment of what or who you are so as to overcome the corollary disposition to rail against the parents, class, fate, past decisions, or world that brought you to this point. Affirm the past, with the suffering that has taught this and that lesson, as a condition of future possibility. Those who resent the world too much are eager to find others to hold responsible for their condition. They easily become punitive and exclusionary.

But, in periodic tension with this recipe, sometimes it is wise or obligatory to work on specific dimensions of our identity. Perhaps you feel viscerally repelled by nonbelievers, while a subordinate strain in you—perhaps Christian love or a stutter in your faith—resists the ugliness of that disposition. You begin to suspect that your negative definition of atheists is even more bound to a visceral desire to preserve the moral superiority of your identity as a devout believer than to the intrinsic character of the Atheist. You may now explore how to mitigate the first disposition in a way that does not place your visceral trust in God too much at risk. You cultivate a modest shift in your embedded habits of feeling and judgment, working cautiously on the self you have become and, sometimes, on constituencies with whom you identify most ardently. The relation between ethics and identity is tricky.

> What if it turned out, to reverse [Charles Taylor's] equation experimentally, that that which threatens breakdown in the self can also bring it closer to the . . . historically contingent character of its own identity? What if a risk of breakdown were bound up with care for difference, so that ethical responsiveness and discovery of deep

identity were not bound together as neatly? . . . Where . . . is it written that the socio-systemic need for the practice of responsibility corresponds conveniently to the deepest structure of human being? (*Identity\Difference*, 116)

To be ethical is often to put identity, to some degree, at risk. The intertwining of identity and difference carries this implication. My sense is that secular theories in the Kantian tradition seek to avoid this internal connection between ethical responsiveness and the disturbance of identity. They do so in part because they believe that some basic authority, command, or contract must be placed above questioning if ethical life is to be possible. But the world may be more paradoxical than that. To be ethical is often to put parts of your entrenched identity at risk, but to place too much at risk at one time would be to lose the ground from which ethical action proceeds.

I do not typically call myself a "postmodernist." That figure is often represented by critics as one who thinks that identity is fluid and ethical life is unimportant. Postmodernists are cool, ironic, and narcissistic because they do not anchor morality in God or transcendental reason. That corresponds pretty well to how Tocqueville defined atheists in nineteenth-century America. On my reading the opposite is closer to the truth. It is not merely that morality can be at odds with our desires or our interests, as Kantians and neo-Kantians also say. It is, again, that to act ethically is often to call some comforts of identity into question. Is that the disturbance critics of "postmodernism" want to squelch? In any event, to connect ethico-life to the structure of identity\difference relations is to disturb the comforts moralists assume when they equate the demands of morality with an identity they already confess.

But perhaps a related charge persists. Must not an ethic responsive to the paradoxical relations of identity\difference acknowledge a source deeper than any affirmed here? The position confessed in this book, it may seem, cannot locate a *common* source *certain or deep* enough to sustain the very ethical perspective it embraces. The performative contradiction again. Does the charge reflect in this instance a too restrictive delineation of possible sources of ethical life?

A philosophy of individuality and nontheistic reverence for existence must identify ways and means to wage a battle against existential resentment and to elicit respect for the diversity of existence while doing so. (*Identity\Difference*, 81)

> Such a counter-doctrine cannot advance itself as a singular truth. It
> must not, for instance, strive to purge doctrines that rest upon faith
> in a true identity or a particular god. It seeks, instead, to give voice
> to a perspective with a reverence of its own and to limit the extent
> to which the voices of strong identity can define the terms through
> which alter-identities are recognized and responsibility is distrib-
> uted. . . .
>
> Such a doctrine treats the positions of its competitors as posi-
> tions it expects to persist on the field of discourse, and construes
> itself as another possibility to be advanced in competition and con-
> testation with them. (*Identity\Difference*, 118–19)

Nontheistic reverence (or gratitude, as I now call it) for the abundance
of being is the most basic ethical source I confess. On my reading, difference is not only that defined from the vantage point of a particular
identity. It includes a second dimension, too: fugitive impulses and energies that exceed the organization of identity\difference relations themselves. The fugitive dimension of difference is pursued in this book
through an engagement with Nietzsche's notion of "life."

Nontheistic gratitude does not take the shape of a divine command
or a transcendental directive, even though it tracks those two orientations in its way by expressing appreciation for that which exceeds human
understanding and helps to enable new possibilities to surge into being.
Its nontheistic orientation, however, does have affinities to some
Buddhist, Confucian, and Epicurean orientations. They, too, often do
not place a personal God at the base or pinnacle of experience. To a
devotee of nontheistic gratitude law, obligation, responsibility, and
rights are not recognized apodictically. These are, rather, second-order
formations, forged out of care for the fugitive abundance of being that
infuses them. That is why ethical life is fragile as well as indispensable.
And why the list of rights can become augmented as time flies by. The
project is to fold presumptive generosity for the plurivocity of being into
the way interests are expressed, responsibilities are affirmed, judgments
are articulated, rights are acknowledged, and actions are composed.

To anchor an ethic of cultivation in nontheistic gratitude does not
reduce it to "mere preference" or "desire." Such formulations reflect the
representation of this orientation by those who have already discounted
its possibility or dignity. Note how Kant talked about Epicurus and
Spinoza, for instance. Or how Augustine defined those pagans who did
not affirm a single god.

I do not think nontheistic gratitude is apt to be proven, though impressive considerations can be marshaled on its behalf. It is, rather, a profoundly contestable faith, about as contestable as several it contends against. You become convinced of it not merely through argument, but also by tapping into an attachment to the abundance of life that may be there already. Such a faith then becomes infused into the way you receive and inflect arguments. The faith of those who confess nontheistic gratitude is not that it can carry us beyond identity, desire, or self-interest, but that we can draw upon it to fold a larger degree of forbearance and presumptive generosity into our desires, interests, identities, anxieties, and negotiating stances. Ethics is not pure, on this reading, floating above desire, sensibility, and feeling. Rather, its periodic power and constitutive fragility reflect how it is mixed into the materialities of life.

Given the large variations of cultural experience, such an existential faith is hardly going to provide sustenance for everyone. It is likely to remain a minority stance, expressed and cultivated by those in various class, gender, and educational positions who (a) find that a personal God is not a live option for them; (b) nonetheless feel surges of religiosity welling up from time to time; and (c) find thin, intellectualist conceptions of ethics and public life advanced by many secularists to underestimate both the density of culture and the importance of the energizing element in ethical life. While the first condition breaks with, say, Augustine, the last two slide closer to him than to Bertrand Russell or John Rawls. Hence my relation of indebtedness to Augustine amid difference.

But the difference is critical. To embrace publicly a nontheistic source of ethical inspiration without claiming universality for it is to support an active *pluralization* of ethical sources in public life. It is to propel another source into public and political life without claiming that everyone must affirm it. It is thus to break both with a secularism that seeks to confine faith to the private realm and with a theo-centered vision that seeks to unite people behind one true faith. It is to bind ethico-political life to negotiations and settlements between chastened partisans more than to common confession of a universal faith or a consensus forged by the putative power of the better argument. The idea is to attend to the persistence of multiple ethical sources in political life while dramatizing the comparative contestability of the candidates, and to work on ourselves and others to affirm, without existential resentment, the contestability of each in the eyes of others.

Such an approach clearly does not seek to eliminate Augustinianism, or other theistic faiths. To do so would be to work against a public ethos of deep pluralism. Nor does it shuffle theistic and nontheistic faiths into the private realm to enable secular reason, proceduralism, neutrality, or deliberation to reoccupy the place vacated by a common Christianity. In my judgment, and in Augustine's, no practice of public reason, deliberation, or procedure suffices to govern political life. Today, when distance is compressed by the acceleration of speed in many zones of practice, the way to move is toward negotiation of a generous ethos of engagement between a plurality of faiths in private and public life.

Perhaps a further word should be said about the idea of "contingency" as it plays itself out in this book. I contend that identity\difference relations are contingent formations, some of which are deep or entrenched contingencies. They might have been otherwise, given different mixes of tradition, child rearing, the shape of dramatic public events, and so on. But it also follows from what has been said about the comparative contestability of nontheistic gratitude that I do not expect everyone to accept my reading of the deep contingency of things. Many existential faiths, perhaps most, refuse such a view. It is, again, not acceptance of deep contingency that is critical to a generous ethos of engagement but coming to terms affirmatively with the comparative contestability of the faith each constituency brings to politics. In "On Passing By" in *Thus Spoke Zarathustra*, Zarathustra felt this so palpably that he finally had to "pass by" the "ape" who affirmed Z's view of the deep contingency of things while foaming at the mouth against those who denied that "conjecture":

> "By everything in you that is good and strong, O Zarathustra, spit . . . on the city of compressed souls and narrow chests, of popeyes and sticky fingers—on the city of compressed souls and narrow chests . . . where everything infirm, infamous, lustful, dusky, overmusty, pussy, and plotting putrefies together . . ."
>
> Here, however, Z interrupted the foaming fool and put his hand over the fool's mouth. "Stop at last!" cried Z; "your speech and your manner have long nauseated me. Why did you live near the swamps so long, until you yourself have become a frog and a toad? . . . I despise your despising; and if you warned me, why did you not warn yourself?" So Z "passes by" the foaming ape, who expresses a potential voice in himself. "For all your foaming is revenge, you vain fool, I guessed it well."

I also find it noble to treat one's own faith as contestable in one's own eyes, not just to affirm that it is so in the eyes of others. Strive to render oneself a question to oneself, while appreciating that your efforts will meet with partial and limited success. But I do not contend that everyone must hold this view for a positive ethos of engagement to emerge. It suffices if numerous partisans appreciate the contestability of their faith in the minds and souls of others, and struggle to overcome resentment against this persistent feature of the human condition. For, again, when existential resentment becomes intense, others who constitute living proof of the actual contestability of your faith are apt to become targets of your revenge in the name of morality.

To insert a stutter in one's faith is noble, then, in my eyes. But it is also to implicate oneself in a series of paradoxes and limitations. Nietzsche, James, Kierkegaard, and Levinas all saw this, the first from a nontheistic vantage point, the next two from within Christianity, broadly defined, and the last from within Judaism. Such a stutter does not enable you to render everything in your faith perfectly transparent. Each existential faith comes to terms with itself in relation to a specific set of alternatives historically available to it. Much in the faith you share with others, then, will remain opaque to you and them. But it is nonetheless noble to sustain a certain torsion between the nourishment your faith provides and the periodic call to probe dimensions of its comparative contestability. You study comparative religions and ethical theories enough to come to terms with sore points, tensions, and mysteries in yours by comparison to a similar litany in others. Roxanne Euben's book *Enemy in the Mirror: Islamic Fundamentalism and the Limits of Modern Rationalism* provides a fine example here; she calls her book "A Work of Comparative Political Theory."

On the reading advanced here, an existential faith takes the form of a *problematic* replete with paradoxes and other difficulties. The temptation to convert difference into heresy often flows from the effort to conceal uncertainties in one's faith or identity, projecting them onto others as evils. These same difficulties and uncertainties processed through another mood, however, sometimes become materials through which a new conversion is set into motion. Augustine went through several conversions—who knows whether another might have occurred if he had lived a vibrant life for another forty years. Augustine and Nietzsche are siblings under the skin; each encounters and regulates voices in himself that prevail in the other.

> By "state" I mean the political dimension of the entire order—individuals as citizens and taxpayers, electoral campaigns and processes, public officials, lawmaking institutions, executive and enforcement agencies, rhetorical modes of consolidation and division, and so on. The primary targets of state negation are most functional if (a) they can be constituted as evils responsible for threats to the common identity, (b) their visibility might otherwise signify defects and failings in the established [civic] identity, (c) they are strategically weak enough to be subjected to punitive measures, and (d) they are resilient enough to renew their status as sources of evil in the face of such measures. (*Identity\Difference,* 206–7)

On this reading, capitalist processes of production, investment, and distribution are unlikely to become targets of negation through which the collective identity of the American state is ensured; welfare recipients, guest workers, same sex couples, unwed mothers, and members of minority faiths are highly eligible for such an assignment. The vilification of a constituency that does not threaten your survival is apt to be proportional to its political vulnerability and the disturbance its mode of being poses to the self-confidence of dominant identities. So the political success of welfare in the United States resides in its failure as a series of economic programs. This combination shores up the comparative self-confidence of those who have jobs but still find it difficult to make ends meet in the current order, or those who are doing well but seek to give themselves alone credit for that achievement. The persistence of a welfare class needing economic support enables insecure members of the middle class to credit themselves for the income they earn, to blame welfare freeloaders for high taxes, and to exempt other systemic arrangements in which they are implicated from responsibility for the production of an impoverished class. Welfare forms part of the tissue of identity\difference politics.

In other texts, most recently *The Ethos of Pluralization,* I contend that programs with the best chance to reduce economic inequality are those that support the economic security of the large middle class. At the same time, I support programs of equalization most consonant with an expansive cultural pluralism. There are tensions between pluralism and equality, but they set conditions of possibility for each other even more than they pose contradictory political agendas. Hence, drives to reduce economic inequality in the domains of health care, retirement, education, tax levels, transportation possibilities, and housing arrangements are periodically ambushed by advertising how enemies of the cultural Right would be included in the program. Drives to expand diversity in the domains of gender, faith, ethnicity, and sexual affiliation can also be stymied by claiming that these are luxuries only the affluent care about. To lift up the bottom economic tier would be to diminish the force of these arguments.

> One is implicated ethically with others, first, through sharing an identity with some of them, second, through the stirrings of unpursued possibilities in oneself that exceed one's identity, and third, through engagement with pressures to resent obdurate features of the human condition. Reflection on these connections can also encourage one to reflect on how life overflows the boundaries of identity. You could not be what you are unless some possibilities of life had been forgone ("to do is to forgo"). And you now depend upon the difference of the other for your identity. Recognition of these conditions of strife and interdependence . . . can flow into an ethic in which adversaries are respected and maintained in a mode of agonistic mutuality, an ethic in which alter-identities foster agonistic respect for the differences that constitute them, an ethic of care for life. (*Identity\Difference*, 166)

The most pressing question of ethico-political life is not how to get people to do what common moral understandings already call on them to do. "Thou shall not kill." "Honor your mother and father." Mobilizing energy to do what we already concede we should do is important, but the most fundamental issues of ethico-political life arise when interdependent partisans confess different sources of morality and follow somewhat different directives. Attention to the paradoxical character of identity\difference relations encourages you to come to terms with this paradigmatic condition of politics. Cultivation of some "stirrings of unpursued possibilities in oneself that exceed one's identity" is often pertinent to this situation.

I do not talk much about "agonistic democracy" in this book, even though some have placed it under that generic label. Rather, I explore the benefits of folding *agonistic respect* into identity\difference relations in a democratic state. The difference is critical. "Agonistic democracy" could be interpreted as a model in which no positive social vision is enunciated and contestation takes priority over every other aspect of politics. I doubt that anybody actually endorses such a view. "Agonistic respect," on the other hand, is a civic virtue that allows people to honor different final sources, to cultivate reciprocal respect across difference, and to negotiate larger assemblages to set general policies. *Agonistic respect is a reciprocal virtue appropriate to a world in which partisans find themselves in intensive relations of political interdependence.* Agonism is the dimension through which each party maintains a pathos of distance from others with whom it is engaged. Respect is the dimension through which self-limits are acknowledged and connections are established across lines of difference. But the old question arises again in a new form: Must not respect for difference, to *be* respect, flow from a common source?

That is what Augustine and Kant thought, in their somewhat different ways. It is because we recognize ourselves as *homo duplex,* with one foot in the phenomenal world and the other in the noumenal, that we can evince respect for one another, regardless of cultural differences. Kant called this "respect for persons," with the person set above other entities in the world because it is the only being in the world with a foot in the noumenal realm. The effect of this conceit on human relations with the rest of nature has been pernicious. Augustine locates the noumenal in the experience of God, and Kant in the apodictic recognition that morality takes the form of universal laws we are obligated to obey. Where does respect come from on my reading?

My claim is that respect is not deep respect until those who bestow it acknowledge the dignity of those who embrace different sources of respect. Faith in *homo duplex* is one among several contestable cultural perspectives, not The measure through which the claims of contending perspectives are authoritatively assessed.

According to the *particular* existential faith I embrace, respect grows out of a care for life and the earth that precedes and nourishes it. That faith, as we have seen, is neither commanded into being nor given apodictically. It expresses a strain coursing through most people—if they have not been beaten down too severely by the world—and it is then cultivated further. I respect *agonistically* those who draw respect from alternative faiths, such as the Augustinian and Kantian traditions within Christianity. I do not accept the claim that this dimension of their faith must be affirmed by everyone. That is where agonism enters respect. In relations of agonistic respect between, say, Augustinians, Kantians, Rawlsians, Habermasians, Islamists, Buddhists, and neo-Nietzscheans, respect itself flows from different sources: God, reason, public reason and an overlapping consensus, the counterfactual assumption of a possible consensus, exercises to purge the grasping self and release the energy of compassion—and nontheistic gratitude for the earth and the abundance of life. Agonistic respect carries the expectation that you may contest one another on the source of respect, particularly when one party insists that eligibility for respect itself requires you to accept the universal it affirms. It also includes the possibility that something said or done by others may nudge you to reinterpret your existential faith, or draw you toward conversion to another.

On this reading, appeals to different sources of respect may be given public expression, as the occasion requires, though there is no need to advertise one's faith loudly every day. The sharp distinction between religion and philosophy that secular academics have labored so hard to sustain now becomes blurred, as it already is for those who approach western philosophy from the vantage point of non-western faiths that expose its Christian background more vividly. When the range of comparison is broadened beyond the compass of European philosophy it becomes easy to see how faith already enters philosophy and how argument plays a role within religion. Only a few secularists, mostly academics, still purport to leave their existential faiths at home when they enter the public realm. That is because they do not yet acknowledge secular confidence in the sufficiency of public reason (or one of its surrogates) to be a contestable public faith. Most citizens concede that they carry elements of faith with them into the public realm. To appreciate that point, without resentment, is to take a step toward folding respect into agonism and connection into difference.

Tolerance and agonistic respect are kissing cousins, but they are not equivalent. In Euro-American societies tolerance is often taken to flow either from Christian love or Kantian and neo-Kantian revisions of Christianity. Agonistic respect, as a relation of connection across difference, does not entail the consolidation of a majority identity around which a set of minorities is tolerated as satellites. It is more compatible with a network model of pluralism. In a predominantly Christian culture, the public dimension of faith can easily escape attention, at least to practicing Christians and to secularists more bound to Christian conceptions of will, responsibility, evil, and freedom than they may realize. But once you see Christianity, Judaism, Islam, Buddhism, Kantianism, Rawlsianism, Habermasianism, and Nietzscheanism as contestable existential faiths, rather than either merely private faiths or contenders to provide the public matrix in which private faiths are set, the limits of tolerance become more visible. Each faith has a public dimension, and none sets the unquestioned matrix in which the others are situated as private. As I argue in *Why I Am Not a Secularist*, the hubris of secularism is its presumption to define the sufficiency of reason, contract, procedure, or deliberation as the *common matrix* in which contending faiths are enclosed. I like tolerance well enough, but agonistic respect is both more expansive as a civic virtue and more appropriate to the fast-paced world of late modernity in which people of multiple faiths increasingly occupy the same political territory.

Agonistic respect flourishes most when it becomes a reciprocal virtue cultivated by interdependent partisans. This condition, however, is not unique to it. It operates as a constraint on every candidate for public virtue. If religious fundamentalists press hard to universalize the dictates of their faith, a limit is posed to secular tolerance, and vice versa. The question is whether agonistic respect is more appropriate to democratic culture under contemporary conditions of speed, mobility, and plurality; and whether it has a better chance to be negotiated than mere tolerance. I believe it passes muster on both counts. Why? One reason is that the invitation to it contains a confession of the comparative contestability of the faith those issuing the invitation bring to the table.

We can speak of a regulative ideal here. Not one that looks forward to a world of unity, consensus, or solidarity, or one that points to a minimal state presiding over a regime of regular individuals in a market economy, but one directed toward a world in which agonistic respect becomes reciprocal between chastened constituencies who find themselves entangled in the pleasures, tensions, and risks of identity\difference relations.

Agonistic respect is not the only virtue appropriate to an expansive ethos of pluralism. Its twin is critical responsiveness. While the first virtue speaks to relations between already crystallized constituencies, the second speaks to the relation a crystallized constituency pursues to a disqualified minority struggling to migrate from an obscure or negated place below the register of legitimate identity to a place on that register. I did not pose critical responsiveness as a civic virtue in this book, waiting until *The Ethos of Pluralization* before appreciating its importance to the politics of becoming.

The politics of becoming is that recurrent, fugitive politics by which a new constituency or event surges into being from below the threshold

of tolerance, justice, or legitimacy. Before that rocky migration is negotiated it falls below the reach of justice, because its injuries are widely
interpreted to be imaginary, the fixed effect of biology, reflective of narcissism, or expressive of civilizational necessity. The element of paradox
in the politics of becoming is that before success a new movement is
judged by authoritative constituencies in disparaging terms; upon success a new identity emerges that exceeds the energies, aspirations, and
judgments that fomented it. Critical responsiveness negotiates these discordant pressures in a presumptively receptive way. It helps to usher a
new identity onto the registers of justice and legitimacy, doing so in contexts in which the established measure of judgment is insufficient to the
emerging phenomenon. Christianity, secularism, democratic citizenship, feminism, gay rights, and doctor-assisted suicide exemplify a
diverse range of movements that have participated with some success in
the dicey politics of becoming. A *critical* element in critical responsiveness is the effort to read whether a movement promises to support or
curtail the spirit of pluralism. The element of *responsiveness* is a spiri-
tuality of presumptive receptiveness, a disposition to listen with new ears
to a movement that may jostle elements in your identity as, say,
Christian, Male, Heterosexual, or Secular.

So the ethos of pluralism supported here does acknowledge the
necessity of setting limits. *It simply insists that we often do not know
with assurance exactly what those limits must be.* The history of western political thought is littered with the debris of final limits and consummate criteria of inclusion: Platonic Forms, Christianity, an ecumenical God, metaphysical faith in *homo duplex*, secularism, the counterfactual assumption of a rational consensus, western civilization . . . all
have been presented at some time as final measures of what is to be
included and excluded. On numerous occasions, however, many retrospectively conclude that the authoritative principle in question must be
subjected to painful reappraisal or reinterpretation because of hubris
flowing through its enunciations of universality, necessity, normality, or
justice.

To embrace critical responsiveness as a civic virtue is to suggest that
such reappraisals are not about to come to an end. They will recur as the
pace of social reorganization accelerates, throwing up new and surprising grievances and movements imperfectly appreciated by established
codes of judgment. The recurrent need for critical responsiveness
exposes the extent to which a positive ethos of political engagement

exceeds the reach of any fixed code, austere set of procedures, or settled interpretation of moral universals.

> **Why do I, a posttheist living in the last decade of the twentieth century after the birth of your Christ, write to you, the consummate postpagan living between the fourth and fifth centuries? . . . I write to probe a legacy of power, confession, and piety still lodged within modern life.** (*Identity\Difference*, 123)

As already indicated, there are things I would modify were this book to be written today. Major among these is "A Letter to Augustine." Some have read that letter as an effort to purge myself of a Catholic upbringing. In fact I was raised by parents who broke with Protestantism and Catholicism before I was conceived. My engagement with Augustine came late, starting in the mid-1980s. When I read him I felt I was encountering a primer on how to translate differences that disturb the faith you confess into heresies to be banned or corrected. The Augustinian production of heresy corresponds in form to Foucault's account of polemicism in the academy.

The problem is that the strategy I adopted to mimic and expose the code of hereticalization ran the risk of reinscribing it. I was aware of the risk. But I do not think, in retrospect, that I negotiated it well enough. I stand by the critique of Augustinian tactics of hereticalization in this book, but I am happier with the mood of engagement I expressed in *The Augustinian Imperative* a couple of years later. Agonistic respect balances critique with an invitational style of engagement. It seeks to simulate in academic life the ethos it solicits in public life. Laughter in common can be one way to communicate appreciation of mystery and a mood of modesty across contrasting codes of piety. It sometimes stirs up "unpursued possibilities in oneself that exceed one's identity," allowing us to modify some privileges in which we have become encased. It speaks to a thick network of connections forged across multiple differences rather than to the dream of secular thinness, ecumenical community, or a world of national enclaves. A critical task today is to foment laughter across multiple lines of difference.

> **Let us laugh together, on principle.** (*Identity\Difference*, 120)

FOR FURTHER REFERENCE

For further discussion of the fluidity or stickiness of identity, see "Power, Politics, and Ethics: A Conversation between Judith Butler and William Connolly," *theory & event*, http://muse.jhu/journals/theory_&_event/ v004/4.2butler.html.

For a fine essay that compares Confucianism to Thoreau and Foucault as an ethic of cultivation, see Brian Walker, "Thoreau on Democratic Cultivation," *Political Theory* (April 2001): 155–89. The essay should be read in conjunction with Jane Bennett, *Thoreau's Nature* (Thousand Oaks, Calif.: Sage, 1994; second edition, New York: Rowman and Littlefield, 2001).

For an argument against those who think the claims of economic equality must trump those of plurality, see William E. Connolly, "Assembling the Left," *boundary* 2 (Fall 1999): 47–54. While there are persisting tensions between equality and plurality, each nonetheless sets a more dramatic condition of possibility for the other.

For an excellent engagement with the strengths and limits of tolerance, see Wendy Brown, "Reflection on Tolerance in an Age of Identity," in Aryeh Botwinick and William E. Connolly, eds., *Democracy and Vision: Sheldon Wolin and the Vicissitudes of the Political* (Princeton: Princeton University Press, 2001), 99–117.

For a study that explores the ontological dimension of several political theories and probes the political import of the contestability theme in my work, see Stephen White, *Sustaining Affirmation* (Princeton: Princeton University Press, 2000), chapter 4.

The Problem
of Evil

The Second Problem of Evil

The fundamental unfairness of life. Everyone encounters it, in the innocent child who dies, the highly reflective woman in a world that restricts intellectuality to men, the man with instincts of a warrior in a bureaucratic order, the indispensable class condemned to a life of misery, an entire people subjected to genocide because of its religious or political identity.

Within the framework of theism this experience is called the problem of evil. If a god is omnipotent and good, who or what is responsible for evil? When the issue is transcribed into this question, its center of gravity shifts, even though it still bears a recognizable relation to the general experience from which it issues. The question why now assumes priority over the issue of how. And some of the paradigm examples also shift. Why must I die? Why does an unbaptized infant go to hell if it dies? Why would a good god allow evil to exist in the world?

The question "Why?" is bound up with the issue of responsibility, so tightly that once this question acquires primacy the primordial experience of suffering in life threatens to fall out of the category of "evil," reducing evil things to a smaller class of cases to which the question of responsibility is pertinent. Now, before suffering can be called evil, some agent must be responsible for it. This may be a fateful shift. It simultaneously exerts pressure to exclude some injuries from the category of evil and to intensify the search for agents who can be said to be responsible for those forms of suffering we most abhor.

[1]

So perhaps transposition of the primordial experience of suffering into the theistic problem of evil compounds the issue of evil in some ways. Maybe monolithic conceptions of identity and difference, historically authorized by monotheism, locate responsibility for suffering in ways that first create a new problem of evil and then conceal the terms of that relocation. And perhaps some secular doctrines, cutting off the god of theism at the head, retain too much of its body in the ideals of identity, responsibility, and difference that they pursue. Even if certain contemporary theologies have ambiguated these ideals, several contemporary secular doctrines have constructed themselves out of the debris of broken theologies.

I cannot establish these suggestions with assurance in this book—partly because of limitations in my exposure to alternative possibilities of thought, partly because of gaps between the obstacles facing reflection on this rocky terrain and the limited resources to overcome them. Nonetheless, these suggestions do provide this study with much of its energy and direction. Secular philosophies and political theories constitute my primary targets of examination; my selective forays into theistic conceptions aim primarily to bring the primary targets into sharper focus.

Manicheanism, a postpagan sect in a larger constellation called gnosticism that itself moved ambiguously within and against the hegemony of Christianity, responded to the problem of evil by positing a duality in divinity itself. It posited a cosmic force of light haunted by a powerful secondary force of darkness. The force of light lacked the ability to expunge darkness in the first instance, but it radiated with the possibility of subduing it in the last. These opposing forces were held to compete both in the world at large and within the interior of the self; and the redeemer, assuming serial earthly manifestations including Jesus of Nazareth and Mani himself, helped those who heeded its words to attain deeper *gnosis* or insight into the truth of transcendence and salvation.

Augustine, who had himself been a Manichean for several years, who was haunted by the *aporia*s of that doctrine throughout his adult life and who was accused late in life by Pelagians, of covert Manicheanism, resolved the ambiguous threat and attraction of Manicheanism by condemning it as a "heresy," a "baneful teaching" advanced by people "so far gone in folly that they do not listen to what the Lord has said."[1] The bishop of Hippo and saint of the church, with considerable help from his friends, constituted a new evil to solidify the identity of his new faith.

But why could these two cults not engage in agonistic competition within the same church, or, at least, within the frame of the same civilization, each contesting the other because it answers fundamental questions differently and each admiring the other as an essential adversary because it draws its faith and speculations from the same pool of existential mysteries? Some gnostics occasionally approached this possibility, by emphasizing the allegorical character of scripture and its inherent susceptibility to multiple modes of interpretation. But Augustinian Christianity did not. The official reasons were, first, that the divine dualism of the Manichees denied omnipotence to god, second, that this projection of a cosmic/microcosmic war between divine principles weakened the logic of human responsibility to the point of enervation, and third, that the idea of serial redeemers was an affront to the uniqueness of the one Jesus. These Manichean themes were condemned as heretical because they deviated from fundaments of a true faith.

But such an answer only poses new questions—unless they are stifled by the institutionalization of a set of dictates themselves not to be questioned within the faith or the church. What, though, are the compulsions that drive a church, a state, a culture, an identity to close itself up by defining a range of differences as heretical, evil, irrational, perverse, or destructive, even when the bearers of difference pose no direct threat of conquest? What is it in the terms of interaction between competing identities that fosters the probability of this response by one or both of the contending parties?

To pose this question is to reterritorialize the problem of evil. It is to engage the problem of evil residing within human structures of personal identity and social order. Anyone who poses a single, simple resolution to it will almost certainly get it wrong. Perhaps it is important to try to problematize some assumptions that have traditionally guided reflection here.

Every culture seems to contain some themes that are both indispensable to it and inherently problematic within it. The pressure of their indispensability works to conceal their problematic character. This sometimes becomes clear retrospectively after the indispensability of a theme has been lost or compromised; then *aporias* within it flood into the open, making contemporaries wonder how their forerunners could ever have entertained such superstitious or absurd ideas. But this very portrayal of superstitions of the past increases the probability that the problematic character of indispensable themes in the present will not be probed vigorously.

The Homeric idea of the individual as a social center of competing "little selves," with only a weakly centered experience of self-unity, seems strange to modern selves constituted as responsible agents. And the early Christian idea of original sin has for many shifted from the status of an indispensable belief to that of a bizarre idea. Perhaps contemporary ideas of identity and responsibility will someday undergo a corollary shift, with a new set of problematic indispensabilities replacing the set in which we are currently entangled. This "perhaps" is hypothetical and vague; but it may be laudatory to entertain it, even if no one is now in a position to extrapolate very far beyond its bare suggestion.

Certain themes became *indispensable* within Augustine's thought. Augustine tried to save his god from any trace of responsibility for evil while protecting that god's omnipotence and its capacity to promise the possibility of eternal life. He never said it would be easy. A necessary condition of success in this venture was the identification of one moment when a small but definitive wedge was driven between the responsibility of an all-powerful god and the willful act of the first human created by that god. It was indispensable to establish this gap in a way that isolated the god from any taint of evil.

It seems simple. Adam, the first human (Eve is unimportant in Augustine's account), freely chose to disobey his god. He disobeyed a simple command that was extremely easy to obey, and he thereby opened up that fateful gap between the responsibility of his god and the performance of evil. This single, perfect instance of sin through pure will created the indispensable gap; after it was opened in this pristine garden the inheritance of sin and the necessity of grace could be wheeled into place to complicate the exercise of will for all future humans. For the purity of will was needed only once to fulfill the cosmic task assigned to it.

Once the locus of the gap is identified, new questions do arise. But because the gap was indispensable, these questions were posed as if they were either matters to be resolved through simple demarcation or mysteries beyond the powers of human reflection, rather than signs of fundamental difficulties in the doctrine.

Consider but one such question. How could this fateful act have been one of pristine will? If Adam was already given sufficient density of character to render him capable of deliberative choice, how could Augustine's god escape all trace of responsibility for the act flowing from that character? If, on the other hand, Adam lacked density of character before this act, how could it be classified as a willful act of disobedience? This question emerges not only for the act of Adam, but somewhere in every doctrine of responsibility through free will, even in those that, like Augustine's, emphasize the obduracy of bad habits once the self has willfully installed them in itself. For the early actions that install the bad habits must be construed as acts of will. The question is just as pertinent to Kant's doctrine of radical moral evil (where every sin is equivalent to an original sin) and Sartre's doctrine of radical choice of the self. The fact that the issue is present in each act for these thinkers but purely present in only one act of one human for Augustine might seem to diminish its importance in the latter case. But it only concentrates and intensifies the importance of that pivotal moment for the entire doctrine of responsibility.

Augustine first responds to this issue by displacing it. In the *City of God*, he shifts analysis of it from Eden to a discussion of fallen angels who defected from their god, where its explosiveness may be less apparent. Here he defines the issues clearly enough. The created angels who fell must have acquired a certain density of character before they could be said to be governed by pride, but this pride must be said to come from their own wills and not directly from the character the creator invested in them:

> The true cause therefore of the bliss of the good angels is their adherence to him who supremely *is*. When we ask the cause of the evil angels' misery, we find that it is the just result of their turning away from him who supremely is, and their turning towards themselves, who do not exist in that supreme degree. What other name is there for this fault than pride? . . . If you try to find the efficient cause of this evil choice, there is none to be found. For nothing causes an evil will, since the evil choice is the evil will itself which causes the evil act, whereas there is no efficient cause of an evil choice; since if anything exists, it either has, or has not, a will.[2]

The fallen angels *must* have chosen, out of pride, to forsake Augustine's god. Augustine supports this judgment by showing its necessity in the context of the prior conclusion that "God is not to be blamed for any fault or defect which offends us; he is to be praised when we contemplate everything that exists in nature."[3] In the context of this necessity, the indispensability of attributing free will to the bad angels emerges. That this indispensable attribution is also a true representation of the angels' moral personality is not demonstrated, however. Take the angel who was tempted by the devil. The question now becomes: Did the temptation cause the act, or did the angel freely consent to the temptation? Augustine now becomes an analytic philosopher, presenting the hypothetical case of two men who converge on everything except the choice of good or evil, as a means to clarify the difference between good and bad angels:

> Now if both experienced the same temptation, and one succumbed and consented to it, while the other remained unmoved, *the only way to solve the difficulty is evidently to say that one refused and the other agreed to lose his chastity.* What other reason could there be than his personal decision, given their dispositions were precisely the same, in body and mind?[4]

Once it is established that the fallen angels are responsible for their own fall, it is then argued that the good angels cannot be said to be singularly responsible for their own beatitude, because god alone is responsible for everything good:

> Those other angels were created good but have become evil by their own bad will; and this bad will did not originate from their nature, which was good. It came through a voluntary falling away from the good, so that evil is caused not by good, but by falling away from good. Either they received less grace of the divine love than did the others, who continued in that grace; or, if both were created equally good, the one sort fell through their evil will, while the others had greater help to enable them to the fullness of bliss with complete assurance that they will never fall away—a point we have already made, in the previous book.[5]

"What other reason could there be than his personal decision?" "What other name is there for this fault than pride?" "Either they received less grace . . . or . . . fell through their evil will." These questions and assertions summarize a series of arguments by elimination, but they work only after one set of compulsions has been inserted into the subtext in a way that renders another set of responses untenable or unspeakable. For there *are* alternative answers in principle available to Augustine here. He might have adopted the Manichean position, or some variation of it, saying that a force of darkness gained the upper hand in some cases and not in others. ("What other reason could there be but the force of darkness?" "What other name is there for it than an evil principle in being itself?") He might have concluded, alternatively, that while the principle of will is indispensable in the system to which he is committed, it contains so many difficulties that it must not be taken too literally or too seriously. Or he might have adopted a "pagan" stance, affirming some version of Greek thought. That is, he might have compromised the hegemony of will by speaking, even metaphorically, of forces or demons that enter into the soul to push it in one direction or another—as in the Greek tragic poets, who, in George Steiner's words, "assert that the forces which shape or destroy our lives lie outside the governance of reason or justice. Worse than that: there are around us demonic energies which prey upon the soul and turn it to madness or which poison our will so that we inflict irreparable outrage upon ourselves and those we love."[6]

These latter possibilities sound superstitious to some modern ears, so it is well to remember that Augustine himself believed in angels, demons, and assorted spiritual forces. A modernized version of Augustinianism, dropping those beliefs, concentrates on the primacy of the will, treating deviance from the standard of self-responsibility as some form of mental illness. But a modernized version of Manichean and tragic visions might treat references to "forces" and "demons" as signs of persistent insufficiencies in the categories through which we construct our understandings of identity, action, responsibility, and deviance.

Such possibilities of interpretation are occluded by Augustine. He is pressed to give primacy to the will to protect his conception of an omnipotent, benevolent god. Why must he protect that conception? We will take up the issue in Chapter 5.

Once this conception of god is set in stone, the primacy of will emerges as the best means to create the gap between god and evil. And that which provides the gap between god and evil also clears the ground for fixing the human being as a deep, confessing self and a responsible agent. Now the notion of will becomes indispensable to both the faith and the self-identity of the faithful. Once this strategy becomes indispensable, any position that might compromise the conviction of its universal necessity or intrinsic truth becomes a threat to the internal integrity of one's faith and identity.

Manicheanism now appears not as an external affront to a faith that has attained internal coherence and unity but as an alternative possibility of faith that must be constituted as heresy to protect the integrity of the self-identity it threatens through its existence. The indispensability of one conception of divinity, evil, and will is established by defining what deviates from it as a heresy that must not be entertained as a counter-possibility. Humans drawn to paganism or Manicheanism must be made to suffer in order to vindicate the self-identity of those who find their deepest hopes disturbed, destabilized, or threatened by these alternative possibilities of interpretation. In a more general sense, Augustine's solution to the first problem of evil both delimits the sites at which responsibility can be located and intensifies the demand to identify agencies of responsibility. We are still living out the effects of this legacy.

Let me call this effect the site of a *second problem of evil*. The second problem of evil is the evil that flows from the attempt to establish security of identity for any individual or group by defining the other that exposes sore spots in one's identity as evil or irrational. The second problem of evil is *structural* in that it flows from defining characteristics of a doctrine as it unravels the import of its own conceptions of divinity, identity, evil, and responsibility; but it is a *temptation* rather than a necessity because it is juxtaposed to other interior elements—such as, in Augustine, the orientation to mystery, a certain presumption in favor of leaving judgment to his god—that could be drawn upon to disrupt or curtail it. It is a temptation rather than an implication, and a structural temptation rather than simply a psychological disposition.

The Augustinian definition of Manicheanism as heresy and of Greek polytheisms as paganism provides two exemplifications of the politics of identity and difference. That politics contains the second problem of evil moving silently inside the first one. The question now becomes: Is it possible to counter the second problem of evil without eliminating the functions served by identity? That is one of the defining questions of this study.

Of course, the story I have spun could be told in a more familiar way, with a certain gain in plausibility flowing from its familiarity. The story would start with the internal quest of Augustine to achieve communion with his god, and move from there to his findings and his faith. My version is told from the vantage point of a perspective operating at least partly outside the terms of that quest. It is told from an external vantage point that is contestable, just as the familiar version is told from an internal perspective that is contestable. Perhaps such a process of experimental defamiliarization enables reflective detachment from received identities. Such an approach may be needed to encounter and disrupt the problem of evil inside the politics of self-identity.

Plausibility is not a sufficient criterion of judgment when one is engaging the transcendental egoism of a hegemonic self-identity, when one is struggling with the tendency of an identity to seal itself in a higher semblance of truth or necessity because one is it and it is one. The criterion of plausibility draws too much of its power from the force of familiarity and the drive to self-reassurance. It deserves to be compromised and contested by other considerations. To engage the second problem of evil, it is necessary to practice the arts of experimental detachment of the self from the identity installed within it, even though these are slippery, ambiguous arts hardly susceptible to full realization. For it is probably impossible and surely undesirable to be human without some sort of implication in a particular identity, yet it is how an identity is experienced and how it defines itself with respect to different identities that is crucial to engagement with the second problem of evil.

The Paradox of Ethics

The consolidation of identity through the constitution of difference. The self-reassurance of identity through the construction of otherness. Augustine is neither the first nor the last to follow such a course. Polytheists, theists, and atheists before and after him pursue similar tactics. The definition of difference is a requirement built into the logic of identity, and the construction of otherness is a temptation that readily insinuates itself into that logic—and more than a temptation: a temptation because it is constantly at work and because there may be political ways to fend it off or to reduce its power; more than a temptation because it typically moves below the threshold of conscious reflection and because every attempt to come to terms with it encounters stubborn obstacles built into the logic of identity and the structural imperatives of social organization. To come to terms with one's implication in these strategies, one needs to examine established tactics of self-identity, not so much by engaging in self-inquiry into one's deep interior as by exploring the means by which one has become constituted as what one is, by probing the structures that maintain the plausibility of those configurations, and by analyzing from a perspective that problematizes the certainty of one's self-identity the effects these structures and tactics have on others. These same tactics apply when *we* encounter the problem of evil in *our* identity.

In exploring some ways the second problem of evil works, and in struggling to find ways to subdue it, I owe my most salient debts to Nietzsche and Foucault. Not to Nietzsche alone or Foucault alone, but to each as a complement and corrective to the other. Especially to Foucault as a response to the heroic conception of self-responsibility and the disdain of democracy in Nietzsche. Nor do both together suffice as correctives to each other. A critical extrapolation from this combination is needed after one has linked Nietzschean affirmation of the "abundance of life" to Foucaultian care for identity and difference.

As I "read" the combination that emerges from placing these two in conjunction, Nietzsche and Foucault do not ask "Why be ethical?" or "What is the transcendental ground of ethics?" But neither do these refusals disengage them from ethics. Together, Nietzsche and Foucault expose a persistent paradox of ethicality as it operates in a variety of settings. In a world where hegemonic claims to identity are always already permeated by ethical dispositions and marked by proclivities toward moral self-righteousness, they devise strategies for cultivating care for identity and difference in their relations of discordant interdependence. Not *why* be ethical, then, for if someone really (rather than hypothetically) poses that as the question to be answered first, he or she is probably beyond the effective reach of ethical concern. Not *what* is the epistemic ground of ethics, for the unrelenting demand for an answer to that question fosters either a passive nihilism in which one becomes immobilized from action or an aggressive nihilism in which cracks or fissures in the answer endorsed are suppressed to preserve its sanctity. The primary quest is not for a *command* that answers "why" or a *ground* that establishes "what" but for *ways* to cultivate care for identity and difference in a world already permeated by ethical proclivities and predispositions to identity. They oppose to the authoritarianism of the various command ethics that have populated western thought an ethic of cultivation.[7]

Such an ethic of cultivation requires genealogy as a mode of reflection and democratic politics as its privileged mode of public life. These two must function together to draw agonistic care for difference from the abundance of life that exceeds any particular identity. In the contemporary world, where practices of child-rearing, intimate relations, tactics of self-improvement, gender re-

lations, administrative regulation, therapy, work-incentive systems, medicine, advertising, election strategy, and political dissent
are all legitimized or delegitimized through the theorizations that
help to constitute them, the modalities of genealogy and democratic
agonism must infiltrate each other if either is to make a difference of
note anywhere.

Genealogy and democratic agonism foster the experience of contingency in identity amid the contrary pressures lodged in the
inertia of language, imperatives of social coordination, the drives
within us to find external justifications for existential suffering, and
the desire to transcend the paradox of ethics. They are also dangerous practices, sometimes threatening to backfire.

A further elaboration of these themes, or rather a reflection that
invokes them, is best left to the chapters that follow. What, though,
is the paradox of ethicality that Nietzsche and Foucault together
help to expose?

If one keeps in the back of one's mind that uneasy combination of
self-responsibility through will and inheritance of original sin inaugurated by Augustine in the fifth century, a set' of documents
introduced without much comment by Foucault in the twentieth
can provide a sense of how this paradox functions. In 1835 a
troubled young man, shortly after killing his mother, sister, and
brother in a small village in France, presented authorities with a
memoir entitled *I Pierre Rivière, Having Slaughtered My Mother, My
Sister and My Brother.*[8] Pierre clearly committed an atrocity, but the
memoir exceeded and confounded at every turn the cultural terms
of analysis available to the authorities. Was Pierre a "responsible
agent" or a "monomaniac"? If he was neither, the authorities and
local people lacked terms through which to identify and respond to
the act. For these two categories exhausted the available set. If the
case of Pierre were forced into one of the two available terms, a
strange sense would arise that a secondary injustice was being
perpetrated through the very enactment of justice. Most of the
authorities (lawyers, doctors, judges) called upon to render a judgment, though differing among themselves as to whether he was a
responsible agent or a monomaniac, agreed that he was one or the
other. A few confessed themselves to be confounded by the conjunction of this case and these categories.

This was a pivotal moment, when the modern duality of the
responsible offender and the sick criminal was being formed and
consolidated. Can one hear in this nineteenth-century dualism

echoes of the earlier one enunciated by Augustine? At any rate, these new categories were neither as refined nor as sedimented into practice as their progeny have become today. So the case of Pierre enabled the constructed character of categories of identity, responsibility, and punishment to glimmer for a moment or two for a few people in this particular place. Then the "case," a local happening in any event, slipped into obscurity.

Similar instances occur every month in every locale. Each instance sows seeds of doubt and disturbance among a few people for a few moments. And then it is dropped. There are powerful pressures working upon everyone—theorists, journalists, doctors, judges, lawyers, citizens—to treat such instances either as cases to be drawn without loss into established categories or as modest anomalies that call for slight modification in the categories. Such instances are not allowed to accumulate to expose a more general paradox of ethics that flows beneath the self-confidence of a culture of justice.

Here is one formulation of the paradox: Without a set of standards of identity and responsibility there is no possibility of ethical discrimination, but the application of any such set of historical constructions also does violence to those to whom it is applied. Such standards are indispensable constructions rather than either disposable fictions or natural kinds. And though some constructions are better than others in the circumstances of their application, that point, too, is compromised when people insist upon treating the set that prevails as if it were intrinsically true, as if the intersection it established between the imperatives of social life and the terms of identity/responsibility corresponded to an intrinsic design of human being itself. Though there are universal elements in these historical conjunctures, that circumstance does not exempt them from the terms of the paradox either.

Foucault and Nietzsche, far from fostering the flabby historical relativism that some transcendentalists foist upon them, treat such disparate events as the case of Pierre and the flowering of Greek tragedy as moments when a general, persistent paradox of ethicality can be discerned and engaged. Genealogy seeks and probes such moments, and it probes the pressures that push them back into forgetfulness. It invokes a second-order ethicality to counter the moral pressures that would suppress the paradox of ethicality.

It is tempting to bury this paradox through a variety of ontotheological strategies, such as a myth of the contract, an elabora-

tion of transcendental proofs, a fictive standard of rational consensus, or the discernment of a harmonious *telos* in being—and then
to try to seal this burial by insisting that one cannot even recognize a
paradox of ethics unless one is "implicitly" committed to one of
these strategies as the ground of ethicality. But Nietzsche and
Foucault resist these responses, *not by pretending they never find
themselves implicated in them*, but by pursuing compensatory strategies to compromise, loosen, attenuate their hold on the cultivation
of ethicality. They strive to expose the paradox of ethicality and to
cultivate an ethic of agonistic care for identity and difference. Who
or what guarantees, they ask, that ethics must escape the condition
of paradox?

   This study works within and against the terms of the paradox,
wagering that it is better to expose it than to suppress it, and placing
a second bet that a counter-ontological projection may open up
productive possibilities of reflection in this domain. It concurs with
the later Heidegger and the early Derrida that *différance* enables,
disturbs, and compromises every system of identity and difference.
"This does not mean that the *différance* that produces differences is
somehow before them, in a simple and unmodified—in-different—
present. *Différance* is thus the non-full, non-simple, structured and
differentiating origin of differences."[9] But this study also recognizes that even this fugitive presentation of *différance*—which emphasizes its nonbeing outside a network of practices, its nontheistic
character, its distantiation from teleological ontologies, its general
affront to "ontotheology"— even these negative determinations relocate *différance* (and its functional equivalents in other antimeta-
physical texts) in the metaphysical tradition it strives to unsettle.

   So the strategies of "deconstruction" are not actively pursued
here. While I strive to expose the contestable character of opposing
ontological projections by working against them from the inside,
the counter-interpretations advanced here overtly evoke a social
ontology challenging those that have implicitly governed the matrix
within which much contemporary political reflection occurs. My
interpretations invoke a set of ontological projections open to contestation. Attempts are made to subject them to self-problematization even as they are being advanced. And I insist upon treating
alternative interpretations in the same way.

   It is not that historical considerations cannot be advanced on
behalf of the projections I endorse. It is rather that no interpretation
can proceed without at least covertly invoking some fundamental

presumptions currently underdetermined by reason and evidence. Nor is it that the interpretations advanced here are immunized against deconstruction. They are eminently susceptible to it: even deconstruction is susceptible to it, as Derrida shows in the case of Heidegger and reveals through the recurrent shift of terms through which he himself proceeds. It is just that deconstruction is not the only activity needed in town, even by those concerned about the terms of closure in established discourse and appreciative of the need to disturb it. If one suspects that experimental detachment from the dominant terms of debate is an element in the cultivation of freedom and care, then the detailed elaboration of an alternative interpretation may be a viable way to proceed. For every detachment from a particular mode of thought is also attachment to another.

The idealization of politics advanced in this study constitutes an attempt to build recognition of the unavoidability of fundamental presumptions and the unlikelihood of secure knowledge of their truth into an ideal of political discourse itself.

This book examines how diverse theories of deep identity, singular responsibility, contingency as opportunity for mastery, individuality as a modality outside the sphere of politics, and communion with an intrinsic harmony in being all contain the temptation to suppress the paradox of ethicality. It explores an alternative in which people strive to interrogate exclusions built into their own entrenched identities. It pursues an agonistic ethic of care that ambiguates assumptions it itself is often compelled to make about the truth of the identity it endorses. It probes the idea of a politicization of difference, in which conventional standards sealed in transcendental mortar are tested and loosened through political contestation. More hesitantly yet, it explores the ethicality of a politics that refuses to resign itself unambiguously to limits imposed by the structural requirements of any particular order, a politics alert to a tragic gap between the imperatives of organization in the order it idealizes and admirable possibilities of life that exceed those imperatives.

Though each of these efforts, I think, feeds into the others, they do not sustain one another without internal tension. Yet at least one set of charges conventionally brought against efforts of this type might be countered now. Engaging the paradox of ethicality by cultivating the experience of contingency in identity does not entail the celebration of any and every identity. It does not open itself to a politics of racism or genocide, for instance. For identities that must define what deviates from them as intrinsically evil (or one of its modern surrogates) in order to establish their own self-certainty are here defined as paradigm instances to counter and contest. They stifle cultivation of care for the ambiguous relations of identity\ difference through the way they constitute good and evil. So, in another way, do academics who define evil as relativism.

The agenda is not to develop from scratch an entire philosophy of identity and difference. In a world always already saturated with operative relations of identity and difference, such an agenda is neither possible nor desirable. The agenda is instead to intervene from a distinctive perspective in theory-imbued practices of identity and difference (always) already in place.

In this study explorations of identity and difference at the level of individual and group relationships outstrip those at the level of interstate relations. The academic division of labor between political theory and international relations theory is one that I have not escaped, even as I now recognize the imperative to scramble it. There is a need to rethink the intersection of democracy and sovereignty as defined in realist/idealist readings of "domestic" and "foreign" politics. The realist confines democracy to the internal politics of a few territorial states, while the idealist dreams of a sovereign place extending beyond the current parameters of the state where democracy can flourish. But, or so I see it, territorial democracy in the late-modern time requires supplementation through nonterritorial democratization of global issues by movements that cross state lines and exert external/internal pressures upon states to revise their priorities. I begin to think about this issue in the present study, but the words break off before the pertinent questions have been pushed far enough.

This remains an interim report, then, containing the wish to defer its final version to a later date.

CHAPTER ONE

Freedom and
Resentment

Freedom and Mortality

We secularists, it seems, know where we are going. We're on the road to nowhere. It can even be sung. No illusions about eternal life. No need to pass a new battery of tests to qualify for immortality. No worries about infinite boredom haunting the afterlife of a disembodied soul. Perhaps we compensate by clinging to an ethic of health and longevity. Perhaps some of us have even transfigured the promise of personal salvation into a doctrine of collective progress. Still, these secular dreams and consolations seem innocent enough.

Appearances deceive here, though. For a pattern of secular insistence about the relation life must bear to death spawns illusions about the circumstances of contemporary life. Contemporary social theory contains within it a set of secular reassurances that compensate for those lost through the death of God.

To think critically about these compensations is to think about some commonalities that bind several contending theories of contemporary life into a frame held together by that which is unthought by many of the participants. And it is, perhaps, to identify troubles and dangers on the horizon that are obscured by the terms of contestation within this frame. I will call these background assumptions the unconscious phenomenology of life and death in late modernity. My strategy will be, first, to summarize this phenomenology as if it were explicitly articulated by social theorists today, second, to lend greater credibility to the thesis that it contributes to the unconscious of contemporary thought by outlining an alternative reading of the late-modern condition that disturbs parameters of contestation within the frame it provides, and third, to probe more carefully the boundaries of this frame and the unthought that governs thinking within it. The idea and experience of freedom, as it is interpreted at each of these sites, will provide the organizing instrument of this endeavor.

The unconscious phenomenology of life and death is significant, partly because its constructions contain indispensable insights, partly because it screens out important shifts in the contemporary experience of freedom and unfreedom. Its song might be relatively familiar, since it draws into its melody strains from thinkers such as the early Heidegger, Sartre, Merleau-Ponty, and Hegel. The following summary, however, drains it of nuance, variation, and complexity so that it can be reduced to a cultural stereotype.

Recognition that life is short encourages the self to contribute to the crystallization of its own individuality. Since, as Heidegger says, no one, however rich or powerful, can pay or order another to substitute for him in this performance, foreknowledge of death can encourage a human being to establish priorities in life, to consolidate the loose array of possibilities floating around and within one into the density of a particular personality with specific propensities, purposes, and principles. Nudged by the prospect of death to ponder life, you may struggle to establish distance between yourself and the common stock; the common good does not, after all, own you completely if its continuation is punctuated by your death. Since it is your death, you may be ready to assert that it must, to some degree at least, be your life too. Pondering these issues, you may become more insistent about your importance in the order of things, even about your intrinsic significance despite the order of things. Those ways of life that strive to absorb the self completely into the body of the community would not have to devise such demanding rituals of commonality if the prospect of death did not stir up, among other things, powerful drives to individuality.

The relation of individuality to foreknowledge of death creates an ambiguous context for the exercise of freedom. If I lived forever, I could be a philosopher, a professional basketball coach, a concert pianist, a transvestite, and a corporate lawyer. If there were time for every possibility, the language of freedom would become extremely slippery. For freedom involves choice in a setting where it

is impossible to pursue every valued option concurrently or serially; it presupposes a contrast with unfreedom that could not be
maintained in a world without the constraints of time. A free
mortal forecloses alternative possibilities when it chooses to do or
become *x*; and every act of freedom is therefore bound up with the
possibilities it must forgo.

The actualization of a life is ambiguous because the process of
becoming an individual with specific skills, memories, propensities, prospects, and liabilities rules out whole sets of options
previously hovering in front of one. Hence anxiety, self-doubt, and
even rage against the human condition often accompany the actual
exercise of freedom. Some try to defer choices indefinitely to avoid
the experience of foreclosure. Others try to do a little of everything
and accomplish little of anything. Time weighs upon many bearers
of freedom because, more generally, implicit foreknowledge of
death slips into every decision that defines one in some fundamental
way. The very structure of freedom and individuality is pervaded
by the relation they bear to the self's implicit anticipation of its end.

But foreknowledge of death also connects the individuated self to
a larger world that enables and disables it. One dimension of this
relation is conveyed by Hobbes. The fear of early, violent death
becomes a tool deployable by the sovereign to regulate otherwise
unruly, restless, variable, and unreliable beings. Hobbes piles on
top of the individual's inclination to avoid death the obligation to do
so, so that suicide becomes a sin against the law of nature and its
god. He fears that the pull of individuality will overwhelm the
dictates of an order strong enough to protect individuals from the
constant threat of violent and arbitrary death *unless* the episodic fear
of death itself is converted into a reliable weapon in the service of
civil order. Thus the same foreknowledge of death that encourages
the self to assert its individuality also becomes an instrument enabling power to restrict, domesticate, and regularize the self.

Fear is not the only means by which the prospect of death can
connect the individual to the larger world in which it is situated.
Gratitude (or something akin to it) plays a role too. When we
confront the ambiguity of freedom we also realize that an open
society, housing diverse ways of living, enables us to cope with this
ambiguity. A fortunate individual, acknowledging the distinctive
possibilities this world opens to her and to those she loves, recognizing that she might have been thrown into a hellhole of one sort or
another, allows a diffuse feeling of identification and gratitude to
infuse daily transactions. So does he.

If one ponders child-rearing, work, tax payments, writing, political action, tax cheating, and associational membership in the context of one's own finitude, it eventually becomes clear that one's life efforts do not redound only to one's own detriment or benefit; each, after life, bestows a legacy upon those remaining. You can't take it with you, nor can you consume every product or effect you have engendered before the onset of death. Thus, in ways the radical individualist inadequately acknowledges, the very individuality of death connects us in life to others and to a future that continues without us after death. This preliminary connectedness to a larger way of life means that we implicate ourselves through specific, daily performances in the destiny of the order to which we belong. Our current contributions connect us to a future that stretches beyond us. Maybe those we raised will remember us with pride; maybe a future generation will remember and respect the effort and sacrifices of the present one. Connectedness to a future that stretches beyond my life and our lives provides me with pride in the present and consoles me somehow about the end that awaits me. We seek this consolation, and our pursuit of it enters into readings of the future we participate in preparing.

Freedom and Dependent Uncertainty

This abbreviated phenomenology of freedom and death illuminates ambiguities in the self's relation to order and to its own individuality. Individualists tend to accentuate some of these elements, while communitarians emphasize others. The contemporary debate between them can be located in this space of contestation over the appropriate terms of accentuation. But the disputants also share assumptions forming the common pool from which these alternative pails of theory are drawn. For this phenomenology presupposes a relatively stable and serene context of self-identity, social practice, state and interstate relations, and temporal projection.

The links it forges between life and foreknowledge of death, individuality and connectedness, choice and foreclosure, individual and collective life in the present and projections of future prospects for both, presume, first, a close alignment between the identity the self seeks to realize and socially available possibilities of self-formation and, second, a shared sense of confidence in the world we are building, a confidence that links the present to the future through effort and anticipation at one time and memory and appreciation at another. If these connections, sentiments, and projections become severely attenuated, the serene phenomenology of freedom and finitude also becomes strained and anachronistic. To retain it would then be to cling insistently to a picture of the world belied by individual and collective experience.

I think something like this is occurring today. The secular drive to domesticate the prospect of death without immortality functions today as a filter to theorization, sifting out features that discipline individuality, disturb connectedness, and disrupt the ambiguous exercise of freedom. This compensatory code of secular reassurance screens out disciplines and dangers residing in contemporary experience. It contributes in its own way to the dangers it seeks to contain.[1]

Three characteristics of contemporary life disturb and unsettle this phenomenology. There is, first, an intensification of the experience of owing one's life and destiny to world-historical, national, and local-bureaucratic forces. There is, second, a decline in the confidence many constituencies have in the probable future to which they find themselves contributing in daily life. There is, third, an even more ominous set of future possibilities that weigh upon life in the present. Each of these developments is distinctive enough, in its newness, its intensification, or the extent to which it is inscribed in lived experience, to be treated as a defining dimension of contemporary life. The time is distinctive enough to be given a name. Let's call it late modernity.

The first experience (of owing too much of one's life to world-historical forces) is so close and pervasive that its political effects tend to escape explicit attention. It consists of an exacerbation of elements necessary and desirable in smaller proportions. Many young people, facing the exigencies of life as a career or a job without one, feel it dramatically; so do many older people, preparing for "retirement."

The identity available to the late-modern self remains bound up with historically received standards of self-responsibility, self-discipline, and freedom. Individuals are responsible not merely for particular actions, but, to varying and shifting degrees, for the character they develop, the stability of their mental lives, the careers they nurture, the quality of their love lives, the way their children turn out, the level of income they "earn," the social recognition they attain, and so on. Background notions and institutions of love (where each chooses the other free from traditional constraints), self-responsibility (where one is held accountable for what one does and becomes), equal opportunity (where one's career and income flow from one's own ability, effort, and luck), individual freedom (where the consequences of one's actions are linked at least loosely to intentions that go into them), and citizenship (where each plays a part in shaping rules and laws governing all)—each of these practices is enabled and confined by relations it bears to the others.

But while these standards of identity and responsibility remain intact, the institutions in which they are situated have become more highly and pervasively organized. One must now program one's life meticulously to meet a more detailed array of institutional standards of normality and entitlement. If one fails to measure up to one (or more) of these disciplines, one runs a high risk of entrapment in one of the categories of otherness derived from it: one becomes defined through a reciprocal category of delinquency, irresponsibility, dependency, criminality, instability, abnormality, retardation, unemployability, incapacity, obsolescence, credit risk, security risk, perversity, evil, illness, or contagion. And these latter categories of abnormality license bureaucratic correction, discipline, regulation, exclusion, conquest, help, conversion, incentives, or punishment. The more tight and extensive the disciplines become, the more deep and widely distributed become the deviations to be dealt with. This is the irony: the intensification of social discipline fosters the proliferation of differences defined through multiple categories of subordination, inferiority, incapacity, and de-gradation.

In late modernity old standards of freedom and responsibility impose a new set of hard choices. One can either treat one's life as a project, negotiating a path through a finely grained network of institutionally imposed disciplines and requirements, or one can struggle against those disciplines by refusing to treat one's life as a project. To follow the first route is to be indebted to the institutions in which one is enclosed: one's office space, self-esteem, income, merit, mobility, power, family, and personal identity now depend on microconformity to pervasive norms that come with the territory. And this remains so whether those standards are established democratically or imposed from above. To select or be selected by the second path, on the other hand, is to be shuffled out of the good life available and to increase one's susceptibility to one of the categorizations that license institutional discipline from another direction. "The choice," as we say in tones overtly celebrating freedom and covertly attacking the other, "is yours."

When the self experiences itself as penetrated too densely by disciplinary powers and standards, even the benefits it receives begin to indebt it too much. One begins to experience uncertainty, contingency, and fragility residing in the status, power, and opportunities bestowed upon one. For anything given might also be taken away. A stock market can crash; a technical education can become obsolete; a liberal education can become irrelevant; a normal standard of family life can become abnormal; an avenue of mobility can become closed; a standard of merit can be reconstituted; the principles of self-respect can be modified; a hilarious sense of humor can be redefined as sickness; a previous pattern of affection can be redefined as illicit. Every newly institutionalized reward for attaining a current standard also creates new possibilities for deviant conduct and new possibilities for future revisions or extensions of old standards. And the very intensification and temporal extension of the typical life project decreases the probability that future standards of success will mesh with those projected by youthful pursuers. The late-modern definition of life as a project first demands intensive self-organization and then produces dependent uncertainty—dependence upon a more refined set of institutional standards and disciplines, uncertainty about the temporal stability of established rules of dependence.

Dependent uncertainty fosters a character type whose explicit consent to its way of life is laced with generalized resentment. The reactive attitudes of gratitude and resentment are intimately linked already in personal life, as Nietzsche knew. If you are grateful to me for my help, you know that I know you were recently in a position of need or vulnerability. You can easily become resentful over actual or imagined misuses I might make of this knowledge.

A similar logic applies in social life. Those who experience themselves as penetrated too thoroughly by disciplinary powers and standards resent even benefits they receive. Here, though, the object of resentment becomes less easy to fix; indefinite gratitude toward a way of life slides imperceptibly into floating resentment against its requirements and contingencies. Those burdened by this new weight are unlikely to bear new responsibilities lightly; they are also likely to evade old ones not tightly bound to their job descriptions.

Generalized resentment (as I shall call it) finds expression in a

diverse set of practices today, ranging from drug use through litigiousness, "mindless" violence, teenage suicide, and high divorce
rates to tax evasion and "work according to rule." But it receives its
most revealing and politically active expression in the hostility of
those in positions of official independence to the complaints of those
in officially recognized conditions of dependence, such as third-
world countries, convicted criminals, mental patients, welfare
claimants, affirmative action candidates, coddled athletes, minorities, teenagers, illegal aliens, and privileged college students—
hostility, that is, to every constituency appearing to putative beneficiaries of prevailing institutional standards to whine about their
treatment within officially defined arrangements of tutelage, punishment, assistance, dependence, or privilege. What gives these
"others" the right to complain when many struggling to measure up
to the demands of life as a project already face as much self-
discipline, dependency, and uncertainty as they can handle?

The second and third shifts in the context of contemporary life
sharpen characteristics already elucidated. When people devalue
the legacy the present bestows upon the future, they divest selectively from common life in the present. This personal economy of
divestment, achieving variable weight within any self at different
points in the life cycle and each definable constituency at various
sites in the order, lodges itself in gender relations, child-rearing, job
performance, the character of political coalitions, strategies of investment, and tax payment. In each domain the claims of self and
immediacy gain leverage over those of connectedness and the future. And as economists of psychic investment are fond of iterating
and reiterating, once divestment establishes itself in a few places
and constituencies it becomes more irrational for others to withstand its temptations.

What are these anxieties about the future? It seems probable that
affluent states of late modernity will be unable to protect their
privileged position in the future without extending disciplinary
control domestically and fomenting recurrent hostilities abroad.
More pervasively, late modernity is a time when the worldwide web
of systemic interdependencies has become more tightly drawn,
while no political entity or alliance can attain the level of efficiency
needed to master this system and its effects. This fundamental
asymmetry between the appropriate level of political reflection (the
world of late modernity itself) and the actual capacity for collective
action (the state and various regional alliances of states) cannot be

transcended by any discernible means. Nonstate terrorism, the internationalization of capital, the greenhouse effect, acid rain, drug traffic, illegal aliens, the global character of strategic planning, extensive resource dependencies across state boundaries, and the accelerated pace of disease transmission across continents can serve as some of the signs of this contraction of space and time in the late-modern world. Together they signify a widening gap between the power of the most powerful states and the power they would require to be self-governing and self-determining.

This condition renders increasingly anachronistic and danger-ous, I think, classic-modern conceptions of the state as a sovereign or self-subsistent entity that enters into "foreign relations" or—within the frame of the democratic ideal—as a self-sufficient, dem-ocratically accountable political entity with the efficacy to control the collective destiny. No state can be inclusive enough to master the environment that conditions it; but the ideal of the modern, democratic state, as the consummate agency of collective freedom, is predicated on the assumption of this capacity. As long as this gap is treated simply as a deficiency to be rectified, the drive of late-modern states to close it will constitute a danger to global survival.

The size of this gap between world systematicity and state efficacy helps to explain the extension of discipline in late-modern states. The late-modern state is becoming a medium through which world-systemic pressures are transmitted to its most vulnerable constituencies as imperatives of domestic discipline.

This prognostication of the future is embedded in the percepti-ble dispositions of many constituencies, even though it remains underarticulated politically. It finds covert expression in the inten-sification of a national chauvinism designed to close the gap be-tween actual power and self-determination and in the corollary pretense of public debate that persisting deficits in state efficacy flow mostly from the political failings of particular leaders. It finds expression as well in the hesitancy to discuss publicly a more ominous set of contingencies, global contingencies residing in the black hole located between the drive of late-modern states for mastery and the world-systemic effects generated by it.

The belief in the state as the site of collective freedom and mas-tery is sustained today by a failure to confront the *globalization of contingency* that haunts late modernity. Thus climactic changes gen-erated by late-industrial society may eventually sink large chunks of inhabitable and arable land under the sea; crises in essential supplies of oil or safe water or good soil or oxygen may flow from the effort to industrialize the entire world; state and nonstate terrorism may escalate into a condition of continuous insecurity and violence unconfined by state boundaries; and the impotency of a late-modern state or a nonstate fragment may produce a nuclear exchange that destroys civilization or removes human life from the face of the earth.

The globalization of contingency is the defining mark of late modernity.

But even to draw up a brief list of global contingencies (that is, of possibilities and potential emergencies that might be resistant to control) is to recite a series of banal truisms. These are more like idle words than political enunciations because they are only precariously linked to a public discourse that might state them as issues or problems susceptible to compromise or resolution within the state-centered frame of political debate and action. This banalization of political reflection on global contingency is itself a sign of the gap between the globalization of contingency and the efficacy of states in late modernity, between intensification of the organizational drive to world mastery and the creation of contingencies that endlessly push this objective out of reach.

Each possible scenario of future waste or destruction is linked ironically to priorities definitive of the modern epoch, especially to the drive to organize the state, the economy, and self so that the world itself can be subjected to more thorough mastery. These scenarios of possible reversal expose how the end of eliminating contingency recedes as the means to it become more refined and perfected. The project to master microcontingencies and the globalization of macrocontingency advance together, while the organization of state-centered political discourse celebrates the first effect by banalizing the second.

In late modernity, the contingency of life and the fragility of things become more vivid and compelling, while reflection on the issues posed by this condition is shuffled to the margins of state-centered discourse. Established disciplines and rules become experienced more often as arbitrary restraints insecurely linked to the future that justifies them. Resentment becomes more generalized and acute, and more actively seeks available targets of vilification. Politics becomes less attuned to the future and more locked into claims of the present, less attentive to claims of the suffering and more willing to discipline those whose suffering cannot be ignored.

The late-modern condition compromises the individual's bond of affection to the common life, disciplines individuality, disconnects present decisions from care about the future they engender, and disrupts stable contexts in which the ambiguous exercise of freedom occurs.

What is the experience of freedom like in such a condition? Perhaps Milan Kundera, writing in a more extreme setting, can clarify certain elements in this one through magnification. Kundera thinks specifically about Czechoslovakia after 1968, where collective memories are expunged from public records and media, where the reputations of patriotic rebels are systematically ruined, where traditional rules and ethical guides become irrelevant to new circumstances, and where the state apparatus absorbs everyday gossip into a system of police surveillance. He teaches more generally, though, about the disturbance introduced into the phenomenology of freedom when ruptures are opened between intention and result, personal identities sought and those validated by the order, the self and its tie to the common life, the present and the future it prepares. If an act of resistance and courage in photographing Russian invaders later becomes a source of information to authorities rounding up dissidents, what does that teach retrospectively about the unstable context of individual freedom? If an entire epoch finds itself facing new and dangerous contingencies after spending centuries trying to master contingency, what does that teach about the structure of collective freedom?

Kundera thinks about the paradox of freedom in a condition marked by structural binds and personal contingency: "Human life occurs only once, and the reason we cannot determine which of our decisions are good and which bad is that in a given situation we can make only one decision; we are not granted a second, third, or fourth life in which to compare individual decisions. . . . History is similar to individual lives in this respect."[2]

Kundera revises Nietzsche's teaching of eternal recurrence. In this new condition the freedom depicted by the serene phenomenology could be established only through Nietzschean recurrence with a distinctive twist. If each lived life over many times, recalling in each new cycle what followed previous decisions and knowing that the only new agency to be introduced into the recurring setting would be one's own newly informed decision, the freedom of each individual and state would increase with each cycle of recurrence. Radical contingency, as we might call a condition in which the mastery of microcontingencies accentuates global contingency, could be contained by using the past to prophesy future results of current alternatives. But individuals and states actually go around only once: "living only one life, we can neither compare it with our previous lives nor perfect it in our lives to come."[3]

When the background presupposed by the serene phenomenology of freedom and mortality is destabilized, each of its elements becomes disrupted. The experience of freedom is drained from the exercise of choice; the experience of choice is wrenched from the requirement to convert life into a project; the assurance of temporal stability is withdrawn from the time covered by a life project. People often do what they want, but their uncertain, disciplined, and dependent condition unravels freedom even as they do so. The anticipation of death, which was to foster individuality and connectedness, becomes prized loose from a stable context in which these consolations are assured.

A paradoxical element always operative in the practice of freedom now becomes intensified: I can often do what I want or what I think will promote my long-term advantage, but my implication in an organized system of available life projects means that one or another institution might itself fall under pressure to transform the standards I have striven to meet; we can act together in a state to domesticate local contingencies, but the cumulative effect of such actions by a variety of states generates global contingencies resistant to mastery; late modernity replaces acceptance of blind fate with the mastery of contingency, but it creates global contingencies that haunt it with a new fatefulness.

Just as the serene phenomenology of life and death idealized the world in which it located the ambiguous practice of freedom, the revised phenomenology presented here purifies an emergent world by adopting alternative principles of selection. It is an exaggeration, designed to crystallize elements simultaneously squeezed out of the first account and newly elevated by the late-modern condition.

Freedom and Necessary Contingency

Contemporary politics should seek to mitigate generalized resentment and respond to historical contingency. But what understanding might inform this response? Many political theorists today seek to resuscitate individualism or, among those who find that response repugnant, to establish an equally familiar ideal of community. Both are apolitical ideals in their dominant formulations. The first position promises to reduce state pressure on the individual by enabling self-reliance, thereby relieving the politics of resentment; the second promises to elevate the experience of connectedness to a larger community, thereby dissolving resentment into a solution of common identifications. But each of these alternatives also complements the other. The first concentrates disciplinary pressure in the privately incorporated economy; the second lodges it in an anticipated community that establishes harmonious norms and ends for all. Together they license a lot of discipline. But perhaps the contemporary crystallization of dependent uncertainty, generalized resentment, and global contingency provides an occasion to rethink the terms of this familiar debate. Perhaps it enables us to look with new eyes into the mobile idea of freedom.

As a prelude to such a reflection we might note the multifaceted character of the term "contingency" itself. By contrast to the necessary and universal, it means that which is changeable and particular; by contrast to the certain and constant, it means that which is uncertain and variable; by contrast to the self-subsistent and causal, it means that which is dependent and effect; by contrast to the expected and regular, it means that which is unexpected and irregular; and by contrast to the safe and reassuring, it means that which is dangerous, unruly, and obdurate in its danger.

Many contemporary theories of politics strive to reduce the threat of contingency in two ways. First, they select one or two dimensions in this loosely associated set of elements and treat them as the defining character of contingency. Second, they implicitly adopt a social ontology that allows them to domesticate the selected elements while defusing the threat of those ignored. Alternative theoretical strategies for the domestication of contingency and the corollary glorification of freedom mirror alternative political strategies competing for hegemony in late modernity.

Heidegger, in "The Age of the World Picture," suggests that the competing ideals of individualism and collectivism, as well as those of negative and positive freedom, arise together in the same time.[4] They share, amid their visible opposition, a contestable picture of freedom. The debate Heidegger alludes to has by now evolved into at least three positions, each with several alternative formulations struggling for hegemony within it. Call them the individualist, collectivist, and communitarian pictures of freedom.

The first two parties concur on a central thesis. Individualists and collectivists agree that we can master a world that is indifferent to us, that we can convert it into a deposit of resources amenable to our use. Mastery is the route to freedom. The individualist thinks that civil society is the road to world mastery, that freedom for the individual involves control over personal destiny, and that control over personal destiny is perfected to the extent that the impersonal structure of civil society succeeds in subjecting nature to human purposes. The collectivist agrees that freedom involves mastery over nature and insists that its highest locus of expression is the collectivity (a state, a people, a class) that establishes a settled plan to achieve it. The individual is a member of a collectivity, and we achieve freedom together through collective mastery.

A third doctrine opposes these two quests for mastery. It sees more than indifference in nature; it discerns a bent or direction in the world to which the self and the community must strive to become attuned.[5] The self becomes more free by becoming more attuned to the deepest purposes inscribed in its community, and the community becomes more free by becoming more attuned to the bent of nature in the self and the world. Freedom involves above all attunement to a higher direction or harmony; it is fulfillment and harmonization. Artists drawing this picture then debate among themselves how many concessions to individual diversity should be made in a realized community.

With respect to the idea of freedom these three positions can be located in the same frame. A matrix, in which the categories across the horizontal axis are mastery and attunement and those on the vertical axis are the individual and the collectivity, creates space for four theories of freedom.[6] The permutations can then expand indefinitely as compromises are forged by theorists of mastery who create a little room for attunement, theorists of individuality who give more credibility to the state as a site of collective freedom, theorists of community who concede a little more to the dictates of mastery, and so on. But these contending theories share certain affinities.

First, across the horizontal axis, the doctrines linking freedom to mastery and attunement share a pattern of insistence: each demands, through a set of presuppositions about self and nature providing the measure against which all other assumptions and standards are to be assessed, that the order of things be susceptible in principle either to human mastery or to a harmonization that approaches the highest human essence. The world, at least in the final instance, must be *for us* in one way or the other. It—including external nature and the human material from which unified selves are constructed—must be either formed for us or plastic enough to be mastered by us.

Ontological narcissism—as we might label views that demand dispensations from within the world to replace the loss of a personal, willful, and powerful God located above it—allows each of the contending parties to domesticate the protean idea of contingency: each of these orientations invokes ontological assumptions that domesticate contingency as the unexpected, the dangerous event, the obdurate condition that resists effective intervention, the inevitable outcome accidental only in its timing, the resistance to detailed design lodged in the human animal and nature. And perhaps each masks the conversion of a world of microcontingencies into a world of global contingency by its insistence that the world itself must be predisposed to us in one way or the other.

Second, along the vertical axis, each position tends to deploy its idealism within the terms of the problematic of sovereignty. Either the state is the highest embodiment of freedom and democracy, or it is the site of constitutional protections that guard space for individual freedom. None of the positions within this frame strives to rethink the problematic of sovereignty itself, probably because each thinks that any effort to do so would take away the essential precondition for democracy in the territorial state.

It is not easy to think outside the frame of these debates, and I do not claim to be ready to do so in any finished or refined way. But it may be important today to try to push against these boundaries. For within the terms of these debates the appreciation of incorrigible or necessary contingency is stifled in thinking about freedom. Freedom becomes restricted to the confines of the sovereign state because only there can the institutionalization of democracy be established. Freedom becomes bound up with mastery or attunement because the world is treated (at least implicitly) as if it must be susceptible to one aspiration or the other: *it* owes that much to *us*, for god's sake. When these bonds of insistence between the contending parties are discerned, we may also be in a position to locate the impulse to serenity inside the phenomenology of life and death summarized earlier. Perhaps a secret plea for secular consolation binds together the contestants in these debates. If God (with a capital letter) is dead (or at least severely wounded), then the World itself must be for us in one way or the other: it *must* be susceptible either to our mastery or to our quest to become attuned to a harmonious direction installed in being. And perhaps that plea, inscribed pervasively in the twin projects of mastery and realization, simultaneously exacerbates dangers and disciplines residing in late modernity and screens out interpretations that might dramatize them more cogently.

The contemporary experience of disruption in individuality and connectedness might encourage some to challenge the frame in which these debates are set. The contemporary condition, brought initially into focus by the engagement between Nietzsche and Heidegger over the sources and implications of modern nihilism, and crystallized by contemporary thinkers such as Foucault and Kundera who reflect on that debate, encourages a rethinking of the modern demand that the world be predisposed to us in either of these ways. Each of these latter thinkers, at least at his best, resists consoling assumptions about the plasticity or providence of the world. Each thinks about freedom while confronting incorrigible discrepancies, resistances, and disjunctions between the world and the most magnificent human designs. Each, demanding less from the world, suggests connections between these modern strategies of freedom and the emergence of dependent uncertainty, generalized resentment, and dangerous systemic contingencies. Each seeks to subdue existential resentment.

Suppose internal and external nature contains, because it is neither designed by a god nor neatly susceptible to organization by human design, elements of stubborn opacity to human knowledge, recalcitrance to human projects, resistance to any model of normal individuality and harmonious community. Suppose these elements of dissonance enter into the unities and concordances established, creating disturbances in the designs we pursue. Each worthy design of the normal self, the common good, and justice, while realizing something crucial to life through its patterns of connectedness and interdependence, encounters resistances that inhibit its transparency, coherence, and responsiveness and impede its harmonization with the other elements of life to which it is bound. Each design engenders new contingencies while subduing old ones. The more perfectionist the demand imposed by any design, the more discipline must be applied to the selves called upon to achieve it.

Some with a low tolerance for ambiguity may hear only discord, resistance, disruption, and strife in these formulations, but it is essential to the idea of freedom I am trying to develop that the element of connectedness, receptivity, interdependence, and belonging be heard too.

In any case, with these suppositions, a revised idea of freedom becomes discernible, at least in rough outline, an idea appreciating that in the self and the world which is opaque to knowledge and resistant to organization while affirming the necessity and desirability of social designs in human life, an idea folding respect for dissonance and contingency into its picture of freedom while insisting that freedom cannot be reduced to a wholesale struggle against any and every social form given to the self or the world in which it resides.

Such a perspective might support a three-pronged effort to relieve discipline and to curb generalized resentment—first, by tracing the deepest well of resentment to the modern quest to eliminate contingency from a world not susceptible to its elimination, second, by attending to that in the self and its world which is defeated or subjugated by contemporary standards of normality and the common good, and third, by relaxing modern dreams of bringing everything under control or into attunement.

Freedom, Heidegger suggests, "is that which conceals in a way that opens to light . . . lets the veil appear as what veils."[7] I interpret the phrase "lets the veil appear as what veils" as standing in opposition to modern enframing—where everything is drawn into a pattern of knowledge and stands in reserve for organized use. It does not mean that we lift the veil created by enframing to expose Being as it is in itself; it does not mean that we find a higher direction in Being that tells us to stop dominating nature in order to enter into some new relation of harmony with it. It means that enframing veils veiling, failing to appreciate the incorrigible discrepancy between the world it reveals and that concealed by its mode of revealing. Every revealing conceals. And a veil must always be in a world neither designed to correspond to our capacities for cognition nor comprised of plastic material perfectly susceptible (even in the final instance) to human organization. The phrase, then, calls us to appreciate the difference between our ideals and the world we draw upon to realize them without purporting to elevate that difference itself to a higher standard or metaknowledge.

One stands in a more free relation to one's own ideals when one affirms that the world might never be exhausted by a single perspective or a constellation of contending perspectives. The world is always richer than the systems through which we comprehend and organize it. Necessity now becomes more particularized, while contingency becomes universalized; contingency becomes invested with necessity because every particularity must create and encounter it.

My Heidegger (there are several) calls upon us to relax the drives to mastery and integration by giving more room to elements in the self and the world that deviate from them. This room becomes more conceivable as we acknowledge that projects that would squeeze contingency out of the world do not correspond to any actual or possible principle in Being. And this enlargement of ontological space identifies new points of unfreedom in organized space.[8] In a way of life defined according to principles of gender duality, for instance, the presumptive rights of "the hermaphrodite" become enhanced after we glimpse ways in which this demand of duality defines and disqualifies a human whose body does not fit into its artificially defined slots of "male" and "female" and whose contingent formations of sexuality do not fit into its conceptions of "masculine" or "feminine" either. A new claim to freedom is introduced here, one that challenges the last refuge of teleology lodged in contemporary theories of the body, one that opens up suggestive possibilities in other domains and for intermediate cases in this domain, one that can make its case in contestation with other standards and restraints operative in the common life.[9]

Thought in this way, the quest for freedom, though it does so obliquely and imperfectly, strives to create more room for difference by calling attention to the contingent, relational character of established identities. It does so not solely by extending tolerance, but, as we shall see in later chapters, by extending a politics of agonistic respect into new corners of life—a politics in which one of the ways of belonging together involves strife and in which one of the democratizing ingredients in strife is the cultivation of care for the ways opponents respond to mysteries of existence. This is an idealism, of course, one that expects to enter into relations of contestation with alternative ideals, one that informs assessments of the counter-idealisms of realists, neorealists, communitarians, and individualists with whom one enters into agonistic dialogue in interpreting actuality, projecting future possibilities, and identifying present dangers.

The most general (and idealistic) idea is to subdue the politics of generalized resentment by moving on two fronts—first, by removing social injustices that exclude a large variety of constituencies from the material and cultural life of the whole and, second, by criticizing modes of existential resentment that intensify social dogmatism with respect to identity, responsibility, and otherness. These two "fronts" are neither separable nor fully harmonious within this vision. They are interdependent in that a politics of freedom cannot make much progress on either without making some on both. They enter into strife in that each can easily become a staging area for infringements upon the other. In the chapters that follow I try to keep one eye on the first front while attending most closely to the second. This more or less reverses the emphasis I have followed in the past.[10]

The thinking that refuses to engage the second front can often be identified through its unwillingness to explore necessary injustices in its own ideals. An unnecessary injustice is an undeserved injury done to some that can be removed within the existing order of things. A systemic injustice is an undeserved injury not removable in the existing order. A necessary injustice is an undeserved injury that cannot be entirely eliminated without the introduction of another injustice. Perspectives on theory and life that do not come to terms with systemic and necessary injustices in their own ideals have, according to the perspective endorsed here, concealed the pool of existential resentment that animates them. Of course, whether and when this is so is always contestable, as is the more general perspective through which the issue is posed.[11] But still, this perspective provides a timely test to pose to oneself in one's most rhapsodic theoretical moments: what injustice may I be concealing in my ideal so that I can dream my dream of a world without injustice?

When thought attends to subterranean modes of resentment that operate below the threshold of explicit formulation, it may become more responsive to differences between human formations and that which deviates from them. It may also treat historical variations in forms of selfhood, normality, and otherness as signs of the element of contrivance and contingency in each historically hegemonic formation, thereby multiplying sites at which the issues of freedom and unfreedom can be posed in late-modern life: the time of late modernity itself (as a system of interdependencies without a collectively organized agent), the state (as a center of collective agency and social discipline), the normalized self (as the center of individual agency and self-discipline), the external other produced by this standard of normality, and that in the self which resists normalization (the internal other). Each of these becomes a potential site of freedom and constraint.

It is impossible to bring each of these sites and its claims into neat alignment with the others. The idea of freedom is thus most fundamentally a political one in which each site of freedom enables and confines, complements and opposes, each of the others. A political theory of freedom now becomes one in which each claim is drawn into engagement with others, in which priorities are contested in a setting where many participants understand in advance that the world is not predisposed to establish perfect alignment among these interdependent and contending elements. Such a reflection authorizes a theory in which the idea of freedom becomes intimately bound up with the idea of politics.

Today, it seems to me that the first and last two sites deserve special attention, partly because the middle two have dominated discourse to this point and partly because these polar sites together manufacture much of the generalized resentment plaguing contemporary politics. To focus the eye of freedom where world-systemic effects escape collective control and where difference resists normalization is to look with new vision into the spiral of demands to improve, correct, aid, control, perfect, treat, test, or deter individuals in the name of self-realization or state rationality. It is also to rethink the perverse relation between the late-modern experience of global contingency and the modern drive to master contingency through the intensified organization of life.

CHAPTER TWO

Global
Political Discourse

Discovery of the Other

In 1492 Columbus sailed the ocean blue. Then he discovered
America. He did not discover a world as it existed in itself; nor
could he have. He discovered a world of otherness, a world of
promise and danger, utopian bliss and barbaric cruelty, innocence
and corruption, simplicity and mystery, all filtered through a late-
medieval culture of perceptions, conceptions, aspirations, faiths,
anxieties, and demands. His discovery was an encounter, an encounter that took the form of clashes between his cultural predispositions and unfamiliar beings—strange words, alien acts, surprising appearances, uncanny responses. For instance, once he
played martial music to welcome heretofore peaceful natives pad-
dling to his ship, and they replied with a hail of arrows.

Columbus's discovery was essentially ambiguous, neither the
recognition of a new world as it was in itself, nor the pure creation
of a world out of nothing (in the manner of one of the strangest gods
ever invented), nor a preliminary map to be filled out gradually and
unproblematically with the collection of more information. The
most compelling discovery Columbus made was that of an enigma,
an enigma that resists straightforward formulation while persistently demanding recognition: the enigma of otherness and knowledge of it, of otherness and the constitution of personal identity, of
otherness and estrangement from it, of otherness and the consolidation of collective identity, of otherness and dependence upon it, of
otherness and the paradoxes of ethical integrity.

The simple word "discovery," then, does not capture the relation between Columbus and the world he encountered. Neither does any other single word in English: words like "invention" and "constitution" give too much impetus to the initiating side; words like "dialogue" and "discourse" give too much to a mutual task of decipherment to promote common understanding; words like "conquest" and "colonization" underplay the effects of the encounter upon the self-identities of the initiating power. All these words, in their common ranges of signification, reflect one or another of the epistemologies of purity; each projects a "regulative ideal" that seems to me not only unattainable but dangerous to invoke *in any simple or unambiguous way*. I will stick with "discovery," though, allowing its internal composition to shift as we proceed.

Columbus's discovery was not only more than a simple discovery (in the sense of finding what was already there); it was also a rediscovery. Christians before him had made similar discoveries, and explorers before him had landed on this continent. It was, moreover, like those before it, an incomplete rediscovery subject to self-erasure. Augustine (and he too was not the first to follow this path) encountered the enigma of otherness when he found it necessary to invent the shallow, egocentric, conceited self of paganism to promote the deep, confessing, interior self of Christianity. He needed this perception of the other to enable creation of the Christian self. Columbus's discovery of the enigma of otherness was both a rediscovery and a partial discovery because, like most of his predecessors and successors, Columbus protected and refined his own cultural identity by concealing the enigma he had begun to encounter. The enigma was subjected to erasure even as it was being experienced. If this is a familiar tactic of western, Christian culture, with roots in the Bible, the church, medieval political thought, and early-modern thinkers, there are also counterpoints to it in these same traditions.

Perhaps the word "discovery," retaining its established suggestions of adventure, newness, encounter with strangeness, untapped riches, the initiation of ownership and entitlements, advance and progress, may now be infused with the idea of irony—an irony crafted from insight into how forgetting, denial, self-conceit, and erasure enter into the very relation between the discoverer and that which he discovers. Columbus discovered America out of the blue in 1492. But this blue now acquires depth beneath its pure, glistening, innocent surface. The surface and the depth, in this discovery out of the blue, now compromise and confound one another.

It is useful to think of the discovery of the new world as the discovery of a world saturated with textuality, not because that world consisted only of words, not because a single author had written it, not because it could be reshaped or reconstituted at will be erasing some words and inscribing others, not because it lacked real things, natural powers, actual bodies, unexpected events, dwellings and modes of power, but because the early explorers, once they decided to establish entitlements over their discoveries, had no recourse but to read what was there as a strange text that did not mesh well with presumptions, concepts, expectations, and demands they brought to their reading. And because there was no neutral place from which they could represent the new world itself apart from the cultural texts that permeated it. And because there was no master code into which they could translate both their codes and the codes of the new world without violence. And because the new world was susceptible to multiple readings, only some of which were immediately available to them. And because the new world provided a pretext that functioned eventually to redefine elements in the world from which they had come. The new world is a text, and it too is compounded from earlier texts. It's text all the way down and all the way to the top. That means there is always more than any particular textualization encompasses, and that signs of this "more" will reside in subordinate dimensions of the particular text itself—in resistances it encounters, unexpected play in the metaphors it finds indispensable, unassimilated shifts in surface significations that reveal them to contain hidden depths.

"International relations," as we know them, were compounded at that time out of this intertext between the old world and the new. This is a world-historical moment in the history of western intertextuality. It also provides a better "model" of how "international relations theory" is constructed, tested, and revised than any official account of the relation between "theory and evidence" can offer today.

Where is the god who promises to transcend the double edge of intertextuality so that one true account can in principle be given of the world? What should be done with or to those who refuse to believe in this god on the contestable grounds that this belief itself embodies conceit, cruelty, and danger? Must those who locate incorrigible contingency, contestability, and intertextuality in the most fundamental objects of inquiry in international relations also be defined as others who lack the "discipline" (the self-control and the support of an academic field) required for the study of international relations? What is the status of this "must"? Does it reflect ontological, epistemological, ethical, political, or security imperatives? Or does it contain a politically potent combination of them? Certainly this disciplinary "must," proposed variously and repeatedly in the late-modern academy, follows a line of time-honored practices in Christianity when it encounters the other who deviates from the faith that grounds the rest of its faith. There may be something to learn by attending to this line of continuity amid discontinuity.

There are, indeed, parallels between sixteenth-century Christian definitions of internal otherness and the range of contemporary orientations to academic otherness among secular social scientists. There have been shifts in the locus of faith, in the degree to which faithfulness is demanded, and in the treatment of the new heretics, but the discursive strategies by which the core elements of faith are protected reflect a certain consistency. Today, too, the academic other is often constituted as the innocent to be converted, the amoralist to be excommunicated, or the indispensable Jew to be enclosed in a ghetto and used occasionally as a counter to consolidate consensus within the canon.

These microstrategies of academic containment, like their world-historical predecessors, reveal how fragile the established structure of faith is, how compelling its maintenance is to the identities of the faithful, how difficult it is to keep the faith by demonstration, reason, and evidence alone, how indispensable a discursive field of contrasts, threats, and accusations is to its internal organization. These strategies disclose, as does their reversal, some elements in the enigma of identity in its relation to the other.

We have here another intertext, filtering old Christian dualities of faith and heresy, purity and sin, monotheism and paganism, conquest and conversion into the structure of secular academic life through the vehicle of the ambiguous "must": "You *must* presuppose truth in calling it into question; you *must* presuppose morality in accusing it of immorality; you *must* presuppose the deep subject in the act of criticizing it; you *must* presuppose the purity of freedom in opposing it. You *must* . . . , or else we *must* define you accordingly!" Again, what type of imperative governs this "must" today? And why should anyone, yesterday or today, refuse to conform to it?

We might learn something pertinent to today about the power of intertextuality and the enigma of otherness by pondering those questions as they emerged during encounters between the old world and the new in the sixteenth century. These can only be indirect insights, contestable insights, insights that contain riddles. That, indeed, may be one of the insights, the one—particularly, perhaps, in international relations theory—hardest to learn, easiest to erase, most difficult to translate into practical precepts of global politics.

The first of these insights can now be given a preliminary statement: to deny the enigma of external otherness—to treat it simply as the innocent, primitive, terrorist, oriental, evil-empire, savage, communist, underdeveloped, or pagan whose intrinsic defects demand that it be conquered or converted—is also to treat radical difference within one's own church or academy as otherness (as amoralism, confusion, evil, or irrationalism) to be neutralized, converted, or defeated. The definitions of the internal and the external other compound each other, and both eventually seep into the definition given to the other within the interior of the self.

The Enigma of Otherness

Tzvetan Todorov, in *The Conquest of America*, explores the enigma of otherness as it emerges in those early encounters of the old with the new world.[1] Todorov does not try to transcend the enigma by enclosing the relations conquistadors and priests established with the Aztecs inside a universal discourse. He does not invoke the discourse of man, reason, rights, freedom, and truth in their universality to transcend simultaneously the parochial perspectives of the discoverers and those of the discovered. That would subject a previously hegemonic set of discourses—the discourses of the old world—to another, later set that evolved out of them. For the early discoverers themselves thought they brought a universal truth to bear on parochial, primitive, savage, pagan prejudices and superstitions.

Nor does Todorov try, at least persistently or single-mindedly, to transcend the early code of the west by "entering into" the internal perspective of the discovered peoples. For that strategy provides a mirror image of the first one. It supposes that if we cannot fashion a pure universalism (a pure rationalism or a pure empiricism) uncontaminated by the particular culture in which we are located, we must be able to fashion a pure contextualism (a pure understanding, a pure interpretation) that draws us into the perspective of the other as it was prior to western discovery of it. These two familiar and contending modalities also complement each other. Each is governed by a quest for purity of understanding, either as pure particularity or as pure universality; each is driven by the impulse to transparency that impels its competitor. And the common quest for purity erases (while leaving marks and smudges behind) the very enigma of otherness it began to render legible. Universalism subjugates the particularity of the other to its own particular code with universalist pretensions; and internal contextualism subjugates the particularity of the other to the myth of universal transparency through intellectual sympathy emanating from bearers of a superior culture.

Those critics of Todorov, then, who chastise him for not examining the conquest of the Aztecs from the vantage point of the conquered people do not see that he already refuses the grounds upon which their objections rest. Indeed, as we shall see, versions of both the universalist and the particularist strategies were pursued in the early encounters between the old world and the new. These two modalities can support complementary strategies of domination, the first supporting conquest of the other in the name of the universal superiority of its own identity and the second neutralizing resistance to colonization by understanding the customs of the other well enough to launch a campaign of conversion.

Since Todorov contests the sufficiency and political implications of these two codes of inquiry, since he suggests how they function together in the encounters he charts, he himself adopts neither the universalist nor the contextualist code unambiguously. Yet, since he cannot avoid making use of both codes partially and provisionally, his text functions best if it adopts an ironic and problematizing stance to its own mode of inquiry. In place of trying to understand the other (the Aztecs) within a universal code or as they understood themselves, he explores how fixed patterns of encounter available to the western invaders forced some priests into moments of self-doubt, confusion, and creative thinking as they pursued their encounters with the other. He treats western texts of conquest and conversion—the two dominant patterns consistent with the cultural universalism of the west—as if they were the decipherable other to the late-modern west, both because similar texts are still inscribed in us today and because other aspects of these early texts possess the power to disturb us about the similarities. That is, these texts, situated on a cusp between the late-medieval age and the early-modern age, remain close enough to use for discomfort, a discomfort that foments thought about orientations to otherness in the present.

Todorov treats Aztec culture, on the other hand, mostly as if it were an undecipherable, resistant, and inexhaustible text upon which representatives of the west reinscribed their own stories and in which, when pushed to the limits of their own cultural resources, they encountered the enigma of otherness in the other and themselves.

Todorov introduces a zone of intertextuality between late-medieval Christianity and late-modern secular internationality in order to open the present to an interrogation of itself and its past. Christianity posits a *single* god and enjoins a *universalist* religion applicable to human beings *equally*. It thus stands permanently above any religion positing multiple gods and claiming the allegiance of a select people. The medieval Christian groundwork creates its external others and constitutes them as pagans, savages, primitives, innocents, or barbarians. Once this basic orientation is secure, two stances toward otherness might contend for primacy within it. It might be deemed necessary to conquer or destroy those who worship other gods—and who engage in practices such as sacrifice, polygamy, cannibalism, and sodomy alien to Christian doctrine—on the gounds that they are a fallen people who defile god and contaminate the purity sought by Christians. Or it might be thought obligatory to convert them because they too have souls and they too can come to acknowledge Christian faith. Columbus, Cortez, and the priest, Ginés de Sepúlveda embody, in different ways, the first alternative. Bartolomé de Las Casas, in his early writings, joins other priests in pressing the second. In general, conquistadors press the first claim, while certain priests reactively seek to install the second. It is difficult to wander far outside this field of debate (as it is today to wander outside the realist/idealist debate in international relations theory), because the conjunction of universalism, singularity, and equality clamps down upon any Christian effort to do so.

The premises of singularity and universality press against affirming a plurality of gods appropriate to the other in the name of cultural pluralism, while the premise of human equality before the Christian god makes it sinful to practice benign neglect or indifference toward pagan beliefs and practices. If innocent, these others must be converted; if hopelessly corrupted, they must be conquered or eliminated so that the corruption will not spread.[2] Perhaps tolerance can be added to the list of possible stances upon this field, but it must be, as tolerance usually is, a circumscribed and tactical tolerance. Tolerance, in this context, becomes forbearance toward cultural practices thought to be intrinsically wrong or inferior, but also thought to contain a glimmer of truth that might evolve, with proper prodding, into realization of Christian truth. Tolerance emerges as a detour on the way to conversion; it takes the form of Christian charity bestowed upon the other because the Christian, too, is a sinner. For that reason it is not to be equated with the two other modalities (many would prefer even this tolerance if these three provided the only universe of alternatives), but it may not represent the highest human possibility either.

If conquest and conversion are the two authorized responses to otherness, neither engages the enigma of otherness. Both operate as contending and complementary strategies that enable a superior people to maintain its self-assurance by bringing an inferior people under its domination or tutelage. These two modes function together as premises and signs of superiority; each supports the other in the effort to erase the threat that difference presents to the surety of self-identity.

But conversion contains an interior dialectic that can push it to the edge of this field of discourse. Las Casas and Bernadino de Sahagún represent two different exemplars of this possibility. Las Casas seeks to learn more about the Aztecs to convert them, but this deep engagement throws his initial confidence of superiority into doubt. For instance, Christians charge pagans with the sins of idolatry and human sacrifice, but Las Casas eventually concludes that the "idols" stand for a principle of divinity in a manner that draws them closer to Christian representations of Christ and Mary. And while the Aztecs practice sacrifice, it also occurs in the Old Testament, and even Jesus was once sacrificed so that we could be saved. The lines of differentiation now become blurred and temporalized. Las Casas slides from a simple model of Christian conversion to a distributive model of multiple routes to the experience of divinity, all heading in the same vague direction. Both Christians and pagans need to progress further along this uncharted path.

But this new posture is precarious and ambiguous. Las Casas clears a little more potential space for the other to be in its difference by losing a clear voice for himself as a bearer of Christian conscience. Upon this shift in perspective, his voice is no longer heard in Spain. The logic by which he falls into silence while continuing to write and speak may disclose an element within the enigma of otherness: when one remains within the established field of identity and difference, one readily becomes a bearer of strategies to protect identity through devaluation of the other; but if one transcends the domestic field of identities through which the other is constituted, one loses the identity and standing needed to communicate with those one sought to inform. Identity and difference are bound together. It may be impossible to reconstitute the relation to the second without confounding the experience of the first. And that may help to explain the tenacity of resistance to reconstituting the tenor of these relations.

Sahagún plows further into the culture of the other than Las Casas (but not as far as those priests who simply become "renegades"). His voluminous *Historia general de Nueva España* is an encyclopedia of Aztec culture. He tries to give voice to the other without losing his own identity as a Christian. But no appropriate vocabulary is available to him. The key terms embody judgments that affirm Christian ontology, reflect Aztec ontology, or, at the edge of discursive possibility, give birth to some perspective inside neither.

Sahagún must negotiate this field of possibilities and limitations in an effort to respect the identity of the other without forsaking his own identity as a Christian. So sometimes he practices a strategy of naming through alternation, using the term "god" in one sentence and "idol" in another; sometimes he adopts (or invents) a behavioral language of estrangement, describing acts of sacrifice in behavioral terms that neutralize cultural judgment at the cost of betraying alienation from the interpretive systems available in either culture. But these microtextual strategies are contained within an architectural organization that locates god at the top and stones at the bottom of the cosmological hierarchy. Sahagún concludes that Christianity is a superior religion but that the attempt to impose it upon the Aztecs has only destroyed one internally coherent system without enabling the emergence of another. His text becomes an inventory of the cultural devastation created by Spanish policies of conquest and conversion. But this inventory, by the very terms of its articulation, becomes one that his contemporaries in Spain can find reasons to avoid or condemn. By 1577 Philip II has cut off all of Sahagún's funding and forbidden the circulation of his texts. In shifting from the role of adviser to the prince to that of ambiguous articulator of the voice of the other to his own people, Sahagún loses the only audience available to him.

Sahagún and Las Casas invent new voices from which dialogue might ensue, but each loses the ground inside his own culture upon which such a dialogue might proceed.

While Las Casas and Sahagún help to bring out the enigma of otherness, there are differences between their circumstances and ours that provide us with openings unavailable to them. First, we have access to the history they helped to create. Second, we reside in a setting where the ontological closure of Christian culture, partly through the self-critical history inaugurated by thinkers like Las Casas and Sahagún, has been fractured, and where it is now possible to question some of the parameters of the secular culture Christianity helped to spawn. It is perhaps more possible today to expose and combat practices of identity and difference that simultaneously conquer, convert, or marginalize the external other and neutralize internal others who interrogate them. Moreover, we live in a time of recognizable *global* danger that (while it presses in exactly the opposite direction too) provides cultural impetus to rethink the strategies of identity and difference through which contemporary states define and cope with otherness.

Identity through Difference

Todorov concludes his own foray into the issue of otherness with a gesture aimed at the present: "We want equality without its compelling to accept identity, but also difference without its degenerating into superiority/inferiority."[3] The aura shines brightly here, but what it illuminates is not yet clear.

It is not immediately pertinent to question Todorov on the material means by which this goal could be advanced. Before that question can be raised, the goal itself must be made more credible as an alternative worthy of materialization. At this crucial level of intellectual imagination Todorov leaves something to be desired. What would be the status of an identity that established such a relation to other, foreign identities? Would this mean a culture without governing identities for the individual and the collectivity? What, then, could provide the pull for equality? What would provide the basis from which difference could be identified even before it was stripped of its terms of superiority/inferiority? What is "difference" stripped of these terms? Todorov lapses into silence here, perhaps because he thinks that what "we want" is too paradoxical actually to pursue or because he thinks he has reached the point within our culture that Las Casas and Sahagún reached in theirs, the point where the attempt to elaborate a new idea sounds inside the culture either like noise or like collaboration with the enemy.

We (the "we" here is an invitation) might pursue these issues by considering how an identity contains at least two dimensions. First, it might be tightly or loosely demarcated in the dimension of its breadth. Thus a Christian culture might restrict itself to Catholicism, or extend itself to include Protestantism, or extend itself further to include the Judeo-Christian tradition, or extend itself in another way to incorporate a secular humanism with recognizable links to a Judeo-Christian legacy.

An identity, second, can also vary along the dimension of depth. An identity might have ontological depth because it construes itself as the bearer of an intrinsic truth that it knows to be true, or it might have faith in its truth and look forward to a day when the faith will be translated into knowledge, or it might conclude that it must always be founded on a contestable faith in its truth, or it might conclude that it is crucial to its individual and collective bearers but historically contingent in its formation and inherently relational in its form—contingent not because it alone in the world of identities has no ground but because it treats as true the proposition that no identity reflects being as such; no identity is the true identity because every identity is particular, constructed, and relational.

Now, this last position accepts the indispensability of identity and lives within the medium of identity while refusing (while struggling vigorously to refuse) to live its own identity as intrinsic truth.[4] Its bearers may acknowledge a drive within themselves and their culture to naturalize the identity given to them, a drive discernible in the history of their previous relationships to external, internal, and interior differences. But they also struggle to ambiguate or overcome this drive because they think it is ungrounded in any truth they can prove and because they find it ethically compelling to revise their relation to difference in the absence of such a proof.

Such a shift in orientation to individual and collective identity would be significant, but it does not lack precursors and premonitions within western culture. It is far enough away from modern understandings to be distinctive but close enough to currents with-in modern culture prefigured by Las Casas and Sahagún to be a development of that culture. I am tempted to say it stands in that ambiguous space between internal possibility and external chal-lenge best described as "postmodern," but I am also wary of this temptation because of the numerous positions parading under that label today. Let me call it, provisionally then, my postmodernism.

My postmodernism assumes an ironic stance toward what it is and is not even when it affirms itself in its identity. And this changes both the experience of identity and its *possible* range of relationships with other identities. We will consider such possibili-ties in Chapter 6. But perhaps it is pertinent now to indicate how the introduction of a new alternative on the field of discourse can affect the self-understandings of the other candidates on that field, how it enables new terms of comparison and debate that place new pressures upon the established field of actualities and possibilities.

The basic strategy here is well articulated by Nietzsche: "Even the *thought of a possibility* can shake and transform us; it is not merely sensations or particular expectations that do that! Note how ef-fective the *possibility* of eternal damnation was!"[5] One might inter-pret Nietzsche's saying as follows. The possibility of eternal dam-nation shook and transformed thought once it was elaborated. For this particular possibility, once it is known even as a possibility, can by the pressure of its own weight become transmuted into faith. "I had better believe this, for if it is true and I don't, the penalty is infinitely high." And once this thought becomes fixed in belief, thought about what "eternal salvation" or "heaven" could mean becomes effectively immunized against self-critical reflection. Sup-pose, for instance, the promise of eternal life were instead jux-taposed to the threat of eternal oblivion. That would not be quite *so* threatening, and thus some might be encouraged to ponder more carefully and critically just what the eternal life of a soul could mean. Pondering that, one might even conclude that the difference between eternal oblivion and eternal life is not that great. What would freedom be like, for instance, where there is no temporal dimension to the experience of choice? The essence of the Christian promise might have been thrown into doubt a few centuries earlier had the possibility of eternal damnation remained unstated. And the range of relationships established to "pagans" in the sixteenth century might have been broadened had that possibility not already installed itself in faith so effectively.

The power of the possibility of damnation was that it stilled a process of critical exploration before it could gather momentum. The power of the articulation of an alternative orientation to self-identity might be that it opens up inquiry into the restricted range of tolerance within which late-modern discourse about identity and difference proceeds. Todorov suggests such a thought without pursuing it.

A lived conception of identity that takes itself to be both historically contingent and inherently relational in its definition might create possibilities for the strife and interdependence of identity\difference exceeding the models of conquest, conversion, community, and tolerance. Such a conception might stand as far from late-modern conceptions of identity and sovereignty (that is, identity at the level of the state) as the thought of Las Casas about divinity did from sixteenth-century Christianity—that is, outside the usual range of discussion, but not so far as to be incomprehensible. Exploration in this direction, as far as I can see, is the best way to proceed in pursuit of Todorov's aspiration even to *imagine* a world in which a given field of identities might hope to recognize differences without being *internally* compelled to define some of them as forms of otherness to be conquered, assimilated, or defiled. Exploration in this direction might, for example, add the ideal of agonistic respect to the possible set of relations that competing identities can establish to one another. So Todorov establishes a thought to be pursued.

If one thinks, to put the point starkly, that conflicts of *identity* sometimes create and often inflame international conflicts of *interest*, then exploration of a modified way of living identity might be salutary. It seems to me that this is approximately what a group of contemporary thinkers presenting themselves under the rubrics of "postmodernism" and "poststructuralism" are up to. But many of their contemporaries have as much difficulty coming to terms with them as sixteenth-century Spaniards did coming to terms with Las Casas and Sahagún. "Postmodernists" have trouble breaking the molds in which contemporary thought is set, and their critics in contemporary social science have difficulty comprehending what it is they are saying. This is so in part because the identity of each party as a scholar or social scientist is touched by the terms of this debate. The example of the sixteenth-century Christian production of internal others through engagement with the externality of the Aztecs remains pertinent to this contemporary context.

Identity in International Relations Theory

How does contemporary international relations theory fare when it comes to the issue of identity and the enigma of otherness? It does not bring late-medieval perceptions, conceptions, expectations, and assumptions to unfamiliar terrain. It is thoroughly modern in its engagements with the unfamiliar. Perhaps the best way to characterize discourse in this domain, at least in the dominant modes represented by realist and neorealist theory, is to say that it dissolves issues of identity and difference into its categories of theory, evidence, rationality, sovereignty, and utility.

Kenneth Waltz, a leading neorealist, characterizes theory "as such" in the following way:

> The infinite materials of any realm can be organized in endlessly different ways. A theory indicates that some factors are more important than others and specifies relations among them. In reality, everything is related to everything else, and one domain cannot be separated from others. Theory isolates one realm from all others in order to deal with it intellectually. To isolate a realm is a precondition to developing a theory that will explain what goes on within it. If the precondition cannot be met, and that of course is a possibility, then the construction of theory for the matters at hand is impossible. The question, as ever with theories, is not whether the isolation of a realm is realistic, but whether it is useful. And usefulness is judged by the explanatory and predictive powers of the theory that may be fashioned.[6]

A promising beginning. For Waltz insists that reality always exceeds the terms of any theory. Reality is thus not a fixed set of objects awaiting the correct set of conceptualizations to represent them perspicuously, but something that depends upon institutional/theoretical organization to establish its fixity and definition. "The infinite materials . . . can be organized in *endlessly different ways.*" Nietzsche and Derrida immediately come to mind at this juncture, though Waltz forgets to cite them. Consider Nietzsche, for instance, on the relation of "nature" to "living" in the context of Waltz's distinction/interdependence between "reality" and "theory": "Think of a being like Nature, immoderately wasteful, immoderately indifferent, devoid of intentions and considerateness . . . , fruitful and desolate and uncertain at the same time. . . . Living—isn't it precisely a wishing to be different from this Nature? Doesn't living mean evaluating, preferring, being unjust, being limited, wanting to be different?"[7]

It is because theory is indispensable to living and yet never exhaustive of what it organizes that Nietzsche develops strategies to enable discourses, theories, identities, conceptions of goodness and utility to disturb, unsettle, and disrupt the closures toward which they tend. The stolid, steady realist, of course, wants to treat his categories as if they mirrored reality. He is, in his heart of hearts, a philosophical idealist who insists that the structure of the world is predisposed to synchronize with the most fundamental metaphors that flow out of him. "While rapturously pretending to read the canon of your law out of nature, you actually want the opposite—you strange play-actors and self-deceivers! Your pride wants to dictate your morality, your ideal, to nature (even to nature!) . . . ; you want to remake all existence to mirror your own existence."[8] But Waltz, in this first gesture, repudiates the transcendental egoism of epistemic realism.

Derrida enters this alien territory opened up by Nietzsche and Waltz through a slightly different trail. He refuses to characterize that which exceeds a theory or a discourse. For that would be to conceptualize what can only have effects in discourse rather than be mirrored by it. Instead, he strives through "deconstruction" to show how within the rich and dense texture of any theory/discourse there are internal possibilities that disrupt and defer indefinitely its claim to sufficiency or closure. Within the edifice of any theory/text/discourse is the play of *différance*. It glimmers, for example, when one probes the fecundity of metaphors that are both indispensable to a theory and uncontainable within the terms of the theory.[9] That is why Derrida (and other "postmodernists") give special priority to the syntactical, discursive dimension of theories and why they oppose stolid realists who devalue that dimension in perpetual pursuit of a perspicuous language to mirror the world as it is in itself, prior to any discursive organization: "This does not mean that the *différance* that produces differences is somehow before them, in a simple and unmodified—in-different—present. *Différance* is thus the non-full, non-simple, structured and differentiating origin of differences." And again: "Rather *différance* maintains *our* relationship with that which we necessarily misconstrue, and which exceeds the alternative of presence and absence."[10]

But Waltz does not consider the Nietzschean or Derridean responses to the fugitive gap he himself identifies between "theory" and "reality." In fact, when confronted with a critique by Richard

Ashley that draws upon these themes (without, though, showing how Waltz explicitly sets the table upon which they come into play), Waltz responds with a gesture of dismissal. He equates Ashley's critique with that of a critical theory that seeks to replace a "problem solving approach" with a "system transforming approach." "Ashley and Cox would transcend the world as it is; meanwhile we have to live in it."[11]

Has Waltz forgotten the first gesture in his portrayal of theory, the acknowledgment that theory never exhausts "reality"? Not quite. Instead he has allowed a second gesture in the same paragraph to assume complete hegemony. He uses it to erase any operational significance from the first. The second gesture: "The question, *as ever with theories*, is not whether the isolation . . . is realistic, but *whether it is useful*."

Waltz buries the Nietzschean/Derridean element of play in the ground of the useful, in that which is useful to system maintenance and to the interests of key parties within it. Once the useful has been delineated, the domain of "problem-solving" becomes fixed through the categories of sovereignty, rationality, anarchy, and utility that organize both the theorists' representation of international relations and the major actors' own interpretation of those relations. If Nietzsche periodically disrupts the closure of the useful to probe how it constitutes its "useless," Waltz accepts the closure of the useful so that the problems to be solved can be reduced to those recognized within its domain. His second gesture represses density in the syntax of discourse and the enigma of otherness in one movement. Waltz becomes the Sepúlveda of his time, treating our categories as *the* categories to impose upon whatever comes before them. For Waltz, the undeniable basis from which all reflection proceeds and to which it returns is not the truth of the Christian god, but a conception of theory, which allows only the criteria of "explanatory and predictive power" as they are encountered within the prior frame of "the useful" to govern theory construction and reconstruction.

What are the implications of that erasure in this time? I will delay until the final chapter exploring its implications for the relations a state establishes to that which exceeds or is repressed by the sovereignty of sovereignty. Here we can consider its implications for the constitution of the internal academic other—the other whose mode of international relations theory exceeds neorealist standards of reality and utility.

In a recent essay, Robert Keohane, perhaps the most liberal

among leading theorists of neorealism, considers the relation between neorealism in international relations and feminist theory.
"Feminist standpoint theory," Keohane concludes, can inform and
tame the power-laden character of masculinist neorealism because
"from her vantage-point at the periphery, the feminist theorist
offers a critique of theories constructed by men who put themselves
in the position of policy makers." Feminist standpoint theorists—
representing one type of feminism—can moderate the tendency of
the neorealist to identify with the perspective of powerholders.
"The feminist standpoint conception as I use it does not imply that
feminist perspectives are necessarily superior in an absolute sense
to traditional views—only that they contain valid insights into the
complex realities of world politics." This perspective can add another dimension to the analysis of power, by supplementing the
concept of power as control with a concept of power as the ability to
act in concert for shared ends. In the most general terms it can
qualify and attenuate the masculine-neorealist "penchant for absolute and dichotomous categories."[12]

Unfortunately, Keohane forgets to constrain this penchant a few
paragraphs later when he turns to "postmodern feminism." "It
seems to me that this postmodernist project is a dead-end in the
study of international relations—and that it would be disastrous for
feminist international relations theory to pursue this path."[13] Let
us forgo (almost) the temptation to review the roles reserved for
women in this triangle of IR theorists, where the sovereign male
receives assistance from the good helpmate and both together fend
off the postmodern tramp. But how does Keohane constitute this
internal other—this mode of theorizing that both diverges most
dramatically from his own and is the most disastrous for the field?

Nowhere is a text by a postmodern theorist, feminist or otherwise, cited. This epistemic realist, who devalues the syntactical
dimension of theory and seeks to perceive the object as it is in itself,
views postmodernism only through the eyes of standpoint femi-
nists who declare themselves to be its opponents:

> As Mary E. Hawkesworth puts it, 'post modernist insights counsel
> that Truth be abandoned because it is hegemonic and hence, de-
> structive illusion.' . . .
>
> I fear that many feminist theorists . . . may follow the currently fash-
> ionable path of fragmenting epistemology, denying the possibility of
> social science. But I think this would be an intellectual and moral dis-

aster. As Linda Alcoff points out, 'post structuralist critiques of subjectivity . . . threaten . . . to wipe out feminism itself.'[14]

Of course I am aware that social knowledge is always value laden, and that objectivity is an aspiration rather than an accomplishment. But I object to the notion that because social science cannot attain any perfectly reliable knowledge, it is justified for students of society to 'obliterate the validity of reality.' [The footnote says, "I owe this comment to Joan Tronto, who made it in the course of a critique of post-modern . . . thinking."][15]

I concur with Keohane in two respects. First, if postmodernism embodied the self-closure he attributes to it, it would be "disastrous" in any area of theory. Second, the tendency among many self-described postmodernists to defer theory construction forever because every theory can be deconstructed is lamentable. I will consider the first issue now and take up the second later, when we have an actual example to respond to.

Note what thesis has been attributed to the adversary in this strategy of condemnation through refraction. For this constitution of the internal other strips it of the thematic most distinctive of its practitioners. Keohane and his allies take the play of *différance* away from the very postmodernists who press this theme most vigorously. And they do so in a way that has become all too familiar. They first reduce the alternatives to a clean dichotomy: either you appraise a theory by comparing it (following the right method) to the independent reality it seeks to represent, or you focus on the grammar of discursive practices of representation and deny that discourse can encounter any resistances, surprises, or "effects" through this means that upset its preordained patterns. Either/or rears its ugly, masculinist head again.

While Keohane's neorealism is lodged in the stolid epistemology of representation, whereby a theory seeks to mirror the fixed reality that precedes representation of it, it constitutes postmodernism as the inverse of itself—as a form of textual idealism which proceeds as if there were only a vacuum outside the text. Keohane deprives postmodern thought of its most distinctive thematic by constituting it as a very simple idealism. This, apparently, is the debate he wants: "we" believe that theory represents an independent reality, and "they" believe that there is no reality. Given that choice, anyone would choose Keohane's side; for here, at least, a certain minimal criticism of an established theory is possible.

But, of course, this requires a systematic misreading of postmodern slogans such as "there is nothing outside the text" and "where the word breaks off no thing may be,"[16] depriving them of exactly the ambiguity they seek to convey. For the "is nothing" and the "no thing may be" in those statements signify, first, that reality can be given no definition outside a discourse/theory/text and, second, that "the nothing" (Heidegger) functions inside the text to indicate that which exceeds the text *but can be given no fixed form outside some sort of textualization.* First, there is nothing (no fixed thing drawn into a network of identities and differences) outside the text. Second, there *is* the abyss and the abundance of "the nothing" that exceeds the text and leaves its mark within it. Derrida's *"différance"* conveys this crucial ambiguity well, but so do Heidegger's "earth/ world" and "truth/untruth" relations, Foucault's "man and his doubles" and the "fecundity of language," Nietzsche's "nature" in relation to thought and "life" in relation to identity, Kristeva's "desire and language," and so on.

There is no "postmodern" perspective, to my knowledge at least, that fails to invoke some version of this thematic. Indeed, the charge of postmodernism is that realist and neorealist theorists either do not attend to this ambiguity in their own discourses (Keohane) or immediately suppress recognition of it by a second gesture (Waltz).

Neorealism, in suppressing the play of ambiguity in its own discursive practice, disables itself from recognizing the overt thematization of ambiguity in the internal other it constitutes. It allows its univocal categories of "reality," "nothing," "theory," and so on to fend off the other rather than struggling to allow the other to confound the self-certainty it seeks to attach to those categories.

This tendency, so bluntly displayed in the two texts under examination, enables established theorists of international relations to label (usually younger) "postmodern" theorists confused, naive, methodologically sloppy, solipsistic, relativistic, irresponsible, and so on. It enables them to constitute the academic adversary as the other.

These strategies of textual closure cannot fail to have implications for the constitution of the external other as well as the internal other. On the other hand, the fact that representatives of neorealism now feel impelled to bestow these definitions upon the internal other means that they have opened themselves to issues about the grammar of discourse previously buried under debates over the right method to represent the object most perspicuously. Keohane, as a key respondent in this engagement, has opened up a debate that will be more difficult to evade in the future (unless, of course, war breaks out, and so on). In this double sense, Keohane is the Columbus of modernity discovering the postmodern.[17] But what about "postmodern international relations theorists"? How do and can they respond to the enigma of otherness?

Typically, or so it seems to me, they adopt a strategy with respect to contemporary discourse very close to the one Todorov adopts with respect to the sixteenth-century Spanish conquerors. They strive to loosen and problematize the categories through which prevailing discourses in their own culture constitute and organize the other. They follow trails cleared for them centuries ago by Las Casas and Sahagún. Thus Michael Shapiro, in a recent essay on IR theory, says that "to employ a textualizing approach . . . is not to . . . reduce social phenomena to various manifestations of language. Rather . . . , it seeks to . . . discern the representational practices that construct the 'world' of persons, places and modes of conduct and to inquire into the network of social practices that give particular modes of representation their standing."[18]

Let us set aside, for a moment, the question of the status of Shapiro's own representations of those representational practices, an issue lodged within the words "discern" and "inquire into" in the second sentence. Shapiro explores the "sports/war intertext" in America whereby sports discourse helps to constitute the objects and legitimize the presumptions of military practice and military practice helps to do the same for sports. An intertext is formed that enables each domain to draw sustenance from the self-presentations/legitimations of the other, protecting each domain from any need for explicit, independent modes of ethical justification that some academics look for in "prescriptive" discourse. Shapiro loosens the normative grip of established practices by exploring the implicit intertextualizations that help to specify and solidify them.

So far so good. But it is also at this latter level, first, that an embryonic set of internal debates begins to emerge *within* postmodern perspectives on international relations and, second, that the most severe objections are posed by mainstream theorists of international relations. A recent essay by Ashley provides a starting point for thinking about these issues.

The issues are twofold. What risks and promises accompany a "poststructuralist" (as Ashley describes himself) refusal to construct general theories of international relations? And what is the epistemic status of any thematization offered by any post-something-or-other?

With respect to the aspiration to construct counter-theories of international relations Ashley says the following: "Poststructuralism cannot claim to offer an alternative position or perspective, because there is no alternative ground upon which it might be established. By the same token . . . , it cannot refuse theory and embrace history. . . . What poststructuralism can do is invert the hierarchy." And, in the same vein: "The task of poststructuralist social theory is not to impose a general interpretation, a paradigm of the sovereignty of man, as a guide to the transformation of life on a global scale. In contrast to modern social theory, poststructuralism eschews grand designs, transcendental grounds or universal projects of humankind."[19]

Several self-restrictions are lumped together in these statements. These self-restrictions are then generalized to a whole constellation of practitioners designated as poststructuralists. Thus, poststructuralist theory does not "impose" a general interpretation; it does not offer "a guide" to the "transformation" of life "on a global scale." The restriction on seeking "transcendental grounds" for any theory is joined to a restriction on "universal projects," and these two injunctions are joined to another against the articulation of "grand designs." With this set of interwoven self-restrictions Ashley may have reduced "poststructuralism" to one perpetual assignment to "invert the hierarchies" maintained in other theories. One might call this a recipe for theoretical postponism. It links the inability to establish secure epistemic grounds for a theory with an obligation to defer infinitely the construction of general theories of global politics. And it does so at a time when the greatest dangers and contingencies in the world are global in character.

I want to resist the binary oppositions suggested by this recipe of self-restriction. One might seek, not to impose one reading on the field of discourse, but to elaborate a general reading that can contend with others by broadening the established terms of debates; not to create a transformation of international life grounded in a universal project, but to contribute to a general perspective that might support reconstitution of aspects of international life; not to root a theory in a transcendental ground, but to problematize the grounding any theory presupposes while it works out the implications of a particular set of themes; not merely to invert hierarchies in other theories (a useful task), but to construct alternative hierarchies that support modifications in relations between identity and difference.

Perhaps it is helpful here to distinguish dimensions of a theory of global politics in terms of its relation to totalization, constructivism, and generality. A total theory reaches, or aspires to reach, all the way down. It purports, either in its overt self-representation or in the narrative structure that governs its presentation, to be itself a truth that knows itself to be true in its most basic fundamentals, or to be a theory that contains protocols capable of establishing in principle its truth or falsity. A nontotalist theory adopts a more problematic orientation to its own ground.

A constructive theory refuses to confine its task to the deconstruction of the totalitarian moment in established theories. If it pursues genealogy/deconstruction, it combines these critical modalities with the aspiration to interpret specific or general features of global politics; it treats constructive and deconstructive modalities as indispensable elements bound in a relation of dependence and conflict in its practice.

A general theory covers a broad terrain of life. It covers more territory than local or regional theories, though it may grow out of these or even represent a loose network of such theories.

Foucault offers rudiments of a constructive general theory, I think, when he writes about "disciplinary society" and when he speaks of a new subjectivity and the cultivation of care for difference through strategies of critical detachment from the identities that constitute us. But he does not advance a total theory; or at least he does not, as we shall see in a moment, offer a transcendental/total theory of the sort targeted by Ashley's polemic.

My own preliminary exploration of an alternative practice of identity and difference in the previous section also moves in the direction of a general theory, proposing a reconstitution of subterranean elements governing a range of contemporary theories. It is on the way to constructive general theory. And it must stand, fall, or languish in competition with established theories, not only through its ability to expose how they might subvert themselves or how they contribute—from its vantage point—to modes of discipline or danger they explicitly eschew, but also through its ability to defend its affirmative constructions. In this case, it must show how its constructions open up new possibilities in the play of identity and difference and then make a case for the value of this endeavor. It aspires to disturb the sense of necessity that accompanies the established terms of debate in this domain, to weaken the privilege of established partners by contesting common assumptions they seldom call upon one another to defend, and to present an alternative way to read dangers, obstructions, and possibilities residing in the present.

Such considerations, I suggest, stood in the background of Foucault's refusal to label himself a "deconstructionist," even while he practiced its art on occasion. I would like to identify myself with this stance by asserting that there is nothing in the imperatives of a "poststructuralist" or "postmodern" problematic that requires perpetual postponism at the level of theory construction and contestation.

I am uncertain just how great the divergence is between the position I have sketched and one Ashley (or Shapiro) might endorse. Perhaps I have treated Ashley as a straw figure in the interests of making a point. At any rate, I advance constructivism and generality in theory not as the exclusive task of critical thought, but as a project to pursue while attending to rhetorical figures, narrative structure, self-subversive discourse, intertextualities, and a variety of other mechanisms through which modernist and postmodern discourses implicitly foster closure in the terms of political debate.

I think the divergence between Ashley and me on the second issue mentioned above (the epistemic status of postmodernist assertions) is even less, though it does deserve elaboration. What, critics of postmodernism tirelessly ask, is the relationship between the utterances of postmodernism and the ontotheological doctrine of truth (or subjectivity or reason or the primacy of a particular method or a transcendental ethic or an ideal of community) it purports to repudiate? Must it not presuppose with one gesture what it denies with another? We can discern how this question/command typically proceeds by reference again to Ashley's text. For after exposing and criticizing logocentrism—the demand that there be one "pure and originary presence" upon which all discursive claims in principle are grounded—Ashley reverses the usual pattern of "logocentrism" in a way that seems to reinvoke the logic of the position repudiated.

He says: "What is noteworthy about this logocentric disposition is that it imposes upon modern theory and practice a *blindness* with respect to the *inescapable historicity* of subjects, objects and modes of conduct."[20] So although Ashley denies the truth of pure presence in any form, he then seems to affirm the truth of essential historicity, essential opacity in identity, the insufficiency of the rules of reason in discourse, a permanent tension between human projects and the world in which they are enacted. And this is where the modernist grabs his "must" and issues an accusation, an accusation designed to delegitimize the adversary and to pull stray sheep back into the medium of truth.

This last charge—this charge that lasts because the modernist perpetually asserts it *as if* each time were at once the first and the last time it will be needed to refute the opponent—itself contains two components.

There is, first, the context of political assumptions in which the question is posed. The postmodernist contends, in a way that overtly presents the contention as a contestable supposition, that we live in a time when a variety of factors press thought into a relatively confined and closed field of discourse. The persistent drive to personal and collective identity, the way in which a common code of discourse tends to condense and normalize difference, the way in which the ontotheological tradition is encoded in the grammar and terms of language, the intensification of interdependence and the demands of coordination in the late-modern world— all of these elements coalesce to promote closure in discourse, a closure not in which one theory gains hegemony, but in which complementary theories compete with each other in ways that tend to conceal affinities and complementarities between them.

The political task, in a time of closure and danger, is to try to open up what is enclosed, to try to think thoughts that stretch and extend fixed patterns of insistence. That is why Nietzsche, Foucault, and Heidegger do not worry too much about the ethicopolitical problematic of "relativism"—partly because we are already located on a field of discourse that is so difficult to stretch and revise in any event and partly because we live in an age in which so many areas of the world are being drawn into the orbit of late-modern life. The relativist worry is untimely.

The modernist, however, often worries that if a transcendental standard cannot be proven (or at the very least proven to be "presupposed"), then all hell will break loose. The political danger resides not in the closure of identity and difference but in the hell of an infinite openness. We glimpsed that worry in the commentary by Keohane. The appropriate ethicopolitical project, from this perspective, is to resecure the ground of representation, to treat this ground as the one that everyone must stand on or be judged guilty of irrationality. The modernist protects the transcendental "must" by harassing those who ambiguate or defile it.

So, in the first instance we have a subterranean conflict over the nature of language, discourse, and identity that issues in an overt conflict over where the political danger is located in the late-modern period. One side seeks to open up discourses that are too closed and self-righteous and the other to protect established truths it considers threatened. But this ethicopolitical conflict, as I see it, is hardly ever thematized by the modernist in overtly political terms. The opponent is treated as if she shared (or must share, if she is a rational, responsible thinker) the modernist's political starting points, and the ethicopolitical difference is unconsciously translated into a universal philosophical issue with one rational response.

When this tacit level of the debate has been occluded the philosophical translation becomes simple and the answer to the question posed becomes obvious. "Don't you presuppose truth (or reason, subjectivity, a transcendental ethic) in repudiating it? If so, must you not endorse the standard univocally once your own presupposition is revealed to you?"

The simple answer is yes on all counts. Yes, yes, yes, yes, yes. And, though many modernists seem to skip over these passages, Foucault, Derrida, and Nietzsche constantly give that answer after posing such questions to themselves. But because they think within a different problematic, they also find that answer insufficient. While modernists univocally apply the code of integration and coherence to discourse on the basis of the implicit faith that only this code can save us, the postmodernist thinks within the code of paradox, because only attentiveness to ambiguity can loosen the hold monotonic standards of identity have over life in the late-modern age.[21]

The postmodernist thus finds it amusing and strange that the modernist *must* translate the code of paradox back into the code of coherence and then treat this translation as a discovery accepted by every healthy, rational, red-blooded academic. What ontological anxiety provides the energy for this perpetual task of forgetting and translation? We will pursue that issue later in this book.

The postmodernist agrees that in order to say anything she must presuppose some code or other, but she seeks to problematize that relation because there is no necessity that what must be presupposed as true at one moment must then be validated as unquestionable at the next or that what must be presumed in one gesture is unsusceptible to self-problematization in another. Even universal assumptions of cognitive discourse may themselves be confounded by artful devices. That is what Nietzsche meant when he said "we have art so that we will not perish from the truth." Truth is not repudiated here: it is treated as a necessary pursuit *also* susceptible to disturbance by rhetorical means. The role that subterranean rhetorical configurations play in protecting the inviolability of the code of coherence also reveals the role that alternative rhetorics can play in confounding the demand for univocality. The point is both to contest the extension of the "will to truth" to new corners of life and to intensify the endless task of detaching historical particulars from the porous universals to which they persistently become attached. The point is to refuse to curtail thinking in the name of guarding the faith.

That is why the postmodern text is infused with self-irony (a modality that must present itself to the modernist as a certain self-indulgence), with fascination over sites of tension between the narrative structure of a text and the cognitive claims it endorses explicitly, with attention to intertexts between discursive domains that function together to insulate a common set of presuppositions from problematization, with analyses of protean potentialities lodged within a normalized mode of discourse, with disclosures of subterranean links between the most extreme claims of reason and the rhetorical ruses by which those claims are bolstered.

That is why postmodernists often play the fool to the academic priest, to the voice of transcendental piety in the self and the other that insists upon converting every code of paradox into a logic of integration. Such a duplicitous stance is reflected in *The Archaeology of Knowledge*, as I read it, where Foucault closes by launching a dialogue with himself over the status of the claims he has offered in that text. To draw attention to structural parallels between earlier debates over the necessity of faith in a Christian god and contemporary debates over the singular status of western concepts of truth, reality, method, and identity, I will sort the two voices within Foucault into that of the priest and that of the fool or jester, recalling that both voices must be present in any text that seeks to speak to its own culture while contesting some of its patterns of insistence.

The priest: But if you claim you are opening up a radical interrogation, if you wish to place your discourse at the level at which we place ourselves, you know very well that it will enter our game, and, in turn, extend the dimension that it is trying to free itself from. Either it does not reach us or we claim it.

The jester: I admit this question embarrasses me more than your earlier objections. I am not *entirely* surprised by it; but I would prefer to leave it in suspense a little longer. This is because, for the moment, and as far as I can see, my discourse, far from determining the locus in which it speaks, is avoiding the ground on which it could find support. . . . It is *trying to deploy a dispersion* that can never be reduced to a single system of differences . . . ; it is *trying to operate a decentering* that leaves no privilege to any center.[22]

Note that the jester never says that he will simply succeed in his attempts. He is, after all, only a jester.

And then, a few pages later, approaching the last page of the text, Foucault seems to suspend the internal game of thrust and parry between the priest and the jester in himself. He says: "It seems to me that the only reply to this question is a political one. But let us leave that to one side for today. Perhaps we will take it up soon in another way."[23] The later Foucaultian texts, dealing serially with disciplinary society, technologies of the self, and the cultivation of care for life, constitute a political reply to this question. Foucault offers interpretations that in the act of presentation presuppose epistemic grounding. But he also deploys a variety of tactics to problematize the ground upon which he stands as well as that upon which his opponents stand.[24] He acknowledges, or so I think, that life cannot proceed without interpretation, that the general tendency is for contending interpretations to congeal around a fixed set of presumptions taken as unproblematic, and that care for the strife and interdependence of identity\difference requires an effort to devise interpretations that counter and contest this second tendency. There is an implicit ideal of politics flowing through this constellation, as well as a social ontology that both counters the models of mastery and attunement noted in the previous chapter and takes itself to be problematic. We will have to consider these themes further in the chapters that follow.

Foucault stands to late-modern, secular culture as Las Casas and Sahagún did to Spanish political theology in the sixteenth century. As each stretches the limits of cultural thoughtfulness in his time to reconsider settled orientations to identity and difference, his own thinking appears more ambiguous, ominous, and paradoxical to many of his contemporaries. Each thereby becomes vulnerable to neutralization by those unable or unwilling to call univocal patterns of insistence into question. But, provided with histories of such encounters by thinkers such as Las Casas, Sahagún, Foucault, and Todorov, critical thinkers today possess distinctive resources to combat, deflect, and subvert this politics of discursive neutralization. Certainly, the influence Foucault has acquired among scholars in the academy today transcends anything these early predecessors were able to attain in the church. If I have dissented from Ashley or Shapiro on one or two points, then, I endorse their advice to disturb contemporary patterns of insistence by engaging critically the history through which those patterns have been established and naturalized.

CHAPTER THREE

Liberalism
and Difference

The Paradox of Difference

My identity is what I am and how I am recognized rather than what I choose, want, or consent to. It is the dense self from which choosing, wanting, and consenting proceed. Without that density, these acts could not occur; with it, they are recognized to be mine. *Our* identity, in a similar way, is what we are and the basis from which we proceed.

An identity is established in relation to a series of differences that have become socially recognized. These differences are essential to its being. If they did not coexist as differences, it would not exist in its distinctness and solidity. Entrenched in this indispensable relation is a second set of tendencies, themselves in need of exploration, to congeal established identities into fixed forms, thought and lived as if their structure expressed the true order of things. When these pressures prevail, the maintenance of one identity (or field of identities) involves the conversion of some differences into otherness, into evil, or one of its numerous surrogates. Identity requires difference in order to be, and it converts difference into otherness in order to secure its own self-certainty.

Identity is thus a slippery, insecure experience, dependent on its ability to define difference and vulnerable to the tendency of entities it would so define to counter, resist, overturn, or subvert definitions applied to them. Identity stands in a complex, political relation to the differences it seeks to fix. This complexity is intimated by variations in the degree to which differences from self-identity are treated as complementary identitiés, contending identities, negative identities, or nonidentities; variations in the extent to which the voice of difference is heard as that with which one should remain engaged or as a symptom of sickness, inferiority, or evil; variations in the degree to which self-choice or cultural determination is attributed to alter-identities; variations in the degree to which one's own claim to identity is blocked by the power of opposing claimants or they are blocked by one's own power; and so on. The sensualist, the slut, the homosexual, the transvestite, the child abuser, and madness may merely suggest a few of these multifarious gradations at the level of the individual; the foreign, the terrorist organization, the dark continent, and the barbarian do so at the level of culture.

Such complexities suggest political dimensions in these relations. The bearer of difference may be one open to your appreciation or worthy of your tolerance, or an other whose claim to identity you strive to invert, or one who incorporates some of its own dispositions into her positive identity while you insist upon defining them as part of her negative identity, or one who internalizes the negative identity imposed upon it by others, or an impoverished mode of existence (e.g. "madness") you refuse to recognize as an identity, or an anonymous self who resists the pressure to crystallize a public identity in order to savor the freedom of anonymity, and so on. Power plays a prominent role in this endless play of definition, counter-definition, and counters to counter-definitions.

What if the human is not predesigned to coalesce smoothly with any single, coherent set of identities, if life without the drive to identity is an impossibility, while the claim to a natural or true identity is always an exaggeration? And what if there are powerful drives, overdetermined by the very inertia of language, psychic instabilities in the human mode of being, and social pressures to mobilize energy for collective action, to fix the truth of identity by grounding it in the commands of a god or the dictates of nature or the requirements of reason or a free consensus?

If and when this combination occurs, then a powerful identity will strive to constitute a range of differences as *intrinsically* evil, irrational, abnormal, mad, sick, primitive, monstrous, dangerous, or anarchical—as other. It does so in order to secure itself as intrinsically good, coherent, complete or rational and in order to protect itself from the other that would unravel its self-certainty and capacity for collective mobilization if it established its legitimacy. This constellation of constructed others now becomes both essential to the truth of the powerful identity and a threat to it. The threat is posed not merely by *actions* the other might take to injure or defeat the true identity but by the very visibility of its mode of *being* as other.

If there is no natural or intrinsic identity, power is always inscribed in the relation an exclusive identity bears to the differences it constitutes. *If* there is always a discrepancy between the identities a society makes available and that in human being which exceeds, resists, or denies those possibilities, then the claim to a true identity is perpetually plagued by the shadow of the other it constitutes. These "ifs" are big and contestable—big in their implications and contestable in their standing. Anyone who thinks within their orbit, as I do, should periodically reconsider the strictness with which they apply and the status endowed upon them. So, too, should anyone who forsakes them in pursuit of more harmonious, teleological conceptions of identity and difference.

The paradox of difference has several dimensions or formulations. One is that if there is no true identity, the attempt to establish one as if it were true involves power, while if there is a true identity susceptible to realization, the attempt to pluralize and politicize identities militates against achievement of the highest good. If we are not in a position to establish either of these claims with confidence, the double relation of interdependence and strife between identity and difference converts the theoretical problem of knowledge into a paradox of practice. For the practice that secures identity in its truth may involve repression of otherness, while that which problematizes established identities may foreclose the recognition of a true one.

I will not deal with this issue directly here. Rather, I will deal with it indirectly by considering the paradox of difference as it emerges within a philosophy that projects an answer to this ontological "if." A projection is offered because thinking cannot proceed here without invoking, implicitly or explicitly, consciously or unconsciously, a social ontology in the very language selected by it. This perspective is treated as a projection because I cannot now discern a way to prove or demonstrate its truth without invoking it again as part of the proof. I am selected by this particular projection because . . . well, at least partly because the history of teleological theories reveals them to be beset by severe internal difficulties, partly because the relative lack of presence of this alternative in contemporary discourse gives too fixed and secure a status to contending projections that currently exercise hegemony over discourse, and partly because the introduction of this alternative perspective into reflection helps to politicize the ontological dimension of academic political discourse. No affirmative theory can proceed without invoking ontological presumptions; several political theories today conceal their own presumptions while occasionally drawing attention to those of opposing theories.[1]

This projection challenges teleological theories that ground identity in a higher harmony in being and ambiguates transcendental philosophies that treat reason or the normal individual or reciprocal rules of discourse as media sufficient to establish a true identity. It does not deny that it too invokes presuppositions of the latter type; rather, it seeks to problematize them even while making them.

Now, the paradoxical element in the relation of identity to difference is that we cannot dispense with personal and collective identities, but the multiple drives to stamp truth upon those identities function to convert differences into otherness and otherness into scapegoats created and maintained to secure the appearance of a true identity. To possess a true identity is to be false to difference, while to be true to difference is to sacrifice the promise of a true identity.

Thus, for instance, madness as unreason or (in a more contemporary vein) severe abnormality is doubly entangled with the identity of the rational agent and the normal individual: it helps to constitute practical reason and normality by providing a set of abnormal conducts and "vehement passions" against which each is defined, but it also threatens them by embodying characteristics that would destabilize the normal if they were to proliferate. Madness and its corollaries stand in a double relation to normality: they constitute it and they threaten it, and the threat is most serious if the constituted normality is construed as intrinsically true rather than as, say, an entrenched identity containing a particular set of institutional limits, possibilities, and imperatives.

The double relation of identity to difference fosters discursive concealment of the most difficult political issues residing in this relation. The spiral of concealments may be summarized as follows. First, as one's doubts about the credibility of teleological and transcendental philosophies become acute, the suspicion grows that while no social life could be without bestowing privilege upon a particular constellation of identities, most historically established systems of identity veil the element of arbitrary conquest in the differences they create and negate. But then, once this doubt has impressed itself upon thought, a reactive impulse emerges to dissolve the new ethical paradoxes created by this admission. For how, it is asked, is the impression of violence in the formation of identity to be grounded if there is no transcendental basis for discriminating between violence and realization? This new anxiety refuels the quest to endow some identities with transcendental privilege. The first impulse, to expose and respond to violence in the relation of identity to difference, now often gives way to a renewed attempt to vindicate an ethic in which the identity affirmed (the good) is seen as unambiguous, inclusive, and free of dirt.

Thought moves to and fro here. Thinkers accuse each other in one respect to excuse themselves in another. Recognition of the ugly moment in the refusal of transcendence fosters a cover-up of the ugly element in its affirmation, and recognition of the ugly element in its affirmation fosters a cover-up of the ugly moment in its refusal. We might call this the politics of transcendental ugliness.

Such a tendency is discernible in recent responses by Anglo-American theorists to thinkers who refuse to dissolve the paradox of difference in a transcendental solution. Critics treat the quest by Nietzsche, Heidegger, and Foucault to expose paradoxes in the relation of identity to difference as expressions of incoherence or self-contradiction or amoralism in their thought. One set of ethical concerns (to expose a paradox and confront the violence within it) is countered by a moral charge against the carriers of the message, namely, that they are unable to formulate an ethical stance free of violence or self-contradiction or incoherence. Critics translate the code of paradox into the charge of incoherence and easily enough convict opponents of the sin they have defined.

Hobbes, Madness, and Ontotheology

Hobbes responded in one way to this issue when he thought about madness in relation to the individual who could be rational, steady, stable, calculable, and self-contained enough to serve as the building stone of a stable order. His thought in this regard is revelatory because he does not assume, as do some contemporary liberals who are indebted to him, that there is a social form in which the claims of individuality will mesh smoothly with the dictates of a well-ordered civil society. He refuses to bury the political paradox of difference beneath a complacent rhetoric of individuality, plurality, dialogue, tolerance, or harmonization; and this refusal, in turn, draws him toward a transcendental politics many contemporary liberals would hesitate to endorse.

Hobbes deploys the category of madness simultaneously to characterize behavior that deviates dangerously from his norm of personhood, to identify those whose conduct falls outside the confines of protections the sovereign offers persons abiding by their obligations, to warn individuals against falling prey to a madness that haunts the interior life of every human, and to advise the sovereign to dispose of those who become too mad to be governed by other means. His conception of madness expresses the severity of strife in his theory between the dictates of order and the claims of individuality, a strife that has become even more intensified in late-modern societies, where the demands of regularity, calculability, self-containment, and social coordination are more extensive than they were in Hobbes's day.

"The secret thoughts of a man," says Hobbes, "run over all things, holy, profane, clean, obscene, grave and light, without shame or blame."[2] The ghost of madness roams the interior of the self, though only a few selves are overtaken by madness as a condition. It is "want of discretion that makes the difference." This difference, often assuming the shape of "extraordinary and extravagant passion," is caused sometimes by "the evil constitution of the organs," and at other times by the "vehemence or long continuation of . . . pride . . . , self-conceit, or great dejection of mind." "In sum, all passions that produce strange and unusual behavior, are called by the general name of madness. But of the several kinds of madness, he that would take pains, might enroll a legion. And if the excesses be madness, there is no doubt but the passions themselves, when they tend to evil, are degrees of the same."[3]

For Hobbes, it is the duty of all subjects to practice self-restraint so that unruly, lustful, unguided, and extraordinary passions do not render them so unsteady that they fall into madness and "utterly lose themselves." For if the self is lost, if it is overtaken by "vehement passions," it becomes a danger to be disposed of in whatever way the sovereign deems appropriate for protection of the order.

We can hear these several messages inside Hobbes's rhetoric of rationality and madness as he presents his fourth "precept of nature":

> *that every man render himself useful unto others*; which that we may rightly understand, we must remember that there is in men a diversity of dispositions to enter into society, arising from the diversity of their affections, not unlike that which is found in stones brought together in the building, by reason of the diversity of their manner and figure. For as a stone, which in regard of its sharp and angular form takes up more room from other stones than it fills up itself, neither because of the hardness of its matter cannot well be pressed together, or easily cut, and would hinder the building from being fitly compacted, is cast away, as not fit for use; so a man, for the harshness of his disposition in retaining superfluities for himself . . . , being incorrigible by reason of the stubbornness of his affections, is commonly said to be useless and troublesome unto others. . . . Whence it follows (which we were to show) that it is a precept of nature, that every man accommodate himself to others. But he who breaks this law may be called *useless* and troublesome.[4]

It is imprudent to be called useless or troublesome in a Hobbesian world, and this is partly because Hobbes loads both the burdens of difference and the responsibilities for "complaisance" onto the self rather than construing clashes to flow from frictions between the dictates of identity in that order and unexpected modes of difference engendered within it. This latter perspective is suggested by Willie Bosket, a life-term ward of the state and delinquent whose vicious acts of abstract revenge against whoever happens to be closest (his guards) have confounded attempts to explain and subdue him. He says, "I am what the system created, but never expected," refusing to construe himself either as a passive effect of the system or as a defective stone that simply contains the source of its defectiveness in itself.[5]

Every theory (and every society) must develop strategies for dealing with differences engendered by the identities it enables. It is not this necessity—or, in the first instance, the particular strategy Hobbes himself culls from the western storehouse of possibilities—that calls for questioning now. What calls for questioning is, first, the range of imagined alternatives from which particular selections are made and, second, the terms of justification that establish and delimit these possibilities.

Hobbes answers these questions in a way that locates him within a philosophical tradition his theory is sometimes thought to escape. He concentrates on one possibility within that tradition: he treats a significant range of differences as otherness (as madness, drunkenness, atheism, obscenity, sinfulness) that falls below an identity known to be coherent and worthy in itself; he then warns those susceptible to the pull of otherness to guard themselves from it or reform themselves if they have already fallen into it *or else* find themselves conquered or excluded by a power that represents the "dictates" of reason. The pull of the first two demands is bound up with the "or else" clause accompanying them; it, in turn, is justified by a minimalist theology binding the dictates of reason to the commands of an otherwise unknowable God who makes a portion of his Will for humanity discernible through the reason "he hath given them."

These gestures place Hobbes within the ontotheological tradition of the west. To vindicate the conception of madness as a lapse from true identity, rather than a tragic discrepancy between the dictates of an order and certain types of self-formation engendered within it, he rises to the transcendental plane. The sustenance he draws from this source enables him to treat madness as a nullity that deviates from both the rational order and the dictates of true identity. The Hobbesian text gives primacy to the rationalist/containment strand within ontotheology while vociferously opposing its teleological/attunement strand. Of course, Hobbes *himself* may or may not believe in the connections adumbrated in these texts. He may merely think it necessary for others to hold such views if order is to survive. But that possibility is irrelevant to the issue posed here—to the way the relation between identity, madness, and divinity functions within the text.

I borrow the awkward term "ontotheology" from Heidegger, though I do not use it exactly as he does. By it I mean a tradition of thought that demands or presupposes an ultimate answer to the question of being, an answer that includes an ethical principle humans are either commanded authoritatively to follow or internally predisposed to recognize once distorting influences have been lifted from their souls. "Being, since the beginning of Western thought has been interpreted as the ground in which every being as such is grounded."[6] The ground might be the will of a god revealed in scripture or in the dictates of reason "given" by that god, or it might be a *telos* inscribed in the soul or nature or the body or history or language or the community or the principle of subjectivity. The ground must be treated as knowable, either by God or by humanity, either now, in the past, or in the future; and the human link to this ground can be one of faith, intuition, or knowledge. Such theories are grounded by appeal to a higher command (a law, a will) or an internal predisposition (an intrinsic purpose or potentiality), and they function to provide ontological reassurance to those who draw upon them.

Of course, every constructive theory is teleological in some senses of this elastic word. Every such theory endorses some ends, purposes, or goals over others and offers considerations in their defense. A theory is teleological in the more elevated sense I have in mind, though, if it insists that the ends it endorses express a higher direction in being itself and that the closer a self and a "polity" approach to that direction, the more true, harmonious, and inclusive they will be in their inner being and outer relations to each other. A constructive purposive theory might identify resistances, conflicts, disturbances in the very ideal of self, discourse, or statehood it commends, while a constructive teleological theory points to a way of being in which these frictions are minimized without significant repression because the structure of the political order has become attuned to a higher direction (a ground) in being itself.

Some modern pragmatist, utilitarian, and Marxist theories repeal the ontotheological demand for transcendental or teleological reassurance and then refill the vacancy created with assumptions about the predisposition of the world itself to mastery by human communities organized in the most propitious way. They replace obedience to the will of a god with the implicit premise of the responsiveness of the world itself to human use and organization. These latter perspectives are a continuation of ontotheology by other means: they compensate for the loss of transcendental reassurance by loading secular thought with a faith that the world itself is predisposed to be mastered in support of the ends and identities they favor, and then they forget the element of faith operating in their doctrines. They shift faith from God to the world, trusting that the world is *plastic* enough to respond to the drive for mastery without reacting back with a vengeance born from its indifference to their ends and the diversity of forces and energies flowing through it, and then they pretend that the withdrawal of faith from God eliminates faith altogether. They thus secularize the "oblivion of difference" that, in Heidegger's text, is a defining mark of ontotheology.

The demand for a divine authority or for a world predisposed to human mastery does not have to emerge as the demand of a singular, insistent thinker. It is already inscribed in the cultural terms of discourse that carry us along in the late-modern age. If the western tradition of ontotheology is inscribed in established conceptions and assumptions, we might expect a theory that explicitly eschews "metaphysical" and "ontological" reflection to be a particularly effective vehicle for its transmission. When John Rawls says, for example, that "in a constitutional democracy the public conception of justice should be, so far as possible, independent of controversial philosophical and religious doctrines,"[7] he does not escape the ontotheological tradition; he adopts a position within it that defuses its internal controversies. He looks "to our public political culture itself . . . , as the shared fund of implicitly recognized basic ideas and principles," without seriously entertaining the thought that denial and danger might be lodged within those commonalities.[8]

The later Rawls draws liberalism away from its proclivity (in the academy especially, but not only there) to locate a principle or ground in the universal human subject or the dictates of reason, and toward a liberal hermeneutic. This hermeneutic strategy represents an advance over the liberal foundationalism by which Rawls himself was once tempted, and the dialectic by which Rawls has arrived at this juncture might be instructive to a range of rights theorists, rational choice theorists, and economic individualists who have not yet reached this point. But, I want to say, this sojourn of Rawlsian thought is not the consummation of liberalism: it prepares liberalism to engage a debate between those who think a benign hermeneutic can continue within the established parameters of traditional liberal assumptions, demands, and faiths and those who think that this shift prepares liberalism for its next set of engagements. For genealogy, deconstruction, intertextualism, and so on define themselves not just against the structuralist version of rationalism, but also, and equally, against cultural reassurances operative in dominant forms of hermeneutics. By saving his theory from one set of criticisms, Rawls opens it to another set of issues.

Individualism and Individuality

Liberal individualism and liberal individuality are not equivalent. They converge in giving the individual moral primacy over the interests of the collectivity. But individual*ism* presupposes a model of the normal or rational individual against which the conduct and interior of each actual self are to be appraised. This standard of the "stiff, steadfast individual," as Nietzsche would characterize it, provides the ground for a theory of rights, justice, responsibility, freedom, obligation, and legitimate interests.

The doctrine of the steadfast individual (the autonomous agent, the self-interested agent, the normal individual) easily becomes—seen from the standpoint pursued here—a doctrine of normalization through individualization. Its tendency is to reduce the political to the juridical—to condense most issues of politics into the juridical categories of rights, justice, obligation, and responsibility and to treat the remaining issues instrumentally as contests in which individuals and aggregations compete within juridical rules to advance their "interests" or "principles" by rational means. Politics gets bifurcated into a dualism of principle and instrumentality, with one group of individualists (rights theorists, theorists of justice) celebrating the former and another group (utilitarians, pragmatists) insisting upon the incorrigibility of the latter. Neither faction comes to terms vigorously with the constructed character of *both* the virtuous self and the self-interested self or with the extent to which both constructions were valued by their early theoretical designers because of their calculability, predictability, and utility to sovereign power.

For these very reasons—the presentation of a single model of the generic individual, the minimalization of the contingent, constructed character of virtuous and self-interested individuals, and the reduction of politics to the juridical—theories of liberal individualism deflate the *politics* of identity and difference.

A theory of the normal individual establishes its parameters of normality not so much by specific argumentation as by omissions in its generic characterization of the individual. Certainly, once a general characterization of the rational agent as a bearer of rights, virtues, and interests is presented, the presenter is then free to contest a whole series of actual demands of normality imposed upon concrete selves but not required by the generic definition of the self. This, however, is not how such theories proceed. Rather, they insinuate a dense set of standards, conventions, and expectations into the identity of the normal self *by failing to identify or contest a constellation of normal/abnormal dualities already inscribed in the culture they idealize.* One can discern this tendency through retrospective exemplification and by comparing the rhetorical strategies of liberal texts defending the generic individual with those of critical texts interrogating the density of the normal individual.[9] I will merely offer one exemplification here.

In the 1950s in the United States, a topic of debate was whether "homosexuality" (a medical term for a sexual disposition) was a moral fault (the then conservative view) or a personal sickness (the then liberal view). Neither party considered how both sides pre-supposed "it" to be a defect in the self of one type or the other, or how their joint constitution of this disposition as a defect of one sort or the other protected the self-certainty of heterosexual identity. And this example could be replicated across a whole range of issues concerning the normal self. The usual mode of discourse governing individualist theory does not support a problematization of estab-lished standards of normal individuality; the narrative and rhetori-cal designs of its texts do not pose disturbing questions about the dense construction of the normal individual and its abnormalities.

The politicization of abnormality is made difficult in any event by the institutional silences and constraints that typically envelop the formation of normal identities. But the theory of individualism exacerbates these difficulties through its mode of theorization. It is pulled, by its minimalist understanding of how politics enters into the constitution of identity and difference, to consent tacitly to the politics of normal individualization.

A theory of liberal *individuality* is another kettle of fish. It gives primacy to the individual while qualifying or problematizing the hegemony of the normal individual. Here nonidentity with a nor-mal or official self constitutes a sign of individuality. Individuality, indeed, comprises a range of conduct that is distinctive, stretches the boundaries of identity officially given to the normal self, reveals artifice in established standards of normality by superseding or violating them, and brings new issues into public life through resistances, eccentricities, refusals, or excesses that expose a series of contestable restraints built into fixed conventions.

George Kateb has done much, certainly the most in contempo-rary America, to clarify and advance this perspective. His version of the theory is inspired by Emerson, salted by Nietzsche. He celebrates "democratic individuality," insisting, against Nietzsche, that the unsettled character of democratic politics and the enhanced institutional respect for the individual that tends to accompany the exercise of democratic citizenship together provide an institutional context in which any self may express its individuality. Democracy "unsettles everything for everyone, and thus liberates democratic individuality."[10]

Kateb strives to elicit from the lived experience of individuality both a public appreciation of diversity and an enhanced appreciation of the value of existence beyond its encapsulation in any particular network of identities, conventions, norms, and exclusions. For Kateb, those who express individuality and appreciate it in others tend, first, to say no to encroachments by the state into new areas of life, second, to accept responsibility for themselves and their life projects, and third, to "acquire a new relation to all experience, which may be called either a philosophical or poetical relation to reality."[11]

This last formulation speaks to an appreciation of existence as such—gained through the experience of individuality and ratified by its best poets. It emerges less as an argument in favor of individuality than as a solicitation of the moment of individuality in each self, less as a proof that we owe allegiance to existence as such than as a revelation of the attachment to existence already implicit in the appreciation of individuality. It is Wim Wenders' *Wings of Desire* transcribed into prose.

In this way Kateb signals a Nietzschean (and Emersonian) refusal to ground ethics in reason alone, asserting that if there is not already an attachment to existence flowing from the self and overflowing into care for other lives, no rational ground of ethics will ever generate ethical conduct. Foucault's formulation of this thesis is that "care of the self" is an essential preliminary to care for other selves, and care for others emerges from an abundance cultivated by the self. Lawrence Taylor, the talented and controversial linebacker for the New York Giants, expressed one side of this thesis while responding in his own way to a reporter interrogating him about his lack of concern for teammates and fans adversely affected by his drug habit: "A friend of mine recently asked about my driving habits. I told him I don't wear seat belts because if I ever get in a crash at the speed I go, I wouldn't survive anyway. . . . But I also told him what I tell anyone else who asks: If I don't care what happens to me now, can I really think about what might happen to others?"[12] If one lacks care for oneself, one will surely lack the abundance from which care for individuality in others might emerge.

Kateb has placed himself on a plane of reflection that invites comparison with a contemporary mode of thought he sometimes treats dismissively. The link between Katebian individuality and Foucault on power and freedom is forged by Nietzsche, to whom both are significantly indebted.

While Kateb emphasizes the roots of his philosophy in the American transcendentalists Emerson, Whitman, and Thoreau, one element in Nietzsche's articulation of individuality and the resistances to it is particularly pertinent to contemporary experience. This is the first point at which my solicitation of liberal individuality—its paradoxes and possibilities—diverges from Kateb's.

Consider three assertions: (1) Nietzsche is the philosopher who exposes the roots of resentment in theism and secularism and who seeks to elicit a nontheistic reverence for life to combat the subterranean politics of resentment. (2) Liberalism is a contemporary philosophy of rights and justice that has become an object of resentment in contemporary politics. (3) Most paradigmatic defenses of liberalism today refuse to ask whether its doctrine embodies and contributes to the resentment it encounters.

A reconstitution of liberal individuality might begin, then, by ascertaining whether there is something in liberal individual*ism* that expresses resentment and something in it that tends to elicit resentment from many who receive its messages. Such an analysis, indebted to Nietzsche, may help to reveal traps liberal individua*lity* must avoid and directions its supporters might consider.

That contemporary liberalism is an object of public resentment seems undeniable. This is so especially at those points where its welfarism and its individualism intersect, for these determine how freedom and responsibility are to be distributed among the various constituencies of the welfare state. Many liberal-welfare programs inaugurated in the 1960s to rectify injustice have been received by a variety of constituencies as the imposition of new injustices upon them. Programs in busing, aid to dependent children, affirmative action hiring, ecology, criminal parole and rehabilitation, and gun control often encounter virulent opposition, indicating that they touch the identities of the opponents even more than their interests. Juridical doctrines and judgments supporting civil liberties and civil rights encounter similar reactions.[13]

Of course these responses have several sources, but one of them is particularly pertinent here. Many of those asked to bear the immediate economic and psychic costs of ameliorative programs already resent some of the conditions of their own existence. But this resentment is not typically emphasized in the rhetoric or pro-

grams of liberalism: the resentment is accentuated by liberal programs and subdued in its rhetoric.

Think of white working-class males. They are subjected to a
variety of disciplines and burdens that limit their prospects for life,
but liberal programs devised since the 1960s tend to treat them as
responsible for their own achievements and failures. And they are
then told by liberals that many women and minorities suffer injustice if they do not rise to or above working-class levels of attainment.

Liberal representatives inadvertently manipulate the rhetoric of
self-responsibility and justice in ways that assault the identity of
this constituency. By implying that professional and corporate
males have earned their position while asserting that women and
minorities are victimized by discrimination, liberals imply that
only one group *deserves* to be stuck in the crummy jobs available
to it: white working-class males. The liberal glorification of self-
responsibility, juridical justice, and welfare together thus accentuates the resentment of those whose identity is most immediately
threatened by its ameliorative programs.

But why is this resentment often so virulent and volatile? Does
liberalism today simply encounter a resentment it does not harbor?
Or does liberal individualism help to dig a well of resentment that
then flows into the culture in which it participates? I believe that
any effort to reconstitute liberalism must explore this latter possibility. Nietzsche provides clues from which such an exploration
might be launched.

From a Nietzschean perspective, the self constituted as a unified,
self-responsible agent contains resentment within its very formation. The basic idea behind this formation is that for every evil
there must be a responsible agent who deserves to be punished and
that for every quotient of evil in the world there must be a corollary
quotient of assignable responsibility. No evil without responsibility. No responsibility without reward or punishment according to
desert. No suffering without injustice, and no injustice unless there
is a juridical recipe for redressing it in life or afterlife. Life is
organized around the principles of individual responsibility governing a baseball game.

A liberal might think that all freedom, responsibility, and justice
must disappear if the ideals he endorses are linked to a subterranean
demand that these equivalences be established. If the purity of
these principles is sullied, everything else good and admirable will

be soiled too. Perhaps. But to explore dangers and cruelties that may reside within these categories, it may be helpful to illuminate them from a different angle, to lower the source of illumination so that the shadows they throw become more discernible.

At the root of the demand for equivalence between evil and responsibility is a demand that the world contain agency in the last instance. Seen from this angle, these categories embody a modernized version of the traditional Christian demand that there be a responsible agent or purpose for suffering in the world, that human finitude and suffering be redeemed by an agency of responsibility. What Nietzsche called the slave revolt in morality—the formation and consolidation of a new set of equivalences—is not exhausted by the attempt of sufferers held in human bondage to invent a god to hold the masters responsible for their cruelty and indifference. Certainly the invention of this god involves an act of "imaginary revenge" on the part of those whose social powerlessness makes actual revenge untenable. Certainly the habitual practice of this revenge eventually becomes consolidated into the creative demand that everyone acquire the honesty, meekness, industriousness, and virtue "we" are already compelled to assume. Certainly weakness is here transformed into merit, so that what the slave *must be* becomes the standard against which every difference is defined as a deviation to be punished, reformed, or converted. But the early, intense transfiguration of overt resentment into the demand to convert or conquer the other for its own good exposes a more pervasive set of dispositions rooted in the human condition.[14] Otherwise, masters themselves would not become gripped by its attractions. Only a more pervasive human dream of a world without injustice seems sufficient to explain the appeal this system of equivalences exerts upon almost everyone. Humans resent the transiency, suffering, and uncertainty of redemption that mark the human condition. We suffer from the problem of our meaning, and we demand that meaning be given to existential suffering. So when the idea of a purpose in existence residing in nature or a god loses its credibility, the insistence that we are rational, responsible agents comes into its own. For if these previous sources of responsibility are dead, some new agency must be created. We give meaning to existential suffering, then, by holding ourselves responsible for it. "Quite so my sheep," we say to one another, "someone must be to blame for [suffering]; but you are this someone, you alone are to blame for it—*you alone are to blame for yourself!*"[15] It can't be a god who must be protected from responsibility for evil. It can't be nature. It will have to be us, if it is to be. We will have to be the responsible agents. "Quite so my sheep."

The modern normal, responsible individual can redirect resentment against the human condition into the self, first, by treating the rational, self-interested, free, and principled individual as morally responsible for willful deviations from normal identity and, second, by treating that in itself and other selves which falls below the threshold of responsibility as a natural defect in need of conquest or conversion, punishment or love. The modern individual, in short, contains resentment against the human condition in its own identity, and this comes out most clearly in the intensity of the resentment it expresses against any others who deviate significantly from that identity. For such deviations, if they proliferate, make the self-identical self appear to be a sucker for accepting the disciplines and restraints required to maintain itself in this way. Only if these deviations are false or evil can it see itself as true. Resentment against injuries to oneself flowing from the standard of self-responsibility becomes translated into rancor against those whom one construes as escaping the dictates of that standard.

On this interpretation, the modern ideal of the *unambiguous* agent is one of the costs we pay for the demand that there be an ethical life without paradox. And the demand for this set of equivalences, seldom stated overtly but working in the background of modern conceptions of self, justice, and responsibility, is itself nourished by a further set of insistences. The "authoritarian personality" is thus not merely a personality type that threatens liberal tolerance. It is also an internal product of the *individualist* demand for a fixed and pure fundamental identity.

No individualist philosopher has ever proven that the human animal is predesigned to correspond to the shape assumed by the modern normal individual, and thus none has proven that this formation can be forged and maintained each generation without imposing cruelty upon those who adjust to its dictates as well as those who are unable or unwilling (can we ever sort out these proportions with confidence?) to do so. These are modes of categorical insistence from which individualism proceeds. Seen from the perspective of those who endorse subjectivity as an ambiguous achievement while refusing to endorse the fiction that it corresponds to what we naturally are, the subterranean presumption that humans are predesigned to be responsible agents veils elements of cruelty and revenge in the formation of this identity and its differences. The most direct sign that liberal individualism disables itself from discerning cruelty in its own constructs is that the most startling exposés of new cruelties and disciplines in late-modern society have come not from liberal individualism but from Foucault, a left-Nietzschean who detects fateful ambiguities in the politics of "individualization."

Individuality and Difference

My first disagreement with Kateb, then, is a matter of emphasis. I place greater emphasis on the element of resentment already residing in the identity of the normal individual. Liberal individualism thus becomes a more ambiguous ally of liberal individuality than Kateb has acknowledged.

And this in three respects. First, its concentration on the normal individual renders it less sympathetic to the claims of diversity, encouraging it to enclose the space for diversity within a closely defined band of standards of abnormality such as irrationality, irresponsibility, immorality, delinquency, and perversity. Second, its insistence on the standard of normal individuality helps to foment a generalized resentment that tends to disable normal and abnormal individuals alike from affirming an ethic that appreciates, as Nietzsche would say, "the rich ambiguity of existence." Third, its juridical conception of politics tends to downplay the degree of political action, militance, and struggle required to establish space for individuality in a liberal society.

A philosophy of individuality and nontheistic reverence for existence must identify ways and means to wage a battle against existential resentment and to elicit respect for the diversity of existence while doing so. I agree with Kateb, Emerson, Nietzsche, and Foucault that no ethic of individuality (or anything else) can be grounded securely in rational proof, partly because such attempts are always contestable and partly because even a successful proof would not guarantee the production of motives to obey its edicts. But this does not mean that a political ethic is merely a matter of "choice" either—the only alternative the rationalist tends to recognize. Rather, such an ethic is solicited from or inspired in us, first, when we come to recognize the element of resentment in the way extant moralities convert difference into otherness and, second, when we cultivate the implicit attachment to existence already installed in life. Nontheistic reverence for existence redraws the line between secularism and religion by refusing either to eliminate reverence or to bind the element of reverence to theism. Such an ethic has reverence for life because life is never exhausted by any particular identity installed in it. Its reverence is sustained through its nontheism.

Nietzsche's texts divert attention from the role reverence plays in them, first, by presenting this mood typically in the context of a castigation of Christian culture and, second, by expressing it within the ambiance of an antidemocratic ethic. But these formulations can also point beyond the particular convictions of Nietzsche for thinkers who seek to enter into a relation of antagonistic indebtedness to him, for those who seek to construct a liberal politics on the basis of a Nietzschean reverence for life, for those who seek an ethic that expresses reverence for the diversity of existence coupled with appreciation of the impossibility of embodying everything admirable in any single way of life.

The relevant spirit can be discerned in Nietzsche's attack on the early Christian church:

> To shatter the strong, to infect great hopes, to cast suspicion on the enjoyment of beauty, to break down everything autonomous, manly, victorious, dominating, all the instincts natural to the highest and best turned-out type of mankind, and bend it over into uncertainty, distress of conscience, and self-destruction—to reverse every bit of love of earth and things earthly and control of earth into hatred of things earthly and of the earth: *this* was the self-assumed task of the church.[16]

If we shift the focus away from the apparent misogyny and aristocraticism in this passage, the attempt to elicit reverence for the earth because it is a fund of differences not governed by a transcendent law or purpose becomes apparent. This reverence is not treated as a command; it is solicited through exposés of extant identities and moralities that contain or suppress it. And, given Nietzsche's reading of the human condition (that is, the incompleteness of the human animal without social form, the density of language, the quest for closure of identities, and the absence of a sufficient principle of harmonization of difference in being), these struggles will always be necessary because of the multitude of pressures in the human condition to naturalize conventional identities and to reduce difference to falsity or evil. To endorse *this* Nietzschean perspective is not to adopt the particular antagonists Nietzsche selects at the end of the nineteenth century. It is, rather, to claim that a political ethic appropriate to a reconstituted liberalism might draw sustenance from this source.[17]

I realize these comments are sketchy and cryptic. We will return to these issues in Chapter 6. The comments are offered to indicate that I agree with the spirit of Kateb's ethic, even though I dissent from his politics.

While Kateb advances a compelling ethic of individuality, the dilemmas and paradoxes within that ethic cannot be engaged until it is translated into a political theory. To put the point bluntly: *this theorist of liberal individuality offers an ethic of individuality in lieu of a political theory of individuality*, in lieu of a theory that confronts disjunctions between limitations on diversity intrinsic to a specific order and the demand for diversity that flows from an ethic of individuality. Once the outlines of such a theory are elucidated, one must either eliminate those disjunctions by making questionable teleological assumptions or confront a tragic element residing within the institutionalization of individuality itself. Engagement with institutional limits to individuality can be evaded either by succumbing to the teleological temptation or by restricting oneself to an *ethic* of individuality situated in a generically defined culture of liberal democracy.

Kateb pursues the second strategy. It finds expression mostly in silences with respect to the structural limits of late-modern liberal-capitalist society. To the extent that the state leaves the individual alone, Kateb is inclined to believe, to that extent individuality will flourish. And if we do not demand too much from the state, particularly in the area of economic life, it can afford to leave us pretty much alone. So, while democratic politics is a necessary precondition of individuality, a too active and organized democratic agenda will suffocate it. The individual's political involvement, therefore, should be limited, confined, episodic. Kateb quotes Whitman's advice to "always vote," but to limit oneself with respect to other modes of political involvement: "Disengage yourself from parties. They have been useful, and to some extent remain so, but the floating, uncommitted electors, farmers, clerks, mechanics, the masters of parties—watching aloof, inclining victory this side or that side—such are the ones most needed, present and future."[18]

Notice the assumptions of early nineteenth-century America

that form the silent background of this sentiment: "floating, uncommitted electors," and so on, rather than role bearers whose conditions of daily existence enmesh them in corporate and bureaucratic structures imposing refined schedules and norms upon them; a self-subsistent state rather than one entangled in a global structure of interdependencies and conflicts that it is pressed to convert into disciplines for its most vulnerable constituencies; a domestic politics of "parties" from which the individual can be "disengaged" and "aloof" without becoming an object of power struggles over norms, regulations, penalties, and incentives governing the details of life.

Kateb modestly qualifies this portrait of the American past in sketching its implications for the present, suggesting that "a *modern equivalent* would perhaps be the *episodic* citizenship of loosely and *temporarily* associated individuals who seek to protest and end *great atrocities*; or seek to protest and end violations of the Constitution, with special attention to defending the Bill of Rights and to warning against executive and bureaucratic *lawlessness* and overreaching."[19] That is, he reasserts the early American idealization of self-reliance by absorbing contemporary politics into its juridical dimension and by treating political engagement as normally secondary to the pursuit of individuality.

But the past ain't what it used to be. What's more, it probably never was. We do not reside today in a world where individuality can flourish if state, corporate, and associational institutions of normalization are left to their own devices except when they overstep clear constitutional boundaries or commit glaring atrocities. The atrocities that glare most brightly today are undergirded by everyday politics. Constitutional boundaries must be creatively redefined and enlarged through political pressures speaking to new circumstances.

The proliferation of drug tests; the extension of corporate codes into new corners of everyday life; credit tests; the increasing numbers of people subjected to security tests along with the increased number of criteria invoked in them; the bureaucratic definition and regulation of safe, healthy, normal sexuality; the introduction of home detention for convicted felons, allowing definitions of criminality to be extended indefinitely; the computerization of individual files, enabling a variety of authorities and semiauthorities to record the life history of each individual for multifarious uses; the militarization of welfare and scholarships; the refiguration of deviations construed in the nineteenth century as sins or moral faults into psychological defects of the self in need of correction or therapy; and most pervasively, the vague sense that each of one's actions today *might* form part of a record that *might* be used for or against one in the future—these signify a *regularized* politics of normalization through observational judgment and anticipatory self-policing.

Individuality secures space to be through resistance and opposition to these bureaucratic pressures. Gay rights movements; feminism; minority politics; emergent movements to attack the institutionalization of homelessness; efforts on behalf of the elderly in nursing homes; movements to establish prisoners' rights; embryonic drives to resist the universalization of drug tests and other closures in codes of employee conduct; the political struggle to die on one's own terms rather than according to terms set by the state; periodic dissidence among young men and women in military, intelligence, and security agencies; localized pressures to roll back corporate and state disciplines forged under the star of efficiency, productivity, and normality; antimilitarist movements to create alliances with dissidents in second- and third-world regions—these protests and movements, however ineffective they may be on occasion, simultaneously signify a broadening and deepening of institutional investments in the life of the self and a corollary politics of resistances, disinvestments, and subversion on behalf of individuality.

The apolitics of liberal individuality is too easily squeezed to death through this intensification of institutional investments. In a highly structured state, an episodic, juridical politics of dissent against extreme atrocities lapses into a nonpolitics of nihilistic consent to the everyday extension of discipline and normalization—the most ominous form nihilism assumes today.

The minimalist politics of individuality is thus not merely a benign perspective that does not go far enough. It is an anachronism that misreads paradigmatic threats to individuality in latemodern society. These threats reside in the normal operation of a political economy of productivity within a society of increasing surveillance and normalization. They are lodged in the state, in civil society, and in some of the interior dispositions of individuals participating in these arenas. Their accumulation requires a politics in which established definitions of normality and rationality are contested along a variety of dimensions in multifarious ways.

Certainly the politicization of individuality creates costs for individuality itself. But these costs can no longer be avoided. The pathos of distance that individuality prizes can no longer be located in some fictive place, sanctuary or "sphere" exempt from political intrusion. These must become politically created spaces rather than geographical or social or private sanctuaries. In late-modern society the pathos of distance means the politicization of distance.

A mere *ethic* of individuality evades an encounter with the Foucaultian world of discipline and normalization not through the social ontology it endorses—for here the two perspectives are remarkably close—but through the temporal reference it fixes. It eludes the encounter through an ideal of individuality floating in the clouds of a nineteenth-century vision.

The finely grained arrangements of self-regulation operative today must be countered by more sustained, organized, and multifrontal counter-pressures, pressures that interrogate established definitions and intrusions of necessity, truth, normality, utility, and goodness while they identify and strive to reconstitute the larger institutional imperatives that drive the politics of normalization. For a proliferation of deviations, defects, discrepancies, abnormalities, perversities, and sicknesses is not equivalent to the flowering of diversity: these are regular means by which individuality is crushed and deformed under the star of the normal individual.

There is a slippery issue here, lodged in the divergence between the vocabulary of individuality that forms the linchpin of Katebian liberalism and the vocabulary of difference adopted in the present study. The idealization of individuality draws attention to that which is unique or special in any self, that which may not be matched or realized in quite the same way in any other person. The thematization of difference is always pursued in relation to a powerful or pervasive identity or set of identities. It calls attention to entire types and categories of being that are neutralized, marginalized, or defeated by the hegemony of an identity. The language of individuality, when it is given too much priority, can thereby divert attention from ways in which relational structures of identity\difference de-moralize entire categories of life.

The ethic of individuality does not authorize a minimal politics at the endpoint of its analysis; it expresses it in the language through which it defines the pertinent issues. "Individuality" is an apolitical term insinuated into a political problematic ("democratic individuality") in ways that depoliticize understandings of social life. When it is translated into the political vocabulary of difference, the need to politicize the established network of definitions becomes more apparent. Once this category mishap is corrected, the contemporary dependence of individuality upon the politicization of difference shines through.

There is always conflict as well as interdependency between the claims of individuality and the dictates of identity in a particular order. A political theory that admires the first set of claims will support constitutional ways to protect elemental rights to diversity. But it will also develop more political protections for claims that express the paradox of difference in a particular setting, countering and contesting tendencies to naturalize the identities enabled in a particular society, exposing and testing limitations imposed by the structural characteristics of a particular social type, and exposing the pressures to conformity and naturalization that emerge when a closed set of identities is reinforced by the structural characteristics of a political order. Advocates of individuality will strive to interpret from an alien perspective a range of disciplines and intrusions that are made to appear natural or necessary or consensual or rational or normal in established political discourse, striving to politicize those which seem the most cruel or injurious to life. They will acknowledge that individuality cannot dispense with commonalities, but they will also insist that these sedimented settlements must be contested and politicized periodically in order to disturb closures and categorical imperatives invested in them.

When the paradox of difference is confronted in the context of late-modern society, it turns out that an ethic of individuality requires a multifarious politicization of difference in order to sustain itself.

Civic Liberalism

Liberal individualism buries the paradox of difference first by insinuating too many dictates of a particular order into the identity of the normal individual and then by naturalizing the identity it has solidified. Liberal individuality evades the paradox by treating an ethic of individuality as if it were a political theory of identity\ difference. A third scholarly version of liberalism completes the contemporary circle of evasions. Civic liberalism corrects defects in the first two positions by reminding us how a set of identities is defined and enabled within the context of institutionalized commonalities. It then naturalizes this insight by insisting that there must be a way of life, either now, in the past, or in a possible future, where established identities are harmonized through a politics of civic virtue.

Its strategy with respect to difference is this: the paradox of difference must be dissolved into a common good that both enables every form of otherness to reform itself until it fits into the frame of a rational community and enables the community to perfect its terms of inclusion so that excluded constituencies can find a home within it. Civic liberalism fosters normalization through a nonpolitics of gentle assimilation. That, at least, is its regulative ideal, the standard against which actuality is measured and through which it is authorized to characterize the present condition as one of fragmentation, loss of identity, and alienation.

"Civic liberalism" will seem like a category mistake to some. But most contemporary communitarian (or civic republican) theories are variants of liberalism because, first, they provide space for rights and individuality within the context of the harmonies they admire, second, they emphasize the juridical and communal sides of politics over its role in disturbing and unsettling established routines, third, they want the identities and commonalities endorsed to be brought to a peak of self-consciousness and rational legitimacy unimagined in traditional theories of community, and fourth, they maintain a corollary commitment to incremental change by democratic means as opposed to transformation by revolutionary or authoritarian means.

A communitarian strategy typically begins by trying to show how preunderstandings implicit in contemporary life point toward a coherent set of standards that justify a more inclusive and fulfilling good. We are already implicated in the circle of commitments communitarianism articulates and perfects, and our mutual rights, duties, and aspirations will be harmonized more effectively as we are brought to greater self-consciousness of their preconditions and implications.

But the question arises, What justifies the exclusions, penalties, restrictions, and incentives needed to sustain adherence to this common good on the part of those who might otherwise deviate from it? What if some would significantly shift priorities within the sanctified circle of implications if they had the power to do so? What if commonly established assumptions about the capacity for realization of the embodied self in a higher community encounter persistent resistances in many selves to these forms of self-organization?

What if the circle of discourse in which these commonalities are articulated closes out other possibilities that would disturb, unsettle, fragment, ambiguate, politicize the achieved sense of unity if they were to find expression? When such questions are pursued persistently, the hermeneutic circle of mutual self-validation among interdependent components of the culture must have recourse to a supplement; it must appeal to a supplementary "bent" or purpose or harmonious direction in being to which a community can become attuned.

The most reflective civic humanists endorse such a supplement, at least when faced by objections that require either that they do so or that they ambiguate more radically the good they endorse. Charles Taylor is exemplary here. In a recent exchange, while insisting that he rejects the strong teleological assumptions embodied in Hegelian theory, he affirms the presence of a principle of teleology in his political philosophy:

> For what is meant by a "teleological philosophy"? If we mean some inescapable design at work inexorably in history, à la Hegel, then I am of course not committed to it. But if we mean by this expression that there is a distinction between distorted and authentic self-understanding, and that the latter can in a sense be said to follow from a direction in being, I do indeed espouse such a view. And that makes a big part of my "ontology" of the human person.[20]

A "direction in being." Taylor proceeds from a rhetoric of self-realization within community, through a rhetoric of communal realization through harmonization of the diverse parts of an ongoing culture, to a rhetoric of progressive attunement to a harmonious direction in being. The latter is a requirement of his theory. But to say that "we" need such a supplement to ground community, or, more strongly, that others who explicitly reject the ideal of harmonious community nonetheless presuppose a facsimile of this supplement in their own thinking, or, more strongly still, that such a supplement is an inescapable component of social thought as such, is still not to show that a supplemental direction (and a being who provides it?) is available to "us."

Taylor suggests that such a direction is needed if the civic ideal is to succeed, but he then exhibits the possibility of that direction, not through particular arguments, but through textual tropes that presuppose its availability. Taylor's Augustinianism emerges in this dimension of his texts. We are called upon to believe so that we can come to know. "Lord," says Augustine, "my faith calls upon you, that faith . . . which you have breathed into me."[21] And Taylor breathes faith in the possibility of harmonious community into the rhetoric that governs his characterizations.

I do not mean to protest this dimension of Taylor's work as such, for no affirmative theory of politics can avoid some such strategy of reflective projection. But I do mean to call attention to the contestability of the projection he endorses and to note how communitarian texts typically fail to promote reflection on the rhetorical configurations through which they elicit faith in their highest ideals.

The problem is not only that this air is breathed into the narrative and rhetorical structure of communitarian texts, but that the realization of community itself requires that most of its members become attuned to the supplemental direction as a harmonious end that binds them together. The ideal of community itself presses its adherents to treat harmonious membership and consensus not as contestable ends to be interrogated by the most creative means at their disposal, but as vehicles of elevation drawing the community closer to the harmony of being. Communalization is harmonization, and harmonization that is treated as contestable or deeply ambiguous is, well, no longer consonant with communalism.

But can't "we" take this step of faith too? After all, it seems a small step, once the initial web of common preunderstandings governing the culture has been articulated. And the return seems so great: the paradox of difference becomes resolved into a project of assimilation in which those who now fall outside the range of communal identifications are drawn into the folds of a higher, more rational, and more inclusive community. Is it not time at last to be reasonable?

This step must be resisted by those who doubt the faith that sustains it. The gentle rhetoric of articulation, realization, community, purpose, attunement, fulfillment, integration, and harmonization significantly reinscribes the common life, obligating people and institutions to reform and consolidate themselves in ways that may be arbitrary, cruel, destructive, and dangerous *if* the pursuit of consensus and commonality are not supported by a harmonious direction in being. The gentle rhetoric of harmonization must be ambiguated and coarsened by those who have not had its faith breathed into their souls, particularly those moved by nontheistic reverence for the rich ambiguity of existence. We thus return to the "if" from which we never actually departed.

The rhetoric of civic liberalism places too many possible disciplines outside its critical purview, revealing in its persistent folding of experience into its specific modality that the supplement it invokes does not require such a small step after all. It must constantly be tested and contested by those whose hermeneutic draws supplemental sustenance from another social ontology, one in which the fit between human designs and the material drawn into those designs is always partial, incomplete, and likely to contain an element of subjugation and imposition, in which the possibilities of individuality and reverence for existence are enhanced when we refuse to pretend that a god retains enough life to give supplemental direction to late-modern existence, and in which democracy reaches its highest level of achievement when agonistic respect is folded into its politics.

A certain asymmetry in the debate between communitarian and post-Nietzschean thinkers deserves elaboration. Taylor says that the assumption of a direction in being "does not seem to me to be in worse shape than its obvious rivals, certainly not the Nietzschean notion of truth as imposition."[22] Leaving aside the need to amplify and modify the suggestion that truth for Nietzsche is *simply* imposition, the Taylor presumption of a harmonious end to which we strive to become attuned must attain significantly better standing than the alternative projections of his opponents if the ideal of community is to be approximated in life. Post-Nietzschean liberalism requires only that an active minority of the population advance it in thought and action and that the culture more broadly come to recognize it as a competing response to the mysteries of existence worthy of agonistic respect. But such recognition already compromises the highest hopes of community. For existing settlements become politicized if a significant element of the populace credibly and insistently refuses to treat them as natural, thoroughly rational, reflective of a dialogic consensus, or grounded in a higher direction and if another cluster of participants evinces agonistic respect for this orientation even while opposing it. The communitarian ontology must receive a more secure consensus than this alternative picture of agonistic engagement within a culture requires. It must triumph over the perspectives of its opponents (and not merely its post-Nietzschean opponents) if its ideal of community is to be realized. A stalemate in ontological politics is exactly what it must overcome to enact its ideal.

This epistemic asymmetry leads one to suspect that there may be a protective power in being after all. The ambiguity of being protects us from the imposition of harmonious community on the populist grounds that, hey, our faith in the ambiguity of life is at least as good as yours in the ontological preconditions of community. But, of course, the actual terms of contestation can never be quite as simple as this formulation suggests.

The Politics of Paradox

I have contended that liberal individualism, liberal individuality, and liberal communitarianism generate complementary strategies to evade the paradox of difference. How, then, might it be engaged? My response is to acknowledge it and to convert it into a politics of the paradoxical, into a conception of the political as the medium through which the interdependent antinomies of identity and difference can be expressed and contested. This orientation is offered (again) not as a definitive *solution* to the paradox of difference, but as a means by which to contest the affinities and closures shared by dominant responses to that paradox.

This perspective on politics endorses dimensions from each of the theories criticized here. From liberal individualism and civic liberalism it draws the understanding that any way of life that enables people to act collectively must embody a set of norms and commonalities that are given variable degrees of primacy in the common life. From the civic tradition alone it draws appreciation of the hermeneutic character of ethical and political discourse, wherein debate and argumentation proceed from preconceptions and convictions already present in the life of the self and society. From the theory of liberal individuality it draws the understanding that the claims of individuality often clash with the claims of conventionality, order, and normality, emphasizing more than theorists of individuality tend to that both sets of claims enter into the interior of the self as well as into public arenas of discursive engagement. And from the Nietzschean legacy it draws nontheistic reverence for the ambiguity of existence and the (iffy) idea that every identity is a contingent artifice that encounters resistances and recalcitrance to the pressures that form it. In each of these instances, though, it politicizes elements that the single-minded bearers of these insights tend to treat in unpolitical ways.

It may be pertinent to note how, according to the perspective advanced here, each of the other traditions repeals an essential element of politics. Kateb, Taylor, and Nietzsche provide excellent exemplifications. The first seeks to insulate the individual from political intrusions, endorsing minimalism in politics in the name of individuality. The second thematizes politics as a gathering together of disparate forces into a shared purpose realized in common, deflating the corollary idea of politics as a perpetual contestation of established commonalities that prevents injuries and injustices within them from becoming too thoroughly naturalized, rationalized, or grounded in a higher direction in being. The third projects an overman who engages the ambiguity of existence largely outside the reach of politics.[23]

On the model of liberalism projected here, the politicization of identities and commonalities is intrinsic to the ideal itself: the regulative ideal is one in which creative tension is generated between the claims of individuality and commonality, the claims of identity and that in the self which resists those claims, the drive to transcendence and that which is repressed by any particular claim to transcendence, the imperatives of the present and the claims of the future, the existing field of discourse and possibilities latent in its partially repressed history. From this perspective juridical politics, minimalist politics, and communitarian politics emerge as complementary apolitical ideals; each deflates one or more of the dimensions needed to keep the politicization of difference alive.

What, then, is the paradox of politics, and how does it relate to the politicization of identity? It can be given a variety of formulations. Here is one: A politics of the common good is essential both to sustain a particular set of identities worthy of admiration and to enable the public to act self-consciously in support of justice and the public interest as they emerge in the common life. But this politics of public rationality presents an ambiguous face. The very success in defining and enacting commonalities tends to naturalize them, to make them appear as unambiguous goods lodged in nature or consent or reason or the universal character of the normal individual or ideal dialogue or a higher direction in being. If humans are not predesigned, and if they therefore are ill suited to fit neatly into any particular social form, then any set of enabling commonalities is likely to contain corollary injuries, cruelties, subjugations, concealments, and restrictions worthy of disturbance and contestation. Each set of identities will generate differences that themselves need to find a political voice.

Another way to pose the paradox is this: The human animal is essentially incomplete without social form; and a common language, institutional setting, set of traditions, and political forum for enunciating public purposes are indispensable to the acquisition of an identity and the commonalities essential to life. But every form of social completion and enablement also contains subjugations and cruelties within it. Politics, then, is the medium through which these ambiguities can be engaged and confronted, shifted and stretched. It is simultaneously a medium through which common purposes are crystallized and the consummate means by which their transcription into musical harmonies is exposed, contested, disturbed, and unsettled. A society that enables politics as this ambiguous medium is a good society because it enables the paradox of difference to find expression in public life.

This perspective is, of course, a liberalism, an alternative, militant liberalism both indebted to and competitive with other liberalisms and nonliberalisms contending for presence in late-modern life. It is a liberalism in its refusal to choose between revolutionary overthrow and the idealization of traditional culture, in its appreciation of the claims of individuality, in its attentiveness to rights and constitutional protections, in its extension of these concerns to forces that would expand the dialectic of discipline and reactive disaffection to new corners of life, in its skepticism about any definitive resolution of the paradoxical relationship between identity and difference, in its radicalization of liberal battles against the hegemony of teleological and transcendental theories, in the ironic distance it insinuates into the identities it lives and modifies, in the ironic dimension in its politicization of difference in a world in which identity is essential to life, in its insistence on questioning fixed unities even while admiring some more than others.

It is not the best liberalism that can be dreamt, only the highest regulative ideal to pursue if we are incomplete without social form in a world not predesigned to mesh smoothly with any particular formation of personal and collective identity.

CHAPTER FOUR

Responsibility
for Evil

The Question of Responsibility

Responsibility is not a simple universal. In other times and places it was not so agent-centered as it is today: the primary human locus of responsibility was often the family or the clan rather than the individual; when heroic individuals were held responsible, the intentions of the actor often weighed less heavily than the results of the action for the community; revenge and sacrifice were often overt ingredients in practices of punishment and responsibility; and sometimes the gods absorbed a portion of the guilt, if not the responsibility, moderns distribute among themselves.

Thus, to take one example, according to A.W.H. Adkins, the Homeric Greeks convey a world of selfhood, responsibility, and faith quite unlike ours. The experience of a plurality of centers of action in the self was accentuated ("the existence of, so to speak, separate 'little people' within the individual"), while the experience of the unity of the self was weak; self-control was valued less highly than strength and success; shame was given priority over guilt in the regulation of conduct. The understanding that the gods intervene competitively in the life of the self was highly developed; they could cause the individual "to do what he would not otherwise have done, or to perform an action more effectively than he would otherwise have done"; and the consequences of action for the welfare of the highly vulnerable community "carried significantly more weight for assessments of responsibility and merit than did imputations of intentions or motives."[1]

This cultural diversity can encourage us to treat established debates over the terms of responsibility and its proper range of application as a historically specific field of discourse bound up with particular conceptions of self, nature, state, language, god, past and future. To touch one item on this field is to move the others, and attempts to introduce significant changes to relieve a sense of injustice or cruelty in one place are often stymied by the adverse effects they engender at other places on the same field.

If responsibility is not a simple universal, it does nonetheless seem to be something like a porous universal or a primordial element in human life. Thus, even on Adkins's contestable reading, modern themes such as the coherence of the self and the importance of intentionality in judgments of responsibility do play a subordinate role in Homeric Greece; moreover, it is possible to identify a terrain upon which Homeric Greek ideas of self and responsibility may be *contrasted* with ours. Not only does no known culture completely lack the idea of responsibility; it stretches the idea of human life to the breaking point to imagine a way of life that does not include some idea bearing a family resemblance to familiar conceptions of responsibility. Reactive attitudes such as resentment, indignation, gratitude, pride, and love, for instance, embody presuppositions about the responsibility of the self and the other. And it is probably impossible to conceive of a way of life in which this range of attitudes is eliminated completely.

To say this much is not, in my thinking at any rate, to say that the primordial idea of responsibility is easy to articulate or readily defined as an unadulterated good. Perhaps standards of responsibility are both indispensable to social practice and productive of injustices within it. Perhaps, *because* every society demands some such standards, a problem of evil resides within any social practice that fulfills this demand relentlessly. Where is it written that the indispensability of a practice must correspond perfectly to the design of the beings to which it is applied? Perhaps responsibility is a systematically ambiguous practice.

These possibilities, then, place thought on guard. They lead one to suspect that attempts to reconstitute the idea of responsibility so that it can work more perfectly may even be part of the problem. Perhaps such attempts issue in the relocation of the evils that impelled the reform. Perhaps that is why the history of western thought is full of attempts to relocate the locus of responsibility: from humanity to the gods, from god to humanity, from a collectivity to the individual, from the past to the present, and, again, from the individual to a new vision of collectivity.

When one glances, not at the criteria of responsibility, but at the field of conduct to which such standards apply in everyday life, it is clear that a sea change has been underway during the last few decades. Areas of conduct in which judgments of self-responsibility, merit, and blameworthiness were prominent have been evacuated or converted into fields of contestation. Obesity, alcoholism, timidity, aggressivity, promiscuity, hypertension, homelessness, homosexuality, hyperactivity, and insanity provide a miscellany of examples. Indeed, some of these terms nominally suggest the old ideas ("homosexual," "promiscuous"), while others embody newly revised judgments that may contain their own injustices ("hyperactive," "homeless").

In some cases, what was once the responsibility of the individual is now treated as a genetic or contingent predisposition resistant to rectification through individual will; in others, the locus of responsibility has shifted from the individual to the family or "community," or from the direct will of the agent to its will to apply techniques of behavioral change to the self; in others, the conduct has been converted from a moral issue into a clinical concern; and in still others, what was viewed as a moral or clinical concern has now become a political issue in which some constituencies try to reconstitute established standards of normality and abnormality so that the question of responsibility for defect itself becomes moot.

When one looks back at the practices of responsibility preceding these particular changes, they now appear to have been pervaded by harshness and self-righteousness. The alcoholic had to contend not only with the debilitating effects of the disease but with the moral judgment of those who construed it as simply a willful abdication of self-responsibility. The families of schizophrenics had to cope not only with the awful instability of a suffering sibling but also with the clinical judgment that it was created by a "double bind" governing the family life. Gays had to deal (and still must) not only with the experience of a sexuality outside the norm but also with the issue of whether they or their parents were responsible for the abnormality. The person with hypertension had to deal not only with the pressures and risks flowing from her condition but also with the charge that it flowed from willful traits in her character. Meanwhile, the normal types benefited not only from the advantages of conforming to the norm but also from the judgment that the irresponsibility or sickness of the other proved their own generic responsibility, merit, or health.

Perhaps the quest by normals for a sense of moral superiority contributed pressures to define the first set of abnormalities in terms of self-responsibility. Perhaps the demand to hold the other responsible for defects flows to some degree from the demand to treat oneself as responsible for every virtue attained. Maybe such patterns of insistence invade the practice of responsibility, partly because reflection on the ambiguity of responsibility as both indispensable to social life and a depository of secondary injustice poses too potent a threat to the security of personal and collective identity.

Many contemporaries now discern cruelty and injustice in the judgments about alcoholism, homosexuality, schizophrenia, and so on that prevailed in this culture only a couple of generations ago. The challenge, though, is to come to terms with the predispositions that encouraged these cruelties, with the field of understandings that concealed them, and with areas of contemporary life where these predispositions and presumptions continue to operate below the threshold of thematization. Otherwise, reflective judgments in this area will mostly be retrospective in character, and the contemporary relaxation of responsibility in some areas is likely to fuel drives to intensify it in others. For if the drive to responsibility is as multifarious and powerful as I have suggested, if, that is, it is a phenomenon susceptible to overdetermination, it is reasonable to expect that the ambiguation of responsibility in certain areas of life will create compensatory pressures to twist the screws more tightly in others. As I suggested earlier, the contemporary demand that each person convert her life into a project or accept the consequences of marginalization may constitute one such area of intensification today.[2]

Is it credible to applaud responsibility as an ambiguous good while contesting the singular demands that govern its practice? Is it possible to shift the field of discourse upon which the logic of responsibility is located to relieve or redress violence in attributions of responsibility without jettisoning the practice altogether?

Anti-Semite and Jew

The potentiality for anti-Semitism is sunk deeply into the roots of Christian culture. A monotheistic religion with universalist pretensions, launched in response to the exclusive monotheism of Judaism and defined against Pharisaism, centering upon Jesus as the incarnation of god on earth, certainly contains anti-Semitic possibilities. The core of Christianity is implicated in the history and persistence of anti-Semitism. There are also elements in Christianity that combat or neutralize these anti-Semitic predispositions. Which way things actually tilt depends on situational factors.

A strong doctrine of responsibility is one that supposes that every discernible evil must be caused by some agency that is itself blameworthy and deserves to be treated as the embodiment of an evil will. Such a doctrine is rooted in Augustine's solution to the problem of evil, where free will and original sin coalesce in an uneasy combination to locate the ultimate responsibility for evil within humanity. Even the human inevitability of death is something for which the first sinners were responsible. When such a doctrine converges with outbreaks of calamity, the conditions are perfect for persecution through attribution of responsibility. Agents are sought who might be held responsible for the new experience of evil, and among the likely candidates are members of that minority whose ancestors are said to have betrayed the first Christian.

Thus, to take one example, in the mid-fourteenth century in France, when the Black Plague was ravaging the country, a massacre of Jews occurred. The evil was traced to a group that was held responsible for it. Guillaume de Machaut, in *The Judgment of the King of Navarre*, describes approvingly how responsibility was established and the appropriate punishment delivered:

> After that came a false, treacherous and contemptible swine: this was shameful Israel, the wicked and disloyal who hated good and loved every evil, who gave so much gold and silver and promises to Christians, who then poisoned several rivers and fountains that had been clear and pure so that many lost their lives; for whoever used them died suddenly. Certainly ten times one hundred thousand died from it, in country and city. Then finally this mortal calamity was noticed.
>
> He who sits on high and sees far, who governs and provides for everything, did not want this treachery to remain hidden; he revealed it and made it so generally known that they lost their lives and possessions. Then every Jew was destroyed, some hanged, others burned; some were drowned, others beheaded with an ax or sword. And many Christians died together with them in shame.[3]

An evil occurred. Human responsibility was assumed. Guilty agents were identified and punished. The prosecutors convinced themselves that their action was necessary and righteous. They were responding to persecution rather than initiating it.

But that was then. Don't we today possess a germ theory of disease to immunize us against such an interpretive response? And doesn't the experience of the holocaust teach us just how the logic of persecution proceeds?

A compelling account of modern anti-Semitism is provided by Sartre in *Anti-Semite and Jew*, written in 1944 as World War II was ending.[4] It is important both because of the particular subject it considers and because it serves as a conscious or unconscious model for a whole series of accounts of racism, sexism, national chauvinism, and antiwelfarism succeeding it during the last several decades.

According to Sartre, the anti-Semite construes the Jew as responsible for the most demeaning evils he and his nation suffer. This insistence serves essential functions. First, it allows the anti-Semite to dissociate himself from responsibility for those things about himself or his condition he finds demeaning. "The anti-Semite is afraid of discovering that the world is ill-contrived, for then it would be necessary for him to invent and modify, with the result that man would be found to be the master of his own destinies, burdened with an agonizing and infinite responsibility. Thus he localizes all responsibility in the Jew" (40).

Second, it enables him to avoid recognition of how much the world diverges from the harmonious condition he projects into its basic or true structure, for this true harmony could be realized only if the Jew were removed from it. "Underneath the bitterness of the anti-Semite is concealed the optimistic belief that harmony will be re-established once evil is eliminated" (43).

Third, it allows him to defer critical examination of the good he endorses. "The more one is absorbed in fighting Evil the less one is tempted to place the Good in question" (44).

Finally, it licenses him to ignore the law in fighting the evil he has identified, allowing him to humiliate, degrade, or kill the other in the name of the good he refuses to examine. It releases his violent desires from the obligations of self-restraint. Even the ambiguous denotation "a beautiful Jewess" serves this function, identifying an attractive target who invites rape and degradation by her mode of being.

The idea that "the Jew . . . has as much free will as is necessary for him to take full responsibility for the crimes of which he is the author" (39), then, enables the anti-Semite to live a life of "inverted liberty": he is free to accuse the other of every evil, to exempt himself from every responsibility, to take matters into his own hands if the government does not respond to the call of the "real France," and to protect himself from confronting the chasm separating the human condition as he insists it must be and the way it is in reality. "Floating between an authoritarian society which has not yet come into existence and an official and tolerant society which he disavows, he can do anything he pleases without appearing to be an anarchist, which would abhor him" (33).

In a brief, unglossed passage, Sartre suggests that "anti-Semitism has kept something of the nature of human sacrifice" (51). A Christian culture is supposed to transcend the cult of sacrifice, with Jesus on the cross representing the last and definitive sacrifice. But the anti-Semite reenacts this cult. The Jew must be sacrificed so the anti-Semite can inflict cruelty without responsibility. The first must be sacrificed so that the second's vision of harmony can be protected. The other is sacrificed so that the self can project an infantile image of self-identity, national unity, and the human condition.

The institutionalized accusations of the anti-Semite place Jews in an untenable situation: if society is torn by class struggle, they are said to seduce the workers into it; if there is financial crisis, they create it by conspiratorial control of financial institutions; if national chauvinism is insufficiently intense, they control the culture that erodes it.

In such a context of accusation and sporadic violence one response is to subject oneself to constant self-examination so that nothing in one's conduct or demeanor corresponds to the stereotype propagated against one. But this creates a new stereotype for persecution: the cautious, self-demeaning, ingratiating Jew who is inauthentic with respect to himself and all the more vulnerable to new assaults by the anti-Semite.

Alternatively, the Jew may seek assimilation, by accepting the universalistic, democratic doctrine of the liberal who says that we are all humans in essence and no particular identity is essential to one's humanity. The message here is: you can be assimilated as a universal "man" as long as you stop being a particular Jew. And once again the Jew is called upon to purge his own particularity through self-examination and self-reformation. The problem is compounded by the fact that the Jew's official ally (the universalist democrat) lacks passion, while his overt enemies overflow with it.

These two possibilities recall the options of conquest and conversion examined in Todorov's account of the first encounter between Europe and America. The strategies for constituting and coping with the internal other thus mirror those applied to the external other. And in a way that parallels Todorov's analysis of those Spanish priests who tried to transcend these two alternatives, Sartre closes his account of the dialectical relation between anti-Semite and Jew by considering the Jew who actively asserts the "Jewishness" attributed to him. He ends with a stark conclusion: "The situation of the Jew is that everything he does turns against him" (74).

Sartre's analysis of the sources and implications of this double bind is rich in detail and impressive in the insights it discloses. Surely, any account of anti-Semitism must draw upon these riches. But the Sartrean account draws upon a second tier of considerations that threaten to reinstate the very dialectic it has identified and condemned.

There are two poles in the (early) Sartrean model: the absolute freedom of the self to choose its self and the "situation" in which such choices occur. The former makes each self responsible for what it is and does. The latter establishes the specific context in which self-responsibility is enacted. At the level of generality Sartre says, "without respite, from the beginning of our lives to the end, we are responsible for the merit we enjoy" (27). Following this maxim, he is able to conclude that "anti-Semitism is a free and total choice of oneself" (17).

But while everyone has absolute choice and a situation at the abstract level, Sartre locates the anti-Semite and the Jew at opposite poles from each other in assigning responsibility for this condition. He loads narrative weight on the absolute freedom of the self when discussing the anti-Semite and then shifts it to the situation in which freedom is enacted when discussing the Jew. The anti-Semite has freely chosen his self, and the Jew has been enclosed in a situation in which any choice of self is self-defeating.

Why does Sartre not, for instance, construe both parties as living in situations where every viable choice of self is self-defeating? It is easy to imagine how such an analysis might be applied to the anti-Semite. For the anti-Semite often does not fare well when measured according to received standards of culture, intellectuality, social achievement, and social status, and this situation could easily generate a set of alternatives that degrade the self-respect of the agents enacting them. What if the anti-Semite as well as the Jew chooses his life within the grip of a double bind?

Or, why does Sartre not identify self-generated pressures toward inauthenticity (pressures to treat identity as given or true rather than forged or chosen) in both parties, even if to varying degrees? For his abstract theory of the human condition postulates a *general anxiety* about freedom that exerts pressure on everyone to engage in "bad faith."

Neither of these interpretive strategies would reduce or qualify the evil in anti-Semitism, at least not in the primordial sense of evil as fundamental and undeserved suffering. Why, then, not pursue them?

Well, the first reason is that a simple *reversal* of this distribution of responsibility would replicate and intensify the logic of anti-Semitism. And second—particularly for those who insist that moral purity as such depends upon adoption of a single model of responsibility for evil—any *redistribution* of responsibility would make it appear that Sartre is casting blame on the victims for the evil they suffer.

But why are the alternatives available to Sartre reduced to these? Better, why does the theoretical structure governing his interpretation reduce the choices to holding the anti-Semite responsible, holding the Jew responsible, or distributing responsibility between them?

The Sartrean rhetorical strategy implicitly maintains symmetry between the depth of the evil identified (anti-Semitism) and the locus of responsible agency for it (the anti-Semite). The moral demand within that symmetry is this: for every evil there must be an agent (or set of agents) whose level of responsibility is proportionate to the seriousness of the evil. This demand is morally satisfying, but it also contains a strain of cruelty. For it requires Sartre to relocate and recapitulate the structure of accusations the anti-Semite projects upon the other.

Sartre thus stands to the anti-Semite as the *mild* anti-Semite (a figure of importance in his analysis) stands to the Jew. This can be seen by recasting the charges he makes against the anti-Semite. Thus, Sartre's very attribution of singular responsibility to the anti-Semite discourages Sartre from "looking into himself" to ascertain whether the presumption of harmony between the level of evil and the level of responsibility is a form of insistence. This attribution enables him to deflect the question whether his model of self-responsibility contains cruelty within it. Perhaps his demand to "localize all evil" flows from a fear of discovering that "the world is ill-contrived." Perhaps "underneath the bitterness" against the anti-Semite "is concealed the optimistic belief that harmony" between evil and responsibility for it must be discernible once the true model of freedom and situation is elucidated. Perhaps the more exclusively he is governed by this demand in his "fight against evil" the less able he is to place the "good" of singular responsibility for evil "in question." Perhaps the demand for symmetry expresses an "optimistic belief that harmony will be re-established once evil is eliminated."

Sartre may not be entirely unaware that the charges he brings against the anti-Semite can be brought against his own analysis. The concluding chapter of *Anti-Semite and Jew* discloses a certain uneasiness about the diagnosis of evil that precedes it. For while the anti-Semite is still held singularly responsible for the evil he does, Sartre evinces little hope that he could be brought to accept this responsibility. The attribution of responsibility functions to reassure the opponent of anti-Semitism that where there is evil there is equivalent responsibility, but it does not point to a strategy for responding to it. And Sartre's explanation of why this is so tends to vitiate the moral equation that governs the preceding analysis.

He begins with a recollection of the analysis: "We have seen that it [anti-Semitism] is not a matter of an isolated opinion, but of the total choice that a man in a situation makes of himself and of the meaning of the universe." But now the distribution of weight in the analysis is reversed, and it is the situation of the anti-Semite that must be addressed: "If we wish to make such a choice impossible, it will not be enough to address ourselves to propaganda, education and legal interdictions against the liberty of the anti-Semite. Since he, like all men, exists as a free agent with a situation, it is his situation that must be modified from top to bottom. In short, if we can change the perspective of choice, then the choice itself will change. Thus, we do not attack freedom, but bring it about that freedom decides on other bases, and in terms of other structures" (148).

So the charge of responsibility secures moral satisfaction, but it does not provide an efficacious strategy to eliminate evil. And now we receive an indirect admission that the anti-Semite, too, lives in a difficult situation, one that exerts so much pressure on him to construct a "Manichean and primitive world in which hatred arises as a great explanatory myth" (148) that no appeal to freedom, responsibility, authenticity, or decency will move him to transcend it.

Sartre now replaces one exaggeration (the model of singular responsibility) with another (the quest for a world in which unity and commonality nullify the drive to nullify the other). "Anti-Semitism manifests the *separation* of men and their isolation in the midst of the community . . . : it can exist only in a society where a rather loose solidarity unites strongly structured pluralities. . . . Again, anti-Semitism would not have existence in a society without classes and founded on collective ownership of the instruments of labor, one in which man, freed of his hallucinations . . . , would at long last throw himself into *his* enterprise—which is to create the kingdom of man. Anti-Semitism would then be cut at its roots" (149–50).

I would underline a different phrase than the one Sartre has selected for emphasis: "it can exist only" reverses the priority between freedom and situation insisted upon in the moral diagnosis; it promises a world where the situation itself relaxes pressures that engender anti-Semitism and other sacrificial definitions of otherness. The ideal of community projected by Sartre in this last chapter formally resolves the impasse created by the earlier diagnosis, but it does so by confounding central elements governing the first analysis: it now denies that we are thrown into a world ill contrived to mesh with our most demanding drives for identity and harmony and that there is an ontological opacity in our relations with the world, the self, and one another. The shift of narrative emphasis from singular responsibility for evil to the contingent/changeable situation in which evil is generated discloses a persistent demand amid this theoretical oscillation: if responsibility cannot be located in the individual, it must be localizable in the collectivity.

But this new demand for community and solidarity threatens—from the vantage point of some assumptions adopted by Sartre in the earlier analysis and others supported in this concluding chapter—to convert the situation of everyone into one too close for comfort to that of the assimilating Jew in a world of anti-Semitism. One of the situational sources of "Jewish disquietude is the necessity imposed upon the Jew of subjecting himself to endless self-examination and finally of assuming a phantom personality, at once strange and familiar, that haunts him and which is nothing but himself—himself as others see him" (78).

A Jew in a world of anti-Semitism is constantly pressed to observe himself from the perspective of the other, to regulate his demeanor and behavior so that he is not vulnerable to the panoply of accusations the anti-Semite is all too ready to bring against him. This is an intolerable "situation." But if humans are not prede-signed to coalesce with one another in some higher community of solidarity, the attempt to resolve persecution by creating such a harmonious community could have the effect of converting every-one into an agent of constant self-surveillance. Everyone could become "a witness against himself"; everyone could be subjected to the terms of self-examination Sartre so deftly exposes as the condition of the assimilating Jew in a world of anti-Semitism. The world would approximate the conditions of self-discipline and surveil-lance vividly portrayed by Foucault in his analysis of the panopti-con.[5]

Sartre's implicit demand for harmony between evil and the locus of responsibility eventually impels him to project an ideal of community that compromises his own insight into the debilitating effects of continuous self-surveillance. The ideal world he projects at the end of *Anti-Semite and Jew* looks suspiciously like the resent-ful ideal of harmony he insightfully identified as the existential demand at the root of anti-Semitism. For one of Sartre's most compelling insights is that the anti-Semite is driven by "the op-timistic belief that harmony will be re-established once evil is eliminated."

No wonder Sartre understands the double bind of the Jew in an anti-Semitic culture so well. Whichever way *he* turns, he cannot fulfill the demand for a doctrine worthy of his own endorsement. With each turn he perpetuates the logic of sacrifice he opposes, first through the demand for singular responsibility and then through the demand for communal solidarity. Perhaps everyone must come to terms with such a pattern of insistence in one's own thinking in order to curtail or redress the logic of moral sacrifice. In Sartre's case the insistence takes the form of an oscillation between an optimistic belief in symmetry between evil and the locus of respon-sibility and an optimistic belief in the prospects for social harmony once the institutional preconditions for self-responsibility are in-stalled.

The Instability of Responsibility

Charles Taylor advances a critique of Sartre's understanding of identity and responsibility that converges and collides with the one offered here. He criticizes the idea that the individual is an agent of "radical choice," finding it incoherent in a way that inadvertently deepens insight into the logic of responsibility.

When we think of a person as responsible for her actions, we tend also to think of her as responsible for the evaluations that enter into them. But what model of responsibility applies here? Sartre, says Taylor, draws on the model of radical choice, saying that each of us chooses the self he becomes and the evaluations that emanate from that self. Bad faith is the unwillingness to admit to oneself the truth of radical choice.

But the idea of radical choice turns out to presuppose elements it denies. When the young man portrayed in *Existentialism Is a Humanism* is torn between remaining with his sick mother and joining the resistance, Sartre portrays this as a dilemma in which a radical choice must be made, a choice not itself grounded in a prior set of judgments or principles. Taylor agrees that a choice is necessary here, but this is so only because the dilemma occurs in a prior context where both options exert a moral pull on the agent involved; the very fact that it is a dilemma reveals that the agent draws upon a web of prejudgments that constitute his situation and, to some extent, his identity. It "is a dilemma only because the claims themselves are not created by radical choice."[6]

It is the standing of these prior claims that Taylor pursues. They cannot themselves be said to be chosen, for the idea of choice operates only in a situation where alternatives are present, each with some degree of difference from the other. "A choice made without regard to anything, without the agent feeling any solicitation to one alternative or the other . . . , is this still choice?" (293). It seems clear to Taylor that it is not.

Taylor then concludes that something more is going on here. This choice rests upon an implicit structure of "strong evaluation." Strong evaluation occurs in a context of judgment/discovery that one is already deeply implicated in a web of prejudgments that constitute one's identity to some degree and that serve as the porous and inchoate ground upon which one's specific evaluations develop. Choice of self is never truly radical because it always presupposes a prior background that exerts a pull on the self.

So, Taylor says, in Sartre's theory of radical choice strong evaluation "creeps back in even where it is supposed to have been excluded" (294). But does it creep back into the ontology Sartre advances or into the prior formation of self that precedes radical choice in Sartre's theory?

Certainly, the doctrine of radical choice rests upon a fundamental ontology Sartre explicitly advances. For Sartre holds that humans are thrown into a world where there is no higher being or transcendental argument providing a ground for the principles they adopt. They are, finally and ultimately, "responsible" for themselves in some sense of this protean word. Even as the late Sartre progressively attenuated the idea of radical choice through conceptions of serialization, totalization, practico-inert, lived experience (*le vécu*), and, in general, *la force des choses*, he reaffirmed the earlier judgment that there is no higher direction in being available to human beings to articulate or discern. Granted that Sartre often advances this ontology as an announcement not itself open to problematization, once this "strong" judgment has been advanced, the doctrine of radical choice can be seen to emerge as *one* of the possibilities to explore. A set of other alternatives (including Taylor's own) are foreclosed from exploration from the start.

Taylor is right to the extent that he discloses the prior assumptions that favor this doctrine of choice; he is also correct, in my judgment, in his charge that ethical choice always invokes a background only partly under the conscious purview of the evaluating agent. We are not responsible for all of the presumptions under which we act. One might endorse these two points, though, without necessarily tossing out other ingredients in Sartre's ontology. That is, one might repudiate Sartre's doctrine of radical choice, with its implication that one is always thoroughly responsible for the self one is, without endorsing Taylor's particular theory of the self, questioning, and responsibility (294, 296).

Taylor, however, uses this critique of the idea of radical choice as a springboard to endorse an alternative ontology of the self. Here, radical choice becomes subservient to "radical questioning." Strong evaluation is now interpreted as consisting of moral judgment formed against a background of prejudgments that it invokes, crystallizes, and perfects through tests of coherence. While Taylor does not meticulously argue that the deepest element of the self contains an inchoate deposit of prejudgments that bring the questioning self closer to truth as it articulates and endorses them, he does pile ontological weight on the fact that the evaluating self constantly *presupposes* this to be true *as* it evaluates, and he does adopt a rhetorical style that discourages one from exploring ways to question or ambiguate *this* set of presumptions.

Radical questioning itself is enclosed in a set of privileged prejudgments, then. Let's call Taylor's a doctrine of quasi-radical self-questioning. This revised image of questioning is then invoked to endorse a model of deep responsibility for the self not grounded in the idea that the self (radically) chooses itself. Here is how Taylor evokes the counter-doctrine of responsibility he endorses (the emphases, however, are mine):

> There is in fact another sense in which we are radically responsible. *Our* evaluations are not chosen. On the contrary, they are articulations of our sense of *what is worthy, or higher, or more integrated, or more fulfilling*, and so forth. But this sense can never be fully or satisfactorily articulated. And moreover it touches on matters where there is so much room for *self-deception, for distortion, for blindness* and insensitivity, *that the question can always arise whether one is sure*, and the injunction is always in place to *look again.* [294]

> *Our* attempts to formulate what we hold important *must*, like descriptions, *strive to be faithful to something*. But what they strive to be faithful to is not an independent object with a fixed degree of evidence, but rather a largely unarticulated sense of *what is of decisive importance.* . . . It is precisely the *deepest* evaluations which are least clear, least articulated. . . . It is those which are closest to what I am as a subject, in the sense that shorn of them I would break down as a person, which are among the hardest for me to be clear about. [296]

Several points in these two "articulations" deserve notice. First, Taylor's text concentrates its *analysis* on the dependence of explicit formulations upon the inchoate background it invokes and translates into words. This is the terrain where (the early) Sartre is weakest and where the alternative position reveals its greatest strength. But second, Taylor does not then delineate a plurality of conceptions of self and responsibility that might be compatible with such a broad understanding of the relation between reflection and prereflection. He binds these general points against Sartre to a particular ontology of self and responsibility.

The conception advanced recapitulates an Augustinian model at several points: the self is a deep self able to become more attuned to deep truths pursued through an internal process of confession and self-inquiry; the more carefully and honestly one probes the inner self, the closer one gets to one's fundamental identity and the deepest mysteries of divinity; but this truth, because it is infinite and we are finite, is never achieved "fully or satisfactorily"; the self must hence be alert to its propensities to "self-deception" in a condition in which its abilities are limited, its dependence great, and its disposition to "blindness and insensitivity" significant; nonetheless, the self must "strive to be faithful to something . . . , not an independent object with a fixed degree of evidence, but rather a largely unarticulated sense of what is of decisive importance"—that is, the finite self must be attentive to the infinite god to the extent possible; and finally, even amid the limits to self-transparency, the self remains "radically responsible," not so much in its choices (which are secondary) as in its quest to articulate—or the grace that enables it to receive?—the deepest truths about itself.

The power of Taylor's evocations derives from the fact that many of his readers are predisposed to respond to them, making the strategy of evocation more effective than a more prosaic statement of beliefs, arguments, or commandments. Taylor has a long tradition to draw upon, invested in the very terms of discourse he artfully deploys. These include the deep, confessing self; the notion of responsibility as responsiveness to a higher direction or power; the understanding of articulation as always partial and incomplete; the binding together of interior depth and truth; the idea of radical questioning as a probing of deeper truths inchoately residing in the interior of the self; the idea of strong evaluation as a process that includes reception of transcendent truth within it; and the admission that while one can get closer to this inner source of light and truth, one will never reach it fully or certainly.

The rhetorical techniques by which the particular doctrine is folded into the general critique of radical choice deserve attention. For instance, the key terms selected to portray the relation of a self to its internal and external world evoke the experience of discovery and elevation rather than, say, the experience of a socially formed self established upon a raw being partly resistant to its own form. This latter possibility is not considered and contested; rather, the former possibility is inserted gracefully into the mode of presentation as if it provided the only viable alternative to the Sartrean model of radical choice. Taylor's social ontology is carried by rhetorical tropes that are not problematized within his text.

Strategic invocations of "we" and "our" float among these formulations without close specification. They refer variously and indeterminately to a we who agree with Taylor, a we who are implicated in the tradition he invokes, a we who retain faith in the most fundamental postulates of that tradition, a we who often express certain presuppositions when we operate in this tradition, a universal we who must presuppose some notion of truth every time a proposition is advanced, a universal we who avoid the risk of breaking down by refusing to call these presuppositions into question, a universal we who cannot (logically) come up with ways of calling into question at one moment presuppositions necessary at another, and so on.

The "must" in Taylor's formulations functions in a similarly protean way: it may be a moral must at one moment, a logical must at another, and a moral must implicitly treated as if it might be a logical must at yet another. The threat that "shorn of [these deep evaluations] I would break down as a person," for instance, follows and lends energy to the conviction that we "must . . . strive to be faithful to something."

I am not suggesting that Taylor's doctrine of responsibility is false because it draws upon a particular set of discursive strategies. Every such theory, including the one I endorse, invokes rhetorical supports. I am suggesting that too much of the persuasive power of this doctrine moves below the threshold of critical reflection and that the faith it embodies may even discourage efforts to engage its own practices of conversion and confession. This doctrine depends for its effectiveness upon a fundamental, contestable faith, and that teleological faith becomes both more overt and contestable as the rhetorical pores through which it is secreted are opened up.

When one examines Sartre and Taylor *together*, then, it becomes apparent that the idea of "responsibility" itself is a locus of persistent instability and contestation in late-modern discourse. The persistence of instability is indicated by the fact that no single doctrine of responsibility is able to rule the others out while establishing itself securely and by the fact that each doctrine can point to difficulties in the others more readily than it can eliminate them in itself. And this persisting condition, I want to say, should ("must") enter into any particular reading of responsibility.

Each of these doctrines has a long lineage behind it as well, and if I am on the right track, not only the contemporary debate over responsibility but the history of debates preceding it reveal deep instability in western discourse about responsibility.

If Taylor's notion of responsibility is bound up with the Augustinian tradition of will and grace, the very instabilities within that doctrine (its problematic relation to a god, its difficulties in establishing a coherent doctrine of will, its tendency to define the other who deviates far from its core identity as an evil to be conquered or converted) set it up to be the persistent object of doubt, opposition, and contestation. The same is true of the other doctrines encountered here. Sartre himself identifies the stance of the anti-Semite with a form of Manicheanism adamantly opposed by Augustine after his conversion to Christianity. And Sartre's own position is remarkably close to the Pelagian doctrine that the early Augustine entertained and the later Augustine set himself against as a heresy to be suppressed.[7] If one understands a heresy as a temptation a doctrine first creates through ambivalence in its own categories and then condemns in order to maintain its own purity, then Augustine's relation to the temptation he incited and condemned exposes something about the fundamental instability of responsibility in the west.

The Pelagians, as early Sartreans who believed in god, thought each could be saved from sin by her own efforts, but Augustine contended that such a belief would eventually pull believers away from the god who saved them through grace. Sartre has proven him right in this prediction.

Augustine himself needed "free will" in order to save his god from the taint of evil, but he also needed to confine its exercise severely in order to save his theology from fading into a secular doctrine of self-perfection. Original sin as a supplement to the notion of free will filled this bill nicely: free will in its first and only pure expression in Adam established that gap between humanity and god which protected the latter from responsibility for evil, and the inheritance of this original sin thereafter restricted the scope of will in the fallen self enough to make salvation depend on god's grace rather than, as the Pelagians said, human will alone. And Augustine needed both the gap of will and the connection of grace to protect his god's omnipotence.

Original sin provided a place to locate responsibility whenever the judgment of will seemed too forced or peremptory. It served not as a competitor to the idea of free will, but as an indispensable complement that protected the purity of the first idea in its own sphere.

Compare the old pair "free will and original sin" with the new pair "responsibility and delinquency/abnormality." The second members of these pairs play similar roles in their own times: they save the purity of willful responsibility by absorbing those dimensions of life and action that would otherwise compromise the credibility of such responsibility; they deflect the demand to demonstrate instances of free will by producing instances of what it is not; and they allow free will to exist as the residuum. "Free will," it seems, cannot be saved in its purity unless it is joined by a twin that absorbs the discernible impurities that contaminate it.

But in both times the category introduced to serve as the complement to willful responsibility eventually runs into deep difficulties of its own: it loses much of its credibility or its appearance of internal integrity. The dilemma occurs and recurs on two planes: the necessity for a supplement recurrently overturns the hopes of Pelagians and Sartreans for a single, pure model of responsibility; and the inability to secure such a model repeatedly engenders a dualism of responsibility that then encounters grave difficulties in stabilizing itself.

The fact that modern society has found it necessary to introduce a new category to serve functions previously served by the (not quite) defunct category of original sin can be read as a sign both of the persistent instability of responsibility in the west and of a long-term refusal to acknowledge the depths and persistence of this instability. You might picture western practices of responsibility as two poles crossing each other. The horizontal pole consists at one end of a deep identity to be discovered and at the other of a self formed through radical choice. The vertical pole consists of original sin at one end and mental illness at the other. A variety of individuals and groups have been nailed to this cross whenever the problem of evil has become too intense to bear.

The political bearing of the cross of responsibility may be intimated by Foucault when he treats the modern pairing of the responsible offender and the delinquent as a strategic device operating below the threshold of conscious deliberation: "They reinforce each other. When a judgment cannot be framed in terms of good and evil, it is stated in terms of normal and abnormal. And when it is necessary to justify this last distinction, it is done in terms of what is good or bad for the individual. These are expressions that signal the fundamental duality of western consciousness."[8]

Taylor and Sartre offer two contemporary doctrines of responsibility, embodying modernizations, respectively, of Augustinianism and of a heresy (Pelagianism) it spawned. Each of these contemporary doctrines draws sustenance from roots sunk deeply into the rocky terrain of the western tradition. Each root is renewed and reconstituted periodically by frustrations, uncertainties, cruelties, and impatiences generated by the demands or limits of the other. Each periodically finds itself confounded either by its need for a supplement it cannot secure with confidence or by its unsuccessful struggle to establish itself without recourse to that need. And each creates temptations for a heresy (modern Manicheanism) it has limited resources to fend off. Together these doctrines signify the persistence and instability of the western legacy of responsibility.

Much of the harshness in late-modern ascriptions of responsibility lies in the unwillingness of many to acknowledge doubts, gaps, and points of contestability in the specific doctrines they invoke. Sartre and the anti-Semites he depicts exemplify this logic. It is less evident in Taylor's depiction, where injunctions against overconfidence are built into the formulations. On the other hand, the textual tactics Taylor deploys to lift the reader into the faith he endorses are not sufficiently flagged or self-problematized. This enables him to proceed as if his position were the most viable one on a fixed field of discourse rather than a familiar alternative colliding with others on unstable terrain. Argument by elimination, after all, succeeds only when the established field of debate is taken, implicitly or explicitly, to exhaust the range of alternatives.

Perhaps the (re)introduction of another candidate could intensify contestation and productive uncertainty here. It will have to present itself vigorously to establish space on this crowded terrain.

A Pagan Sermon

The pre-Platonic Greeks, Nietzsche suggests, in general agreement with the reading by Adkins cited earlier, drew upon polytheism to relieve and displace a portion of the guilt that would otherwise fall without relief on earthly surrogates. He quotes Zeus:

> Strange how these mortals so loudly complain of the gods!
> We alone produce evil, they say; yet themselves
> Make themselves wretched through folly, even counter to fate.

"Yet," Nietzsche says,

one can see and hear how even this Olympian spectator and judge is far from holding a grudge against them or thinking ill of them on that account: "how foolish they are!", he thinks when he observes the misdeeds of mortals . . . ; foolishness, *not* sin! do you grasp that? . . . In this way the gods served in those days to justify man to a certain extent even in his wickedness, they served as the originators of evil—in those days they took upon themselves, not the punishment but, what is nobler, the guilt.[9]

Paganism, in some of its Greek forms, encouraged the displacement of human guilt, relieving the pressure to identify guilty agents on earth by attributing guilt to contending, limited gods. It held heroic figures responsible for the results of their actions, but relieved them of at least some of the guilt. This is one of the crucial ways Greek cosmology challenges Christian theology. It points the way to a relaxation of the demand for symmetry between the experience of evil and human responsibility for it, a symmetry that remains powerful in contemporary secular culture, with its prehistory of faith in a single, universal, omnipotent, benevolent, omniscient god who must be protected at all costs from any taint of responsibility for evil.

Paganism fostered sacrifice to propitiate the gods. But at least *its* code of sacrifice was overt. And at least its victims were not always held responsible for the fate imposed upon them. Sometimes they were thought to be innocent: they did not deserve what the community nonetheless had to do to them. Sometimes the sacrifice of what was most loved and cherished was necessary to acknowledge a rent in the order of things and to provide hope of repairing it. Such rites, repugnant to my and our sensibility, nonetheless point to the ethical importance of probing gaps between the social indispensability of responsibility and the desert of those to whom it is applied. Once this gap is prized open, it may reveal cruelties concealed within the ambiguous practices of responsibility. Maybe modern sensibility insists upon too much cleanliness in its categories, sweeping dirt under the rug in its own idealizations of responsibility.

Modern life cannot dispense with responsibility, but life exceeds, resists, and overflows the mold of responsibility imposed upon it. Responsibility is both indispensable to life and an artificial construct imposed upon beings never exhausted by its attributions. Responsibility is an indispensable ambiguity, a real fabrication, a constructed reality. In these circumstances it would be foolish and cruel to treat the self as if this organization corresponded to an essential mode of being preceding it. It would be doubly cruel to insist that every transgression that escapes the dictates of responsibility must be treated as a sickness simply because its bearers differ from the ideal in some ways. For this latter insistence redeems the purity and sufficiency of constructed standards of responsibility by treating anything that falls outside their orbit as a defect or mistake in a self predesigned to be a responsible agent. It saves the ideal of responsibility by creating a residual category in which to place everything that might otherwise contaminate it.

Perhaps the late-modern secular culture of punishment, guilt, responsibility, and sickness—formed through a history of engagements with a monotheistic theology—could use an infusion of imaginary paganism, itself secularized and modernized through a history of hypothetical engagements with monotheism. The inoculation might take the following form: We are not predesigned to be responsible agents, but we cannot dispense with practices of responsibility. This is the gap that must be maintained and honored in a *political* theory of responsibility.

From this vantage point, a revealing move in Taylor's argument occurs during one of its moments of reassurance, when he says that it "is precisely the deepest evaluations . . . which are closest to what I am as a subject, in the sense that shorn of them I would break down as a person." Here the pursuit of ethical integrity is tied to the avoidance of personal breakdown, and closer approximation to a true identity is bound to the attainment of ethical integrity.

What if it turned out, to reverse the equation experimentally, that that which threatens breakdown in the self can also bring it closer to the constructed and historically contingent character of its own identity? What if a risk of breakdown were bound up with care for difference, so that ethical responsiveness and discovery of deep identity were not bound together as neatly as Taylor suggests (where "depth of identity" here means discovery of a unity in the self toward which it tends)? Where, at any rate, is it written otherwise? And how solid is the stone upon which this scripture is inscribed? Where, similarly, is it written that the socio-systemic need for the practice of responsibility co-responds conveniently to the deepest structure of human being?

"Must" we maintain these equations because it is too painful to think that the accidents of being establish different conjunctions and disjunctions in this domain? Must "depth" mean the realization of higher harmony? Does avoidance of pain turn out to be the deepest basis of these "musts," so that it now becomes clear why so many theorists of the "must" systematically misread Nietzsche when they condemn his refusal to try to eliminate existential suffering? Might not these reassuring thoughts about depth and truth in identity contain cruelty within them? Why not test ourselves to see how far we can go in exploring less comforting possibilities, on the grounds that whatever is most reassuring in this domain is most likely to be in need of critical reconsideration? Might insistence on this line of equivalence itself infuse dogmatism into the politics of identity and cruelty into accusations of responsibility/sickness?

Deep theories of identity/responsibility/sickness establish a precondition for the production of scapegoats in a world where life flows through and over the structures of responsible agency. If I take my identity to be chosen or deep *essentially*, I am very likely to take you to share these traits to a considerable degree too. There is here a powerful pressure to interpret differences in your conduct through the categories of bad faith, false consciousness, innocence, deviation, sickness, and evil.

Both the doctrines examined here (the Pelagian and the Augustinian in their modern guises) contain enough demands to take these steps. Defenders of these views are thus not yet far *enough* removed from those zealots—the modern "Manicheans," at least as Sartre contestably uses this latter term—who vigorously identify and persecute scapegoats, even when the defenders oppose doing so themselves.

What, exactly, is the insistence within the Augustinian and Pelagian doctrines that arms the Manichean perversion recurrently haunting both? When asked, *Must* we truly have a true identity and a singular responsibility?, each draws upon a logical, rhetorical, and historical arsenal to answer both of these questions in the affirmative. Each refuses to initiate another series of reflections that might call the certainty of this first line of defense into question. Then, when historical crisis, personal uncertainty, or social instability erupt, and cautious advocates of each view are unable to detect a responsible agent accountable for the evil experienced, they are set up by their own doctrines to be accused of weakness, softness, equivocation, or misplaced compassion by modern Manicheans who share their initial conviction of radical choice or deep identity. Finding it difficult to reply convincingly, they may lapse into silence or respond in defensive tones that make it appear all the more that they "lack the courage of their own convictions." They find themselves in a situation where their own efforts to resist are turned against them.

Perhaps the insistence upon the truth of deep identity or singular responsibility simultaneously sets up these accusations and disarms the terms of response available to them.

Must we truly have a true identity? A Nietzschean perspective shares with the Augustinian tradition the conviction that this demand is rooted in an entire array of linguistic, psychological, epistemic, and political pressures built into the human condition. The drive to strong identity and responsibility, to put it briefly, is overdetermined as a disposition of life. What one must refuse to do, one might say to modern Augustinianism and the heresies it spawns, is to invest these dispositions with the blessing of unambiguous truth. One must treat them as entrenchments installed in the self and its world rather than depths that mirror the deepest truths about the world and the self. These entrenchments cannot be eliminated from reflection and action, but they must be excavated and problematized so far as possible in order to confound the singular hold they have over life.

One acknowledges, then, that one also treats these entrenchments as true at those moments when they function as presuppositions in thought. But one strives to place these presuppositions under a critical lens, by gestures that call into question at one moment fundaments one is compelled to acquiesce in at another. One may, for instance, adopt a rhetoric that ironizes the depths governing one's reflections—a rhetoric that problematizes itself even as it elevates its own position to a level above its competitors. One thereby refuses to treat the human fact of entrenchment as a double virtue. One adopts an ambiguous stance toward indispensable constructions and unavoidable fictions, endorsing identity without capitalization and responsibility within a text of ambiguity, in the interests of exposing and contesting the logic of sacrifice built into established doctrines of identity, responsibility, and otherness.

Such a counter-doctrine cannot advance itself as a singular truth. It must not, for instance, strive to purge doctrines that rest upon faith in a true identity or a particular god. It seeks, instead, to give voice to a perspective with a reverence of its own and to limit the exent to which the voices of strong identity can define the terms through which alter-identities are recognized and responsibility is distributed. It seeks to politicize identity and responsibility. [10]

Such a doctrine treats the positions of its competitors as positions it expects to persist on the field of discourse, and construes itself as another possibility to be advanced in competition and contestation with them. It presents itself as a subjugated possibility growing out of the unstable tradition of western discourse about identity and responsibility. It would lack relevance if its competitors disappeared. But it must fend off their efforts to treat *it* simply as incoherent or intolerable or to define it as responsible for discernible evils emerging on the horizon of the western tradition over which they have exercised hegemony. For certain purveyors of deep identity and radical choice will predictably accuse it of nihilism, relativism, or incoherence.

If every extant practice and theory contains elements of mystery, does the charge of incoherence, when pressed vigorously against an opposing theory, mean that the accuser finds *these* points of mystery *intolerable?* Does it mean that the agent finds life too difficult to live within the medium of paradox? Of course, it is appropriate to examine theories that insistently present themselves as exemplars of coherence to see whether they live up to the standard they impose on others and themselves. But what about those that seek to expose paradoxicality in life? These must be appraised, first of all, by the way they respond to the paradoxes they identify.

Identity without capitalization: my identity is entrenched, as well as particular in the sense that no set of universal statements about humanity or reason or rights or the necessity of death can exhaust it; but it is neither chosen in its fullest sense nor grounded in a harmonious direction in being. It is deep in its contingency. It is contingent in the sense that happenstances of genetics, family life, historically specific traditions, personal anxieties, demands, and aspirations, surprising events (the death of a parent, the intrusion of a war) all enter into its composition and give shape to the porous universals that mark me as human. It is deep in the sense that some of these elements become impressed into me as second nature, bonded to my first nature and not readily detachable from it. The attempt to detach them might foster personal breakdown, but that does not mean they are necessarily true. This recognition may enable me to live more of the elements in my identity as contingent formations that do not reflect the truth of being as such. And that in turn, to the degree it is accomplished, can relieve pressures to hold the other responsible for not living up to the hope embodied in my existence.

My identity is contingent and entrenched, and if I am fortunate, it exudes abundance. There is more in my life than any official definition of identity can express. I am not exhausted by my identity. I am not entirely captured by it, even though it is stamped upon me—and even though it enables me. This fugitive difference between my identity and that in me which slips through its conceptual net is to be prized; it forms a pool from which creativity can flow and attentiveness to the claims of other identities might be drawn. Because this abundance is in me but is neither me nor mine, perhaps it can help me to recognize and attend to the claims of the other in myself and to the claims of alter-identities.

The identity most worthy of my respect is the one that strives to curtail the problem of evil installed in the demand for surety of identity. I will hold people responsible for meeting *that* standard, insofar as I can, and this implies that I too cannot dispense with the construct of responsibility. There is a necessary strain of injustice in my sense of justice. I will not punish others for a refusal to see identity and responsibility as I do. Rather, I will strive politically to inhibit them from applying *their* standards to others as if they corresponded to the essence of human being. I will extend "the harm principle," as it were, into the structures of identity and responsibility, while recognizing that no clear or uncontestable line can be drawn between effects that are indifferent and those that are harmful.

This view must include elements of self-irony and paradox. That is the price it pays to combat the logic of sacrifice built into codes of integration. My friends and I will sometimes have to contest elements in your identity, first, because the insistence that it is grounded in truth makes you appear too aggressive and destructive to us, even though you look beautiful and principled to yourself. You are too hellbent on conquest or conversion for our taste. We will try, yes, to convert you to a more modest, contingent view of your own identity, and we will insist that your identity does not give you rights over others simply because they threaten or jeopardize its claim to truth. Our affirmation of the irony in these stances will contain an invitation to you to affirm corollary ironies in your own. Let us laugh together, on principle.

It may be that the quest for unequivocal responsibility and true identity is grounded in existential resentment against the human condition and that a politics that struggles against existential resentment is necessary to modify established ideals of identity and responsibility.

People tend to demand, to put it all too briefly, a world in which suffering is ultimately grounded in proportional responsibility. We resent a world in which it appears that this is not so. But resentment must locate an appropriate object if it is to be discharged as resentment. It thereby seeks a *responsible agent* that it can convince itself is worthy of receiving the load of incipient resentment it carries. Otherwise its existential rancor must be stored or translated into something else. So, part of the drive to insistent attributions of responsibility flows from existential resentment.

Since we moderns lack multiple gods to serve as compensatory agents in this respect, and since the god of monotheism was designed above all to protect it from any taint of responsibility for evil, we invest existential resentment in human beings whom we define as agents. We inflate human responsibility in order to release resentment against the human condition. Or so it seems.

On this interpretation, judgments of responsibility are easily infected by existential resentment or—the afterlife of the same tendency—by insistence that there *must be* symmetry between evil and an earthly locus of responsibility.

If responsibility is both indispensable to life and acutely susceptible to inflation through existential resentment, the best response is to challenge, contest, subvert, and abridge theories and practices that create the environment for such inflationary spirals. The introduction of an alternative code of identity and responsibility is part of this process of contestation. The code of sacrifice through the creation of scapegoats is obstructed by disruption of the insistences and assumptions that express its logic. A doctrine of contingent identity and ambiguous responsibility sits well with an idealization of politics, then. Politics now becomes a medium for the enunciation of suppressed alternatives and the contestation of entrenched commonalities. It becomes a means by which unequivocal practices of responsibility are compromised and confounded.

By combating the self-reassurance provided by theories of neat coordination between the social function of responsibility and the essence of human being, one becomes alert to new dimensions of ethical concern in the relations of identity to difference. One becomes alert to the element of existential revenge lodged within idealizations of identity and responsibility.

In an earlier time the gods served to justify humanity to a certain degree. They took upon themselves, not the punishment, but what is nobler, the guilt. In a postpagan era, where multiple gods no longer flourish, perhaps a portion of existential resentment can be absorbed into those cracks and fissures crisscrossing established constructions of identity and responsibility.[11]

CHAPTER FIVE

A Letter
to Augustine

To the Venerable Priest and Philosopher,
Augustine, Bishop of Hippo:

Why do I, a posttheist living in the last decade of the twentieth
century after the birth of your Christ, write to you, the consummate postpagan living between the fourth and fifth centuries? Do I
wish to demean your world of a sovereign, salvational god, a devil,
evil, demons, angels, miracles, original sin, grace, heresy, schism,
eternal damnation, and eternal salvation? Perhaps, to some degree,
though that neither justifies a letter nor provides assurance it will be
read. You probably found that the most adamant pagans were
unmoved by the scorn you heaped upon their dogmas and scornful
of your accusation that Plato—the pagan you respect the most—
absorbed his best ideas from holy scripture as he was touring
Egypt. Do I wish, alternatively, to place you in the context of your
time so that I might better discern why you adopted this distinctive
position? That is a worthy objective, but not so exclusive that it
rules out other modes of engagement, a point you can appreciate
given your own relationship to pagans and Manicheans. Besides,
contemporary "contextualists" too seldom pay sufficient heed to the
context from which *they* place texts in their contexts. So I leave that
task to others more qualified by training and disposition than I,
drawing on them occasionally to make sense of what first appears
surprising to me.

I write to probe a legacy of power, confession, and piety still
lodged within modern life. I neither follow you in your faith nor

exercise scholarly neutrality with respect to it. Here too I share something with you amid my dissent from you. I admire your willingness to interpret the other openly from your own vantage point. It relieves you from the modern tendency to insinuate one's deepest prejudices into charitable interpretations of the other. This forthrightness takes you halfway down the road to agonistic respect for the adversary. If only you had more resolutely resisted the temptation to convert these relations of strife and interdependence into dogmatic assertions of the superiority of the true faith. But more about that in a moment.

I read your theology as a strategy of earthly power. I want you to hear a couple of the voices in it again. You will not, I'm afraid, see your full figure reflected in the mirror of this letter. I am not a mirror. Nor were you, my friend, when it came to your fellow earthlings.

I write, then, to accuse you, and in doing so to excavate political predispositions in myself and others. To go through myself to you and through you to persistent voices in contemporary secular life. Can a counter-confessional undo the adverse effects of confessionalism? That is surely too much to ask of it. It is impossible simply to dismantle the confessional, and surely it is unwise to try. We would, to take merely one example, never have received the most profound interpretation of memory and its role in identity if you had not perfected the confessional mode. Has it now become a perverse truth with respect to you that "when I call upon him, I call into myself"?[1] I hope you can see that I fall into your debt as well as your shadow.

The spirit of death roams your texts. That revelation may come as no surprise to you. Any contestation of your thought will eventually have to engage death in a way which challenges your treatment.

Consider the *City of God*, for instance. You begin by offering a critique of the pagan gods. You "prove," first, that the introduction of Christianity into an empire previously protected by pagan gods did not cause the fall of Rome and, second, "that the false gods whom [the pagans] used to worship openly and still worship secretly are really unclean spirits; they are demons so malignant and deceitful that they delight in the wickedness imputed to them." Pagan gods sully the moral life, for as long as they lie, carouse, and fornicate, "it may be impossible for human weakness to be recalled from the perpetration of such enormities."[2]

Your guiding imperative is to relieve divinity of guilt and responsibility for abominable acts so human beings can assume these burdens themselves. The human burden is made heavier by treating calamities formerly thought to be grounded in fate as divine punishment for human sin. Even death becomes a continuation of punishment for the original sin.

After converting the pagan gods into demons and increasing the burden of sin in this life, you advance the central charge against paganism:

> Are men such fools as to think in their hearts that the worship of these gods can be of advantage for eternal life, when they realize how futile and ridiculous it is even in respect of those temporal and evanescent gifts which the divinities are said to have in their particular charge? This would be too bold a claim even for those who parcelled out temporal responsibilities to the gods to ensure that they would be worshipped by the unthinking. [*CG*, bk. 6, chap. 1, 228–29]

How base these pagan gods are: too weak even to establish the effective possibility of eternal life. How could a world of multiple, limited, competing gods produce a being with enough power to secure eternal life? How could the single divinity that a few elite thinkers construct hope to do so without the distinctive combination of omnipotence and benevolence you project onto your god? Through a contrast with pagan gods we are informed of the purpose of religion: "in spite of their having no connection with the true God or with eternal life (which is the essential aim in religion), they might have allowed some kind of explanation relating to the natural order" (*CG*, bk. 7, chap. 33, 294).

It does not occur to you to ask whether some pagans were unwilling to pay the earthly price needed to produce a god capable of promising the possibility of eternal life. That is the question, above all, that your questioning mind consistently forgets to pose. Rather, adopting a now familiar strategy, you impose your own demand on faith from the start and then condemn pagan polytheism for failing to live up to it. You speak to the human fear of death by designating eternal life the standard for religion, and you condemn all religions that refuse to be governed by that standard.

While I have not read everything you have written, so far I have encountered no consideration of this question: What is the price paid on earth for insistence upon a religion in which faith *must* be made to accord with the possibility of eternal salvation for human beings? Is it possible that before those multifarious sins of the flesh, such as "fornication, impurity, lust, drunkenness, and drunken orgies," and "faults of the mind" such as "devotion to idols, sorcery, enmity, quarrelsomeness, jealousy, animosity, party intrigue, envy" (*CG*, bk. 14, chap. 2, 549), one should insert "the uncouth demand that a god exist who has sufficient power and care to lift some humans into eternal bliss"? This would be a sin against life and the earth, rather than against your god, of course. For an early earthly victim of this demand for eternal salvation, as several items on your list verify, is paganism, persecuted by Christianity in one way or another for centuries. Many other victims follow in due course.

Christianity itself has paid a high price. The more one looks into the depths of the human condition—and you peer more deeply into this abyss than anyone before and most after—the more it becomes clear how much must be divested from human life and invested in divinity if the very possibility of salvation by a sovereign god is itself to be made secure.

I have a sneaking respect for the relentlessness of your thinking, a relentlessness to which your doctrines of original sin and grace attest. At first you try to protect your god from any taint of evil (this is necessary if he is to be good enough to worry about saving *us*) by attributing free will to every human being. We are responsible for evil because we choose it freely. But this doctrine unaided runs into severe difficulties, difficulties that threaten to condemn everyone to hell through weakness of will or to subtract benevolence from your god or to withdraw supreme power from him. So you modify this theory on the grounds that it does not account for the obduracy of habit in the human or the obdurate tendency of the will to give in to the claims of the flesh. Indeed, Peter Brown, your best contemporary biographer, suggests that, raised in northern Africa where men often exploded into compulsive cursing when crossed by fate, you may have found yourself on occasion unable to eliminate a stream of curses flowing from your own saintly mouth.[3] Would a full embrace of salvation through human will and effort alone not have nudged you a bit closer to eternal torment? Anyway, you yourself emphasize how the male member, after Eden, sometimes rises when unwilled and sometimes remains flaccid when commanded to rise. You even understand how "prohibition increases the desire to commit the unlawful act," adding quickly, to erase the response that leaps to a mind steeped in pagan licentiousness, that "genuine righteousness is never so beloved" as to overcome sin "without the help of God's grace" (*CG*, bk. 13, chap. 5, 514).

After exposing the thinness of any philosophy of self and responsibility that postulates humanity to be in full control of its actions, you invent the most abysmal doctrines to preserve the possibility of eternal salvation. You adjust the demands of your theology to obdurate features of your psychology. That, at any rate, is how I interpret the function of original sin and grace in your thought. Once this psychology of stubborn habit and weakness of will is enunciated, original sin is needed to stick humans with full responsibility for the evils they experience, and grace is needed to elevate some of these "condemned creatures" to heaven. Each of these enunciations implies the other, and both become indispensable if eternal salvation is to be salvaged now. The ghost of death as oblivion haunts each of these enunciations. Answer this question, I pray: Had you been willing to worship your god without the promise of eternal life, would these dogmas have been necessary?

Your Christian opponents, the Pelagians, advance a less profound psychology. They make salvation depend only upon the efforts of the self. Given the thinness of their understanding of habit and their insufficient appreciation of the way important dimensions of our identities are stamped upon us even before we attain the age of maturity, they must eventually encounter a crisis of faith to be resolved either by modifying the doctrine of will, by giving up the demand for salvation, or by concealing discrepancies between life experience and doctrinal enunciations. But I do condemn your eagerness to define those Pelagians—who merely magnify a doctrine you once entertained—as heretics to be excommunicated and exiled. Is this response necessary to preserve your hope or, the same thing in larger compass, your church? If so, is either really worth saving?

I beg you, O Bishop of Hippo, enlighten me where I go wrong here. Fill my mind with a deeper understanding and rid it of those distractions that cloud its vision, I who bear within me my own mortality, and who can only follow the thin shaft of light that leads into your deep soul.

What you challenged in Pelagianism was the shallow psychology it endorsed. What you shared with it was the demand that any doctrine worth conviction must support the hope of eternal salvation. It is what you shared with those heretics that needs to be thought about again, just because the definition of them as heretics was designed to accentuate where you differed from them and shroud the insistences you shared with them. Your theology could not function without its heresies: they mark possibilities spawned by the theology that must be blocked if it is to maintain itself. They are both essential to it and threats to it; "heretics" must be constituted and punished so that the system can maintain itself against the internal weaknesses, gaps, temptations, and diversities it creates—so that it can define itself.

As you see it, god "created man's nature as a kind of mean between angels and beasts, so that if he submitted to his Creator, as to his true sovereign and Lord, and observed his instructions with dutiful obedience, he should pass over into the fellowship of the angels, attaining an immortality of endless felicity, without an intervening death; but if he used his free will in arrogance and disobedience, and thus offended God, his Lord, he should live like beasts, under sentence of death for eternal punishment" (*CG*, bk. 12, chap. 23, 502).

Strong and certain words these, from so humble and pious a confessor. "Man" in the guise of Adam was given free will with the opportunity to exercise it properly and escape death altogether by going without the detour of earthly death directly into the company of the angels. But Adam disobeyed—the original sin—and he was then doomed to die a natural death and face eternal punishment after death. Even death is not a fact of nature on your view, but a penalty imposed on humanity because of the first disobedience of Adam (which your god foresaw). "The condition of human beings was such that if they continued in perfect obedience they would be granted the immortality of angels and an eternity of bliss, without the interposition of death, whereas if disobedient they would be justly condemned to the punishment of death" (*CG*, bk. 13, chap. 1, 510).

But why? Because your god, if he is to be all-powerful and all-good, must not be responsible for evil. The demand that the human fact of mortality itself be considered a "just punishment" for the first sin allows everything else to tumble into place: Adam died; death is evil; evil requires responsibility; god is not responsible for evil; responsibility for evil rests with the agent who brings it into being; Adam had the gift of free will; he brought evil into being by freely disobeying his god. Hence, he is responsible for the evil of death and must pay with eternal damnation. Why is the penalty so severe? Because Adam disobeyed a simple command easy to obey. So he brought a terrible penalty upon himself, proportionate to the severity of the crime and the ease with which it could have been obeyed.

Then you confront the persistent human phenomena, after Adam, of obstinacy of will through obdurate habit and of discrepancies within the density of the will itself. So now Adam's sin must be transferred to us if eternal salvation is to be saved, even as a possibility for some. Our dim memory of a strange happiness we no longer experience confirms this link of inheritance and responsibility flowing from him to us. This link explains how we no longer have free will in its pure form. It was necessary that Adam have free will in its pristine form for a brief moment so that god would not be tainted by limitation—as the Manicheans, those other heretics, thought—or with evil, as the Pelagians come perilously close to implying. None of you Christians want to taint your god with evil—else he might not *want* to save you even if you are good! And you do not want to burden him with limitation—else he may not be *able* to save you even if he tries! Finally, you share with less powerful opponents, though some of them had less inclination in this direction than you, a proclivity to define as heresy any doctrine of the Christian god that diverges very far from your favored view. For a world of Christian plurality without heresy would move too close for comfort to a pagan world of multiple gods. And once those gods started competing in the heavens, it would become too uncertain which, if any, is willing and able to offer salvation. Oh, how demanding this demand for salvation is!

Anyway, Adam committed the original sin, aided and abetted by Eve, his subordinate partner, and we were condemned to inherit the sin they brought into being:

> Those first sinners were sentenced to death, with the provision that whatever sprang from their stock should incur the same punishment. For whatever was born from them could not have been different from what they themselves had been. In fact, because of the magnitude of that offense, the condemnation changed human nature for the worse; so that what first happened as a matter of punishment . . . , continued in the posterity as something natural and congenital. [*CG*, bk. 13, chap. 3, 512]

Evidence that we have lost the purity of free will Adam possessed oh so briefly resides in the experience of bodily movements that escape the control of the will. The issue of the erection again, but many other things too, such as the fact that we will youthfulness, health, happiness, and life and experience aging, sickness, suffering, and death. And so now believers in the promise of eternal salvation are pressed to go along with you. To hold out hope for salvation, given these experiences, they must agree they participate in original sin. Otherwise they are under pressure to attribute these evils to their god who is the creator of everything. So we have inherited original sin.

Now all it takes is the doctrine of grace to fill out the picture of salvation. If we cannot earn heaven through free will alone (a now impious thought), then it can be given to some tainted by sin through the incomprehensible grace of their god. Grace sustains hope of salvation in a world where the strong doctrine of free will has lost its credibility.

All this may sound "implausible" to modern ears, I warn you. But its *functional indispensability* resides in the way it keeps faith in the possibility of salvation while squaring itself with the psychological experience of those who insist that there must be responsibility for evil and that it cannot rest with god. It is not each of the parts in itself that must make sense here; the crucial thing is the way the parts engender one another in an ensemble of insistences.

We moderns are entangled in our own ensembles of insistence, so we should be able to grasp the temptations governing yours. For instance, we have a difficult time holding onto our own ideas of will and responsibility. But we are constantly pulled back to them, not so much because of their intrinsic credibility, but because they seem necessary to a variety of other views about self, morality, and punishment we seek to retain. To assess this theme of yours, then, we need to appraise its function within the pattern of insistences that demarcates it, not its plausibility separate from these other considerations. There are always such other considerations in every doctrine, and they are always relevant. This you understood so well, and it makes your doctrine a joy to read. Correspondingly, to challenge this doctrine it is necessary to disrupt the pattern of insistences that governs it.

Faith and insistence are closely linked, "since faith is only faith when what is not yet seen in reality is awaited in hope" (*CG*, bk. 13, chap. 4, 513). It is better to construe faith as a pattern of insistence that shapes thought and interpretation than as an "act" that supervenes on them. But the earthly penalties and burdens of your faith are extremely high. We must live with the belief that we deserve death, that we are sinners from birth, that most of our bodily impulses and earthly desires are sinful or readily become sins, that we are relatively incapable of controlling ourselves, that we need massive reformation of ourselves, that we require baptism by priests to prepare us for grace, that the church is better equipped to give us the true doctrine than we ourselves, that our prayers for salvation from this pit may never be answered, and that assorted heretics and nonbelievers must be punished or condemned for their sins and impiety in order to protect the rest of us weak ones from their temptations. We must swim in a sea of self-loathing in order to secure faith, that is, hope, in the salvation you promise. We must constantly confess to your god, while constantly confessing that each preceding confession was incomplete.

Still, yours is the most plausible and coherent doctrine of salvation. *If* eternal salvation is part of the essence of religion, your doctrine fulfills that hope of hopes best of all.

Did you confess everything, Saint Augustine? Did you not, even after your conversion, secretly entertain the thought that the evils produced by this doctrine might not be worth the uncertain insistence that there actually is a being willing and able to carry out its plot? Certainly that possibility was available to you for consideration. Some pagans believed in oblivion after death, and they found Christian ideas of creation from nothing, incarnation, resurrection, and eternal salvation barbaric, thoroughly at odds with the refined knowledge of nature they had acquired and, perhaps, too narcissistic to be treated as anything more than mad projections.

Do you, perhaps, owe *us* a confession? Typically, when your texts voice the slightest doubt about some dogma essential to salvation (god's existence, his omnipotence, his interest in our salvation, his exemption from evil, the possibility of grace), you place those thoughts in the mouths of heretics or infidels and surround them with condemnation. That's one of the crucial roles the other plays in a text such as yours. When you do express doubts in your own voice, they are either referred back to your early life of error and sin or posed briefly as questions, to be converted a moment later into intensifications of faith. As when you say: "But how does one who does not know you call upon you? For one who does not know you might call upon another instead of you. Or must you rather be called upon so that you may be known? Yet, 'how shall they call upon him in whom they have not believed?'" and then follow immediately with: "Lord, my faith calls upon you, that faith which you have given to me, which you have breathed into me by the incarnation of your Son and through the ministry of your preacher" (*Conf.*, bk. 1, chap. 1, 44).

There would be a risk, once your strict and demanding dogma has been spelled out, attendant upon converting these doubts and uncertainties into appreciation of a plurality of faiths to be elaborated experimentally and competitively. The god you represent to us demands that doubt be repressed or sublimated into renewed faith exactly at those points where it is most likely to emerge. He would be unhappy with a thinker who, say, converted doubts about responsibility for evil into experimentation with the thought of a god who loved humans on earth but promised them oblivion after death. Or who treated her god as responsible for a portion of evil. Or who denied a singular god in order to affirm the ambiguity of life.

Remember, this is your representation of the essential elements of belief processed to us through your finite mind. So don't those who are condemned on earth by your representation of them as pagans, heretics, or apostates deserve room to construct and live through their cosmic projections too? Do you have anything to confess *to us* about the fears and doubts that govern your definitions to heretics and infidels?

Although you confess how your reflections on time, the trinity, the self, and scripture run into imponderable mystery, you refuse, after the day of your baptism, to gather those doubts together, to consider the horrendous price believers and nonbelievers pay on earth for this doubtful faith of yours, to honor as worthy adversaries those who reject this belief on the grounds of the mysteries it embodies and its barbarous effects on life. You insist upon converting mystery into faith, rather than treating your own stance as a reflective projection into being and encouraging others to enter into discourse with you on this level. Some pagans showed more respect for their fellow humans in this regard than you were able to muster.

Such doubts and possibilities surely continue to surge up within you, even after baptism. The textual signs are evident and abundant. But you refuse to confess them fully and robustly to those on earth receiving your message. You confess only to your god, and let us listen in on the communications. Even while confessing doubt, you tie doubt into transcendental knots. The very structure of a *confession* aimed at an object of doubt is one of them.

Indeed, grace includes as one of its attractions the quest for self-security through a reflexive arc of infinite self-recoverability: "if I cannot stop these supremely illicit doubts from emerging of their own free will," you whisper to yourself and that ambiguous object of doubt and faith to whom you confess, "I will deny them vociferously to the world of believers, heretics, and infidels created by me and project their expression onto others; and I secretly pledge to you, the doubtful one I seek not to doubt, that I constantly struggle to eliminate doubt in myself, so that I might be saved by your (doubtful) grace, though I continue (against my higher will) still to lie to myself and to you in your supreme (and doubtful) self-substantiality." The doctrine of grace buys transcendental insurance for a dogmatist who cannot stop doubting his own dogma.

Do the humble confessions to the doubt you worship not reflect an arrogant refusal to explore the depths of theological mystery more robustly with your fellow humans? After all, there is not such a great spiritual distance between saying that your god's "wisdom is multiple in its simplicity and multiform in uniformity . . . ; it comprehends all incomprehensible things with such incomprehensible comprehension" (*CG*, bk. 12, chap. 19, 497) and concluding that many mysteries are so far beyond human comprehension that it is foolish to project particular powers (such as omnipotence, omniscience, benevolence, and salvation) into a supreme being and then build a coercive theology around them. Or at least churlish to insist that others are sinful unless they share this set of projections. And not only foolish and churlish, but destructive and repressive. Surely such thoughts coast through your soul from time to time. Yet they remain unconfessed.

You are the one who confesses fervently and selectively, so as to sustain the hope of hope that governs your dogma and to capture any thought that might subvert it. There would be no confessional if it were not fervent and selective in this way: if dogma were subtracted, it would become something else immediately—speculation, for instance, of the sort practiced by some of the pagans. But you need both specific faith and generalized doubt, in constant conjunction with each other—faith to secure the rudiments of your theology, and doubt to give the self a constant supply of things to confess and correct.

One thing is certain. You were confident that many would be tempted to turn away from such a doctrine once its severity became clear. So you bolstered it with specific threats and promises. First you threaten eternal damnation for those who forsake god or do not receive his grace, then you paint a blissful picture of heaven for those who turn out to be among the elect. Perhaps these portraits help to put your own doubts to rest too, by placing you on warning of the penalties that may lie in wait for one who entertains such doubts too openly.

The order of your presentation is revealing. The priority given to the depiction of eternal damnation makes the recipient all the more eager to escape it and all the less willing to probe critically the picture of heaven that ensues. You, however, justify that priority differently, saying: "The reason for preferring this order, and dealing afterwards with the felicity of the saints, is that both the saints and the damned will be united with their bodies, and it seems more incredible that bodies should endure in eternal torments than that they should continue, without pain, in everlasting bliss" (CG, bk. 21, chap. 1, 964).

The problem you encounter is that it is difficult for some to understand how a body, finite as it is, could actually burn forever. So some have treated this as a metaphor for suffering of the soul, but you don't like metaphorical and allegorical readings of scripture much, remembering the damage the Manicheans did to the idea of a singular, universal doctrine with their allegorical readings. So you draw upon your god's reputation for miracles and omnipotence to prove that hell is the place described in scripture as "unquenchable fire, where their worm dies not, and the fire is not quenched." By emphasizing the incomprehensibility to us of god's knowledge and power, you easily prove the possibility of body and soul suffering eternal torment together in hell. "I have sufficiently argued that it is possible for living creatures to remain alive in the fire, being burnt without being consumed, feeling pain without incurring death; and this by means of a miracle of the omnipotent Creator. Anyone who says that this is impossible for the Creator does not realize who is responsible for whatever marvels he finds in the whole world of nature" (CG, bk. 21, chap. 9, 985).

Your god's incomprehensibility often serves as a device to explain what is otherwise incoherent to us, but it is never invoked to evince doubt about his omnipotence or interest in human salvation or a host of other points central to your theology. The same goes for his "responsibility." This incomprehensibility and mystery that you wheel out when it suits you is a very selective thing, it seems. Anyway, now fear of eternal damnation tightens its grip. The soul cringes at the thought of its body burning forever; the body faints at the prospect of its soul being tormented forever by the worm of conscience. Did you fear that some might refuse your faith and your church if their souls alone were threatened with eternal damnation?

You advance a political theology of the body in its life and afterlife so that your hope to live forever in heaven can be bolstered by the confirming beliefs of those who surround you—and by the plight of those pagans, Jews, and heretics who deviate from the doctine imposed by your church. Let me call this transcendental egoism.

Transcendental egoism is more extreme than the garden variety of egoism. The latter aims at a few advantages for itself, while the former demands that those whose identity diverges from its own be defeated, excluded, punished, corrected, or converted in order to preserve its own integrity and hopes. It sacrifices the integrity of the other in this life to its own unproven hopes. And it envelops the doubtful character of its own hopes in the language of pious authoritarianism. "The important thing is that we should never believe that those bodies are to be such as to feel no anguish in the fire" (*CG*, bk. 21, chap. 9, 985).

You close one of your texts by making grace not only an undeserved gift from your god but also one he never makes known in this life to those who will receive it. Why is grace always uncertain, dependent in the last instance on the imponderable will of an incomprehensible being? Why not say, "All right, if you seek sanctity, and God makes it clear to you that you are chosen, then, hey, you will enjoy eternal life; if you sin without repentance, or if God makes it clear that you have not been chosen, well, then, your body and soul will burn in hell forever"?

Of course, you give a reason for lifelong uncertainty about the issue that is most important of all to those who regard salvation as the very purpose of religion: finite beings can never know the will of an infinite being. But that does not suffice, for there are plenty of instances where you purport to know plenty about this being and its will: that it created the world; that it gave us free will; that Adam blew it; that we are cursed with inherited sin; that we depend on grace; that this infinite being is omnipotent, omniscient, and benevolent; that it is a savior; and, above all, that there is no way that this being is responsible for evil in the world.

So perhaps there is another reason lurking inside the reason you give? This doctrine of lifelong uncertainty instills doubt, dependency, and anxiety from birth until death. If people knew one way or the other, the political controls of the church (and the state, when the two are allied) would be weakened. People who knew in advance that they were eternally damned might well evade more of the rules you impose upon them on earth, and those who were promised salvation might relax a little, ignoring some of those dictates that civil and ecclesiastical authorities are unable to enforce by earthly sanctions alone. You need grace with uncertainty in your political theology.

Like the doctrines of sin, grace, evil, and damnation of body and soul, the permanent uncertainty of grace instills faith through hope and fear. It is another tactic in a theological economy of bodies and souls. Perhaps its transparency to some who no longer live under its power can help us come to terms with contemporary economies that still cloud the vision of those inhabited by them. Or do I misread you too? Help me to rise above the filth of my thoughts as I strive to pull out of that whirlpool which sucks thought downward, as I go through myself to patterns of insistence constructed by you, and through you to those patterns that tempt me.

Well, after the vision of hell and the uncertainty of grace, you treat us to a picture of heaven. The *City of God* closes with an account of this place:

> How great will be that felicity, where there will be no evil, where no good will be withheld, where there will be leisure for the praises of God, who will be all in all! What other occupation could there be, in a state where there will be no inactivity of idleness, and yet no toil constrained by want? I can think of none. . . . I am not rash enough to attempt to describe what the movements of such bodies will be in that life, for it is quite beyond my power of imagination. *However*, everything there will be lovely in its form, and lovely in motion and in rest, for anything that is not lovely will be excluded. *And we may be sure* that where the will is there the body will straightway be; and the spirit will never will anything but what is to bring new beauty to the spirit and the body. . . . But what will be the grades of honour and glory here, appropriate to degrees of merit . . . ? But there will be such distinctions; *of that there can be no doubt*. . . . And so although one will have a gift inferior to another, he will have also the compensatory gift of contentment with what he has. [*CG*, bk. 22, chap. 30, 1087–88; emphasis added]

There you go again. Invoking mystery in one phrase and filling it in with contour in the next. Now the erection obeys the will to it in a flash, but would any manly spirit ever will anything so unbecoming to the midst of this perfection? What does this combination mean? There will also be a complex order of ranks, with women lower in the hierarchy than men and the less endowed lower than the more. But there is nothing for any rank to do with or for those below and above it. There will be differentiation without function, hierarchy of status without envy or pride, unity of will and body without a project in need of attainment. You never show how these parts and fragments fit together into a complex whole. You present them as a series of coming attractions, leaving it to the incomprehensible being to draw them together into a unified heavenly estate.

Why did you not simply point to the place and say that it is simply incomprehensible to you? I know one reason is that you must claim that scripture presents a true picture that heretics willfully ignore, or else you would not be justified in identifying and punishing them. But still, you are highly creative with scripture when you need to be. Why do you specify the parts in this case and leave the way they fit together a mystery? There must be a political reason.

The benefit, I understand, must be rendered greater than the risk. You are a transcendental utilitarian in the last instance who balances the earthly costs and risks—including the chance that this doubtful doctrine is false—against definite, infinite penalties and rewards if the doctrine is true. You construct an incalculable calculus of faith. The ante must be raised to infinity because any threat to your belief in eternal salvation is infinitely distressing. So you describe heaven and hell in enough detail to make them vivid and then invoke the incomprehensibility of your god whenever the vivid parts threaten to fall into a heap of incoherence.

What is there to do in your heaven, Augustine? How does it differ from oblivion? It seems to be a place where nothing never happens. This effect is merely blurred by the threats and uncertainties that surround the prize.

You've overplayed your hand again, but since you hold the transcendental gun, anyone who calls your bluff risks incalculable suffering later and very specific penalties now. Few are likely to call it openly, for most participate in the theological economy of hopes and fears you help to maintain.

Paganism, heresy, schism, sin, body, soul, error, pride, piety, sacrilege, grace, heaven, eternal damnation, form the operational terms of institutional discipline in your political theology. They incite and magnify the fear of death through a thousand promises and threats. You treat death as a punishment for original sin rather than as a fact of nature; you deploy the threat of death to create the identity of the self and the church; you threaten the self with eternal damnation if it does not pull itself away from the sins you have identified; you promise it the possibility of heaven if it confesses its sins and prepares itself to receive grace, that is, to receive relief from death after life; you deploy death to define interior and exterior fields of otherness haunting the self; and you mount a series of attacks on the life of alter-identities to consolidate the identity built around this fear of death and the hope of escaping it.

You deploy damnation to organize life; you organize life to transcend death; you organize death as afterlife to regulate identity and difference in life.

Yet, you have spoken and many have listened for centuries. This second fact must be pondered. What encourages others to listen to the message you speak?

Some historians point to disappointments accompanying the long delay in the second coming, implying that this delay required the church to come to terms with the way of the world while constructing a more coherent theology. Some of these same historians emphasize the changing place of Christianity in the political arena: it shifted rapidly from a dissident and persecuted cult to a religion backed by the authority of an empire, and it had to come to terms with power, authority, and secular life. Some discuss further the relations between your doctrine of sin/grace and the indispensable role it gives the church in baptism and in establishing authoritative doctrine.[4] Some might think further (Hegel is one who pursues the thought) that the combination of an official monotheistic religion and a world experienced as increasingly abstract, uncertain, and insecure produced a volatile mixture congenial to the spread of this authoritarian piety and "unhappy consciousness." All of these suggestions seem on the right track to me; none of them sufficiently explains your doctrine and its reception.

You speak, Augustine, to an ear located in the interior of the self, an ear that muffles the sounds of death so that it can receive any murmur on behalf of an afterlife, an ear that drowns out sounds that equate death with oblivion, an ear that listens to secret appeals for revenge against a world that is cold and indifferent to the desire to escape oblivion, an ear that would rather hear the voice of the other through a code of heresy, damnation, apostasy, sacrilege, and sinfulness than sacrifice the possibility of eternity.

That's why the mode of the confession governing one of your texts is so perfectly attuned to chords within those mortals who receive its message. You don't so much develop arguments there as attune resonances within yourself to chords of transcendence waiting to be played in the interior of others. You go through yourself to the interior of other selves while constantly stirring up doubts requiring new forays into the same territory.

You embody an impulse to revenge against the human condition. You redefine that condition until it becomes filled with an agency capable of fulfilling the wish for salvation; you then redefine that wish until it squares with obdurate features of the human condition you cannot deny; and finally you accept any punishments for others and debasements for yourself needed to cling to this hope. You speak to us, even when we resist this twist or that turn in your message. We listen because there is much within us that responds to the hopes, demands, resentments, and anxieties you convey. We, too, protest against the fundamental unfairness of life. We, too, are moved by the impulse to find a higher meaning in the existential suffering that marks life.

We must go through ourselves to you because we are haunted by the nonconfessions within these confessions. We are pulled, if not by exactly the doctrine you have propagated, then by those that live on in the afterlife of Augustinianism. But why should we contest the voice you tap within us even as we listen to it with new ears?

Because this quest for revenge against the human condition inevitably turns into revenge against whole classes of others and, ultimately, into revenge against ourselves. It makes no sense to seek revenge against things that are indifferent to life, that can feel no pain and suffer no punishment. If there must be an agent for revenge to release itself against, who else can it be except some of the very ones we ourselves define as the highest agents on the face of the earth? It cannot be a god, or else he would not be an agent of salvation. It cannot be the world, for he gave us dominion over it. That is why there is finally one solution to the problem of evil for those who insist, implicitly or explicitly, that death itself is an evil for which something must be responsible. That solution is us.

Nietzsche, the son of a Lutheran minister, whose thought reflects engagement with thinkers like yourself, exposes this complex when he says: "But this I counsel you my friends: Mistrust all in whom the impulse to punish is powerful. They are people of a low sort and stock; the hangman and the bloodhound look out of their faces. Mistrust all who talk too much of their justice! Verily, their souls lack more than honey. And when they call themselves the good and the just, do not forget that they would be pharisees, if only they had—power."[5]

The hangman and the bloodhound are not simply those others; they haunt us because they also exist as proclivities within us. This you understand better than anyone else. It is what you do with this understanding that I seek to contest. These are the voices in most of us that must be engaged and contested if the logic of existential revenge is to be combated. Or so it seems to me.

Nietzsche remains deeply in your debt even as he subverts much of your message. For the self itself is a complex array of voices, some of which speak in a whisper even while they impose impossible demands. If you perfect techniques to enhance the interiorized self as you confess to your god and encourage us to listen, we must listen with new ears to the message you convey. It is unlikely that it can simply be dismissed at this late date. Those who think it possible to do so are the most likely to be governed by secular variants of the same injunctions.

You are thus indispensable to us; you are even our ally in compelling ways. But lines must be drawn around this unholy alliance, and you may finally refuse to respect them. I am not at all certain about this. Sometimes I suspect that if you returned to earth during the last decade of the twentieth century, you would assume the lead in combating central themes in the legacy you helped to define. You would be in a good position to detect the ramifications of that legacy in the outlines of the present and prospects for the future. But that may be wishful thinking on my part.

Do you deny that a strain of revenge and power flows through your texts? Sure, you grovel before your god as you confess things you know he already knows. But groveling, as anyone dwelling in a large city during the decline of the welfare state can attest, is a posture the weak present to the strong when they want to extract something from them. It is a posture of insistent servility. If only it were dark and they were armed, the grovelers would extract their requests by other means.

This is true of you, Augustine, in relation to your god. You indulge in transcendental groveling. And, yes, you would turn on this god if he showed any sign of weakness whatsoever. He must be omnipotent because you demand so much of him. Take, as a prime exhibit, your thanks to him after Monica's prayers helped you through a sickness that threatened your life before you had received the protection of baptism:

> But you are present in all places, and you graciously heard her where she was, and you had mercy on me where I was so that I regained my bodily health, although still diseased with my sacrilegious heart. . . . Where would have been such mighty prayers, sent up so often and without ceasing? Nowhere, except with you! But would you, O God of mercies, have despised the contrite and humbled heart of so chaste and sober a widow, generous in almsgiving, faithful and helpful to your holy ones, letting no day pass without an offering at your altar? . . . Could you, by whose gift she was such, despise and reject from your help those tears, by which she sought from you not gold and silver or any changing, fleeting good but the salvation of her son's soul? By no means, O Lord! . . . you graciously heard her, and you did this in the order in which you had predestined it to be done. For since your mercy endures forever, you vouchsafe, to those in whom you forgive all debts, to become a debtor by your promises. [*Conf.*, bk. 5, chap. 9, 125]

Flattery filled with insistence: insistence that god be the bearer of grace, that your recovery just might be a sign of god's grace, that you just might be "predestined" for heaven, that no god worth your creation would turn down such a chaste and contrite mother, that devotion and flattery be the key to the heart of your god and that salvation just might be unlocked by the turn of this key. You create your god by praising him to the heavens and castigating yourself by comparison. You castigate us by castigating yourself more thoroughly than we do ourselves. Woe unto this god if you ever conclude that he too falls short of the role you have predestined him to fill!

This is transcendental groveling. It is insistence pressed into the coin of piety and confession; it is power manufactured by converting "I wish it were" into "I demand there be a one who could do it if he would," followed by obeisance to this consummate bearer of agency: "I beg of you, the one who must be as powerful as I conceive you to be so that my highest wish might be done, will what I wish you to will." Through you, O Augustine, the logic of earthly power through transcendental piety begins to unfold.

For pious insistence does not terminate in this relation between you and the heavenly image you draw. You are not the only object of this new power. Your god must be the god of everyone, even those who reject him, if he is to possess sufficient universality, benevolence, and power for your salvation.

> For on that day [of judgment] even the Jews will certainly repent, even those Jews, who are to receive 'the spirit of grace and mercy'. They will repent that they gloated over Christ in his suffering, when they look at him as he comes in his majesty, and recognize him as the one who formerly came in humility, whom they mocked in the persons of their parents; however those parents themselves, who committed that great impiety, will rise again and see him, but now for their punishment, no longer for their correction. [*CG*, bk. 20, chap. 30, 960]

You confess on your knees to the god you create and then promise punishment for the other. The *Confessions* is the prelude to those later epistles aimed at infidels and heretics, with each implying the logic governing the other. Jews, pagans, Manicheans, Donatists, Pelagians—all received your transcendental threats, and often the earthly punishments church and state could offer in anticipation of them.

Piety easily becomes an instrument of transcendental representation. It is a strategy of power—power aimed at securing a set of identities and beliefs so that they cannot be challenged by counterexamples on earth, power that converts counterexamples to its faith into instances of otherness, power that insists that debate and contestation must stop at the points it delineates.

But why this power through transcendental representation? So that you and your kind will not tremble in the uncertainty and ambiguity of existence without a god? But why must counterexamples to your faith be defined as perversity, heresy, or evil? So that there will be no viable counter to challenge the self-confidence of the true identity? So that difference will function not as a counterexample but only as a hard lesson in the truth of the established identity? So that once defined as heresy, apostasy, paganism, infidelism, or sacrilege, these forms can serve as warnings to the faithful about what is in store for them if they diverge from your representation? You say as much:

In fact, all the enemies of the Church, however blinded by error or depraved by wickedness, train the Church in patient endurance if they are given the power of bodily harm, while, if they oppose her only by their perverse notions they train her in wisdom. Moreover they train her in benevolence, or even beneficence, so that love may be shown even to enemies, *whether this takes the form of persuasive teaching or stern discipline.* [*CG*, bk. 18, chap. 51, 833–34, emphasis added]

The stakes are too high to think otherwise, and besides, every apparent evil must be part of some larger, providential plan if your god is to be protected from any taint of evil himself.

Persuasive teaching or stern discipline; conversion or conquest. Piety converts personal faith into social power by duplicitous means, and then commands its recipients to renounce exposure of this duplicity. Have you proven in its fundaments the faith you condemn heretics and pagans for not sharing?

Piety disciplines the playful, metaphorical, and figurative dimensions of discourse; it lovingly insists upon reducing the plurality of readings drawn from its sacred texts to a singular representation, and then it demands, through its loving demeanor, that this representation be treated as the true faith. Too often, the charge of heresy is the judgment piety presents to those who deviate from this gospel of singularity. Where piety is most intense, there sits the temptation to define difference as heresy.

You regard as enemies of faith those gnostics who treated the gospels as insightful allegory, the virgin birth as myth, and the resurrection as metaphorical illumination. You insist against them that the prophetic themes of revelation are fundamentally clear and unambiguous for those who can or will read them carefully enough. "Though there may be direct and clear prophetic statements on any subject, allegorical statements are inevitably intermingled with them, and it is those especially that force upon scholars the laborious business of discussion and exposition for the benefit of the more slow-witted" (*CG*, bk. 17, chap. 16, 746). It is a delicate line you walk here, keeping a certain openness to diversity in the details of faith while maintaining enough singularity so that the texts will radiate with divine authority. For "what does it matter in what direction or by what way the unhappy state of man sets out on its pursuit of felicity, if it is not guided by divine authority?" (*CG*, bk. 18, chap. 41, 816).

This code linking piety and singularity in the fundaments of faith spawns a corollary definition of heresy: "The Devil . . . , stirred up heretics to oppose Christian doctrine. . . . Just so, there are those in the Church of Christ who have a taste for some unhealthy and perverse notion, and who if reproved—in the hope that they may acquire a taste for what is wholesome and right—obstinately resist and refuse to correct their pestilent and deadly dogmas, and persist in defending them. These become heretics and, when they part company with the Church, they are classed among the enemies who provide discipline for her" (*CG*, bk. 18, chap. 51, 833).

"In the hope that they may acquire a taste for what is wholesome and right." Even modern secularists who oppose the capstone of your theology recapitulate elements in its strategy of power through piety. Leave therapists, bureaucrats, party brokers, military evangelists, electoral candidates, and political activists to one side for now. Just listen to an assortment of inside dopesters, epistemic realists, and quantitative analysts in a social science department lapse into this melody when "postmodern" themes of intertextuality, metaphoricity, or the rhetorical determination of empiricorationalist practice get too close for comfort. Suddenly, some of these wheelers and dealers convert themselves into guardians of civilization, servants of truth, priests of western morality, shepherds of something so fundamental that it *must* not be called upon to defend itself in its fundaments. Here the pagan enemy is replaced by the nihilist threat, and the gnostic heresy of metaphoricity by the cult of irrationalism. The self-problematization within the code of these modern heretics and pagans is seldom acknowledged or engaged. Anyone impious enough to propose the ambiguity of self-problematization to the pious themselves is placed on warning that she too may be tarred by the pitch of nihilism.

All too often the pious refuse to open the fundaments that govern them to critical reflection, even when important decisions turn upon the issue. For they equate their identity with the fundamental character of being itself. This is the dangerous thing about piety: its egoism can become so inflated and fragile that it must be concealed under a veil of transcendental idealism. Piety reveals its tendency to egoism through the transcendental tactics by which it elevates and conceals that egoism.

Have you sometimes been tempted to laugh at this wonderfully complex divinity you have crafted? That is, to laugh at yourself while looking into the mirror? Now, that would be a confession worth hearing. Verily I say unto you, piety is a perverse strategy of power; and laughter is a solvent of piety.

It is, then, your legacy that we must consider further. Of course there are few Augustinians running around today, even though in the United States at least 88 percent of the population believes in a god and 84 percent believe Jesus to be the son of their god. Probably only a minority of these accept your doctrine of original sin. Many probably think sin is a result of their own free will alone, that there are fewer sins around now than you once invented, that god helps people who help themselves, and that there are plenty of ways to help oneself in a capitalist society. A smaller number construe faith as a spur to social justice and a call to set limits to state and market intrusions upon individual rights.

Many accept a modernized version of the Pelagian doctrine during reasonably good times. But those who take their theism seriously are likely to revert to a doctrine close to yours when bad times recur. Because, as I said before, your doctrine, among those that link theism, salvation, and responsibility for evil, makes more sense of human psychology than its competitors.

But don't we have separation of church and state, at least in America? Haven't modern states become secularized to a considerable degree? Yes and no. The relation between church and state would be better characterized, not as a separation, but as a series of intersections and interdependencies mediated by institutional distinctions and linkages. Secularism is better conceived, not simply as a counterpoint to theism, but as an ambiguous phenomenon that confronts theism on same planes and absorbs its legacy into secular vocabularies and practices on others. Secularism, in one of its dominant modes, constitutes the afterlife of Augustinianism.

Consider the legacy you have bestowed on us with respect to responsibility and punishment: "The natures which have been perverted as a result of the initiative of an evil choice, are evil insofar as they are vitiated . . . , for the punishment is just. . . . It is just, in that no one is punished for faults of nature but for faults of will; and even the wickedness which has become habitual and hardened into 'second nature', had its origin in choice" (*CG*, bk. 12, chap. 3, 474).

Certainly Sartre, the atheist, could have written these lines in toto, and many, many others would concur automatically in their central thrust. Throughout your intellectual journey, from its early emphasis on free will to the later emphasis on original sin and grace, you retain two themes: the site of responsibility, guilt, and fault is always in the self, either through free will exercised in the present, through habit that embodies free will exercised in the past, or through the inheritance of sin that involved the free will of our ancestors; and the evils for which the self is responsible are extensive.

When evil occurs, look for a responsible agent. And evil is everywhere. These two themes are necessary to your solution to the problem of evil, a problem theism invented when it insisted that existential suffering always had to be a sign of evil, that some agent must be responsible for evil, and that god must not be that agent.

Now, when these themes of individual responsibility and pervasive evil are conjoined with the intrusion of civil and ecclesiastical power into the interior of the self, a potent combination is created. For you hold that power must sometimes push its way forcefully into the interior of the self to ensure that citizens abide by the dictates of truth and become purified in their beliefs and utterances. Even when external enemies have been conquered, there are always internal demons to contend with.

Consider a letter of 418 to your "Venerable Lord and Holy Brother and Fellow-Priest, Worthy to Be Cherished in the Love of Christ," Sixtus, bishop of Rome. You had feared that he was soft on the Pelagians. Their god gave salvation to those who freely will the good, while yours makes salvation depend upon his own incomprehensible decision rather than the free will of puny earthlings. Is there a danger of returning to a time of multiple gods if the former doctrine is allowed to compete with the latter within the same world? Anyway, you are overjoyed to learn that the bishop of Rome too finally condemns Pelagianism, "for what more welcome document could be read or heard than so faultless a defence of the grace of God against its enemies, uttered by one whom those same enemies had boasted of as an influential supporter of their cause?" But Sixtus, it seems, is neither devout enough nor relentless enough in his devotion. You are compelled to give him additional advice, piously of course:

> Wherefore, my venerable lord and holy brother cherished in the love of Christ, athough you do an excellent service . . . , yet this larger duty awaits you of not only having punishment of wholesome severity administered to those who dare with over-much freedom to rave

about that error which is such a dangerous challenge to the name of Christ, but also for the sake of the Lord's weaker and simple-minded sheep of employing with all the vigilance of a pastor the most careful safeguards against those who, though in a stealthier . . . manner, still do not cease to whisper it. . . . *Nor should those be overlooked who under the restraint of fear conceal their opinions under the deepest silence.* . . . Some . . . have suddenly become silent, so that it is impossible to ascertain whether they have been cured of it unless they not only refrain from uttering those false doctrines, but actually take up the defence of the contrary doctrines with the same fervour they showed in propounding error. These, however, call for milder treatment: what need is there to terrify them when their very silence shows that they are terrified enough? . . . For while they are not to be terrified, yet they ought to be taught, and, in my opinion, *this process is easier while the fear they have of severe measures assists him who teaches them the truth.* In this way, after they have learned through the Lord's assistance to understand and love His grace, they may by their utterance refute the errors which they no longer dare to utter.[6]

This alliance between love, truth, and power forms one of the most holy combinations ever invented in the west. You are its most brilliant theorist and one of its early practitioners. The demeanor of love shrouds the dogmatism with which you insist on having your way; it enables you to use fear as a tactical tool to compel the defeated ones to "take up the defence of the contrary doctrines with the same fervour they showed in propounding error." Repression of the other in the name of love provides an insidious strategy by which you eradicate living challenges to the truth of your doctrine. For since your truth is not provable by argument or evidence, it can best be sustained by the fervor of all who fall within earshot of it. Since it cannot be known, it must be validated through general consent. Hence the centrality of conversion and confession in your thought. Would you need to love the other so intimately if you could relax the drive to vindicate the universal truth of your identity?

It might be thought that such tactics are today confined to Stalinism and Maoism. The latter do embody extravagant examples of this practice. But it is a self-serving exaggeration to suggest that your legacy does not operate in liberal societies too. Of course, liberals are committed to freedom of expression, and it is a good thing. But this alliance between love, truth, and power, redefined and redeployed, sometimes operates beneath the threshold of liberal convictions and institutions. These contemporary formations reflect the idea that the individual is the prime and unambiguous site of responsibility, that the most fundamental ends of the civilization—such as an economy of growth and the disciplines conducive to its attainment—are ends outside the realm of political contestation, and that it is intrinsically good for the individual as well as prudential within the existing parameters of the political economy to draw the individual into line with these ends.

This contemporary alliance of love, truth, and power functions to consolidate established identities and to depoliticize modes of conduct that evade, subvert, resist, elude, or oppose them. It is seldom defined as an issue because it functions within a set of presumptions sedimented in the cultural unconscious.

Let me cite, first, a simple example. In an article in the *New York Times* science section entitled "Deep-Seated Causes of Procrastination," the deep sources of this "syndrome" are all located in the interior of the individuals suffering from it.[7] The analysis follows a now familiar pattern. First, the individuals with this trait are shown to suffer considerably; they "have lost their jobs, been sued for failure to meet obligations, destroyed their marriages and family lives, failed to finish their doctoral theses or gone to jail for income tax evasion." Then, this behavior is gathered into a syndrome, allowing it to become a named pattern of behavior subject to dissection, analysis, and cure. After that there is regret and recrimination over the fact that so far there has been "very little procrastination research." Then, the locus of the newly discovered syndrome is announced. It resides inside the self, though its exact configuration within the self is in debate and, yes, still requires further research. Some procrastinators may be "perfectionists who have very high aspirations for themselves. They greatly fear failure or a negative evaluation." But "procrastination can also stem from resistance to control by others . . . ; 'you don't feel free to express your anger directly but you show it by getting things done late.'" Or perhaps procrastinators "fear success" or "get a thrill out of delay" or have a "fragile sense of [their] own worth." Finally, a series of therapies is recommended for individuals who suffer from this syndrome, and further research into the interior of the procrastinator is commended.

This analysis and hundreds like it in areas such as weight gain or loss, drug addiction, criminality, nutrition, personal health, sexual orientation, test performance, hyperactivity, unemployment, humor, corporate dress codes, premenstrual syndrome, aggressivity, and so on rest upon assumptions that established standards of performance are natural or true, that the suffering is due to some deep defect in the self, that the remedy must involve techniques applied to the self by itself or by others to bring it into line, that the true identity of the self will be advanced another step through its more complete integration into established practices. All this empiricism is condensed into the appellation "procrastination syndrome."

Late-modern issues of identity and evil are often dissolved into a solution of individual responsibility for deviation from official standards of being and performance. But other possibilities present themselves, even with respect to the procrastination syndrome. Perhaps systemic changes in performance rules and the pace of productivity, together with the intensification of institutional demands for self-surveillance and self-regulation, have created a context in which what was previously "delay" or "malingering" has now become consolidated into the *deeper* syndrome of procrastination.

Procrastination, on this alternative reading, becomes a systemic effect officially treated as a defect in the self. For many role bearers within this system, the possibilities have been reduced to intensive self-regulation, finding themselves shuffled into a marginal existence through one of the numerous categories of otherness constituted by the order, or ambivalent participation in the order through procrastination and its numerous allied syndromes. Perhaps the procrastination syndrome constitutes a sign—among many others—of institutional double binds whereby, first, the screws of discipline are tightened and, second, a variety of socially constituted deviants are then blamed for stripping themselves of efficacy through deep-seated personal defects.

The typical analysis of such "syndromes" does not define the bearer as an inheritor of original sin, nor does it land solidly on the theme of an agent who sins of his own free will. Rather, it redistributes the oscillation and ambiguity that have governed the Augustinian legacy of responsibility from its inception. It says firmly that the cause is in the self and that the treatment must be aimed at improving the self, and it leaves it poised in productive uncertainty whether the ultimate locus of causation is the free will of the self, obdurate habit for which the self is ultimately responsible, fixed dispositions for which parents are responsible, or an interior illness that no one has chosen. It thereby allows those who deploy it to fill out its contours in accordance with the distribution of emphasis in their own political theology. It depoliticizes the issue of identity and its relation to social power by equivocating between judgments of will and judgments of sickness, that is, by equivocating between free will and original sin in their modern configurations.

The debates spawned by these equivocations mask a set of common operational presumptions: that these norms are true or necessary; that the primary locus of deviance resides somewhere in the self; that if one set of selves is innocent, another set must be guilty; that a rational response must aim at bringing the self into line with established norms and imperatives; that the self realizes itself through interiorization of those norms. And these operational presumptions themselves mask an ambiguity lodged deeply in the tradition of individualism. For the individual is both celebrated as the center of self-reliance through which arbitrary power is restrained and set up as the standard of normality against which innumerable deviations are measured.

The individual absorbs this double role through its dual definition as a center of freedom and a locus of responsibility in a normalizing society. The sign of a normalizing society is not, as critics of this thesis persist in saying in one breath so they can refute it in the next, that everyone becomes the same, but that more and more people deviate in some way or other from evolving standards of normality, opening themselves through these multiple deviations to disciplinary strategies of neutralization. A normalizing society is defined more by its proliferation of failures or near-failures and its tactical orientations to them than by its pristine examples of normality.

This package of equivocations and certainties contains the legacy of Augustine within it, and the power of that legacy allows its bearers to ground these unstable elements in the soil of established intuitions.

The example of procrastination may seem trivial, but trivial examples possess the power of silent accumulation. The late-modern accumulations run along a track paralleling your own lists of sins to which the children of Adam and Eve are susceptible. Moreover, many other examples are not at all trivial, even taken by themselves. Homosexuality (where the theory resides in the term itself), for instance, fit this pattern exactly until it was politicized in the 1970s and 1980s. And the politicization (where it did not replicate the old model by inverting its values) took the form of refusing to endorse the official cause of suffering, locus of responsibility, and hierarchies of identity and difference within which it was constituted.

Your legacy depoliticizes issues of identity and responsibility by locating that which differs from the norms you endorse in the deep interior of the self and by counseling the sick or sinful self to pull itself up to standards and presumptions it must not be so impious as to contest. The drive to sustain this legacy resides, first, in the wish of the self to believe that its identity is intrinsically true, therefore to treat those who deviate it from it as false, hence to look at the other as the source of evil, therefore to treat its own approximation of the standard as a sign of health and self-responsibility, hence to set itself up to be a future target of interior redesign. It resides, second, in the dilemmas that arise when an ordered way of life finds that it must repress some identities to enable others to be within its limits of institutional possibility. It is when the second set of pressures is fortified by the first set of drives that the depoliticization of difference is consummated.

Politicization of identity and responsibility calls these sources of self-confidence into question while identifying an element of cruelty in established identities where only virtues were previously thought to reside.

Perhaps this is an issue around which new confessionals could be organized in the late-modern era. We must go through your insistent constructions to their presence as obdurate demands in ourselves; and we must proceed through these critical engagements to revised readings of the late-modern condition.

Let me say this on my own behalf, I pray. I am not trying to eliminate identity and responsibility, but to problematize and politicize the forms they have taken—to politicize the relation between attributions of responsibility and the grounds upon which those attributions rest, and thereby to problematize established relations between deviation and the locus of responsibility. For these are ways to salute uncertainty and ambiguity, and to expose the cruelties spawned by transcendental egoism.

Let us turn, now, to another area in which your legacy remains potent. Secularism, it is said, gave up faith in the providence of your god and decided to take its fate into its own hands. It would be better to say, though, that secularism repudiated the conviction that the human condition after Adam (Eve is unimportant in your reading) is simultaneously a divine punishment deserved by humans and a sign of divine providence bestowed upon humans who do not deserve it. That would be a better account, though it still underplays continuities between *secular* faith and your legacy.

It does identify, though, two poles in the legacy refigured by secularism, the poles of punishment and providence: punishment for original sin through the introduction of death, labor (for women in childbirth and men in the fields), and a discrepancy between the will in its purity and the will when it allows itself to be weakened by the claims of the flesh; and the providence of a god who created a world of wondrous abundance and developed a plan through which every evil, in ways incomprehensible to us, ultimately contributes to the greatest good. For divine providence is the second, supplementary solution to the problem of evil: though god is not responsible for any evil, he knows in advance which ones will occur, and he deploys evil in the service of a higher and ultimate good.

To come to terms with the secular reconstitution of your legacy, recall the bounteous earth bestowed upon us by the providence of your god:

> Thanks be to you O Lord! . . .
>
> We see . . . this airy space, for it also is called heaven, through which wander the fowls of the sky, amid those waters which are borne as vapors above them, and, on calm nights, also drop down as dew, and those heavier waters which flow upon the earth.
>
> We see the fair expanse of waters gathered together on the fields of the sea, and the dry land . . . , the mother of herbs and trees. . . .
>
> We see humid nature on every side, fruitful of fishes and beasts and birds, for the density of the air, which supports the flight of birds, increases from the exhalation of the waters.
>
> We see the face of the earth, adorned with earthly creatures, and man, made to your image and likeness, and by this, your own image and likeness, that is, by the power of reason and intelligence, set over all non-rational animals. . . .
>
> These things we see, and we see that each of them is good, and that all of them together are very good [*Conf.*, bk. 13, chap. 32, 366–67]

And we are given dominion over this earth. Not mastery, a modern invention (you are far too resigned to the order of things to endorse *that*), but *dominion*, under the watchful eye of your god. We judge how these things of the world are to be used and governed because in our "reason and intelligence" we are made in god's image. You say, drawing upon scripture, that "man . . . has received dominion over the fishes of the sea, and the fowls of the air, and all the beasts, and the whole earth, and all creeping things that creep upon the earth" (*Conf.*, bk. 13, chap. 23, 357).

Do you notice, as you look upon the world today and back to the text you wrote, how solid, fruitful, dense, expansive, clean, nurturing, and maternal the earth is in your portrayal? And how polluted, fragile, and endangered the earth and the things that creep upon it are today? I know you will conclude from this shift that not enough people over the centuries have given themselves completely enough to your god. But some of us see it differently.

You bequeathed a demanding and unstable god to posterity, and as these instabilities unfolded through the ages, the god in whom people had invested their faith became more abstract. His very omnipotence required it, or so the nominalists thought, as they developed against scholasticism one of the strands in your own doctrine. Some reacted by intensifying faith in an absentee lord who limits his interventions in life; others by withdrawing faith from the being and reoccupying the space left by his departure with new patterns of reassurance; others yet by returning to the old god with a new vengeance, repressing any evidence of his instability and blaming nonbelievers for forsaking the legacy they inherited. The first two responses together constitute modern secularism; the third is that huge shadow which continues to stalk it.

With this god lifted higher into the heavens, the idea of human dominion over the earth could now be refigured and intensified by secularists. The retreat of the sovereign god reduced faith in providence and freed humanity from a line of restrictions heretofore governing its dominion over the earth. In the absence of a robust tradition of reverence for the earth itself—grounded in the earth's difference from us and our close interdependence with it—the world could now become a deposit of resources for material use and aesthetic enjoyment. Dominion hardened into mastery, sin condensed into abnormality, and theological economies of life and death congealed into ambiguous secular economies of discipline and freedom.

Note the ways in which you helped to spawn a secularism you would not doubt despise for its optimism and self-pride. First, and most important, *you bequeathed a doubtful, unstable god, projected as the single focal point of faith, reverence, hope, and obligation.* Second, you gave humanity dominion over the earth restricted only by its obligations to this unstable god. Third, you treated the earth as a field of abundance bequeathed by this god. Fourth, you enunciated a fundamentally providential view of the world. Once your god was extracted from this picture, either through rejection, deep contestation over its will and dictates, or benign neglect, modern secularism was released. The only focal point of reverence was taken away, leaving the earth as an instrumental field of human action. Secularism filled in the black hole left by god's retreat with *its* faith in human mastery over a pliable nature.

Only recently have some of the children of secularism begun to discern how much it shares with you amid its vociferous dissent from certain rudiments of your faith. For you insisted that we must be made in the image of your god so that he, through his infinite magnification of us, would possess the interest and capacity to promise eternal life or eternal damnation. And the secularist insists that if your god does not exist for us in this way, then the world must provide us with just compensation. "Nature" must exist for us in its way, by providing a plastic substratum upon which human mastery can be exercised. This was probably an understandable assumption to make, in a culture that first filled the earth with the will of a god and then constituted it as nature after this god had been harassed into retreat. Secularism unties one line of insistence in your doctrine and then draws together other lines already dangling within it.

Disciplinary society, to the extent that it has developed in the late-modern age, is compounded of insistence upon treating the earth as a standing reserve and insistence upon treating any signs of defect in the project of mastery as faults within the interior of resisting selves, a particular economy of life, or both. You contributed to this result through your legacy of a sovereign god, original sin, grace, the interior self, the bountiful earth, reverence owed to god alone, pious authoritarianism, providence invested in the earth itself, and human dominion over the face of the earth.

Your dogmatization of the identity you endorse, grounded in its insistence upon fending off the bird of death, has contributed to a trinitarian history, hopefully with each of three moments to find its day in the sun. Our own ontological investment in the line you helped to inaugurate plays a crucial role in the temptation to remain poised in ambivalence and struggle between the first two moments. Let me briefly spell out all three:

The Augustinian moment: we are fragile; god is perfect; the earth is solid and bountiful; we have been given dominion over it.

The secular reply: we are powerful; the old god is good only for marriages and funerals; nature is pliable and bountiful; we will attain mastery over it.

The posttheist, postsecular rejoinder: the earth is fragile; highly organized human economies are interwoven with its fragility; the *sovereign* god was on balance a destructive construction; the hegemony of the modern project of mastery results in the globalization of contingency; nontheistic reverence for life and the earth remains to be cultivated.

It is too much to hope that the third moment will triumph completely over the other two. Rather, it is imperative to lift it to a new level of efficacy as a counterpoint to its hegemonic competitors, entering into agonistic competition with them and compromising their extremisms through a new political equilibrium of political contestation.

Thus, I do believe in the occasional reality of an afterlife. You live on within us in our theism and secularism, and we confront ourselves as we speak to predispositions within our institutions and you. Those who would cultivate this third moment must focus a telescope on the heavens you have imagined, and thereby magnify the demands of the modern self until they become more visible to eyes that seek to avoid them. We must contest the double legacy of insistence in established theories and practices: attainment of true identity through conquest and conversion of the other, and pursuit of mastery over the earth by treating it as a pliable deposit of resources for human mastery. This is the *counter*-insistence that governs posttheism and postsecularism today.

Because you still reside within us in operative orientations to responsibility for evil, identity as the locus of truth, death as the effect to overcome, the earth as bountiful, and reverence aimed at god or at nothing at all, we go through ourselves to you and through you to patterns of insistence in ourselves. The idea is not to pursue a constantly receding depth where the true self resides, but to excavate patterns of insistence that have become entrenched in institutional structures and self-dispositions. Here argument encounters resonances in the soul that guide its movements, and amplification

of those resonances exposes patterns of insistence that monitor the
field of debate within which familiar positions are defined.

The image of a sovereign, salvational god, heaven, hell, sin, will,
grace, piety, evil, and heresy you constructed provides a route into
the interior of your soul. We may then observe our own doctrines
through the magnifying glass you provide. Perhaps we can thereby
confront lines of insistence established in our thinking and practices, and look with new eyes at the dangers they embody in the last
decade of the twentieth century.

So we learn from you as we contest ourselves, and from ourselves as we contest you. Your own impulses to reverence, questioning, and mystery could contribute affirmatively to this endeavor, as might your understanding of the human domain as a
saeculum in which certainty is absent and plurality advisable.[8] Take,
for instance, your judgment when reviewing the pagan history of
"monstrous" types of humanity, both sprinkled within regular society and forming entire peoples (two-headed people, hermaphro-
dites, humans with too many fingers or toes, and so on). You say:

> The explanation for monstrous human births among us can also be
> applied to some of those monstrous races. God is the creator of all
> and he knows where and when any creatures should be created. . . .
> He has the wisdom to weave the beauty of the whole design out of
> the constituent parts. . . . The observer who cannot view the whole
> is offended by what seems the deformity of a part, since he does not
> know how it fits in, or how it is related to the rest. [*CG*, bk. 16, chap.
> 8, 662]

I confess that I have not pursued these themes in your work in
this first letter, mostly because the demand for salvation in your
texts too severely neutralizes its appreciation of abundance and
mystery. If you could problematize (I do not say purge) this god
who is at once universal, sovereign, and savior, space might emerge
for a more affirmative dialogue between us concerning the political
unconsciousness of secularism today. For, by comparison to the
secular temper, we share a propensity to probe the role of suffering
in wisdom and to appreciate the inexorable excess of being over
structures of interpretation and identity.

While I endorse nontheistic reverence, I acknowledge that it,
too, is a contestable response to the mysteries of existence. There
are theologies that treat god as "absence" in a way that comes rather
close to the position I endorse. Even your theism can contribute to

this discussion when couched in a mode that affirms the deep contestability of the view it endorses. It might concur with contemporary theologian David Tracy in detecting latent affinities between a variety of "fundamentalist and secular" positions today[9] and in asserting that "the claim that only believers can interpret the religions . . . is a position that ultimately robs the religious classics of the claim to truth."[10] And it might treat as worthy of consideration and debate Nietzsche's judgment: "Why atheism today? The 'father' in god is thoroughly refuted, likewise the 'judge' and the 'rewarder'. Also his 'free will'. . . . *It seems to me that the religious instinct is growing powerfully but is rejecting theistic gratification with deep distrust*."[11]

I look forward to any reply you might make to these pleas and insistences.

Faithfully yours,
William E. Connolly

CHAPTER SIX

Democracy
and Distance

The Valences of Identity

The functionality of identity. Reassurance in identity. Habituation to identity. Resentment and violence through identity. How
could one become responsive to each of these elements? How could
the fictive "we"—the we with whom one communes even when its
identity remains cloudy—do so?

Is it possible to think difference without thinking its relation to
identity? Surely not, though some have tried to do so. It seems even
less possible to live with difference outside the space of identity,
even if the identity one lives were to become pluralized, that is,
even if the self were to become the locus of competing identities.
Even if a "way of life" without identity turned out to be possible, it
would still be undesirable. I would not be, do, or achieve anything.
Neither would we. Nor would there be an I or we to criticize for
failure in this regard. Identity, in some modality or other, is an
indispensable feature of human life.

Let's feign these truths to be self-evident: that each individual
needs an identity; that every stable way of life invokes claims to
collective identity that enter in various ways into the interior identifications and resistances of those who share it; that no god created
humanity so that contending claims to identity will coalesce into
some harmonious whole or be dissolved into some stable, recognizable, and transcendent principle; that the singular hegemony of any
set of identities requires the subordination or exclusion of that
which differs from them. How is one to respond to this condition?

How are *we* to respond if—affirming connections to others through ties of identity as well as the abundance of lives not exhausted by the identities that form us—we reject the clean, consistent stance of subjugating difference merely because it is at odds with identities we live and endorse? Here a twofold refusal may be needed: (1) if the identities installed in us achieve social hegemony, we resist repressing difference merely because its existence threatens our self-assurance; (2) if dispositions branded into us are marginalized or repressed by hegemonic identities, we refuse to plot a future revenge in which we vindicate ourselves through simple reversal of the present. This is part of the declaration of independence needed. But what does it mean? To what extent is it attainable in principle? And what work on the self and the order is needed to promote it? In what ways do structural characteristics of the order in which we are situated enable or disable these idealizations?

The issues posed by these questions are more tangled and obdurate than their formulations suggest. For seldom, if ever, does a policy of repression or marginalization simply present itself as such. It typically presents itself as a response to an evil posing an independent threat to goodness or as a regrettable structural necessity built into the order of things. The difficulty resides in the fact that these two paradigmatic excuses are not always simply lies.

So, a response in this domain is usually difficult, and very probably contestable. A response must involve a problematization of the tactics by which established identities protect themselves through the conversion of difference into otherness, an identification of ambiguities in the identity I and we have become, an ironization of some dimensions in my own identity, a politicization of established naturalizations of identity.

None of these slogans can sustain itself in this form. Together they provide an initial inventory in need of specification, modification, and organization. They signal a direction: to affirm the indispensability of identity while contending against the dogmatism of identity; to cultivate care for the agonism of life by disclosing contingent elements in any specific identity; to politicize the ambiguity in human being.

The ambiguity resides, first, in the space between the indispensability of identity and its drive to dogmatism and, second, in the probable inability of any ordered way of life to house together in one harmonious whole all the identities that might otherwise make a claim upon it. No order can enable everything to flower in the same garden: this is a "necessary injustice," as Nietzsche would put it, within the practices of justice. The point is not to deny this ambiguity but to struggle against the denials and simplifications it tends to engender.

It is impossible, for example, to support equally the claim to close, mutually sustaining, and extended kinship ties and the claim to equal opportunity through the extensive mobility of individuals. For the same market institutions and affirmative action programs that enable the second inevitably compromise the first. It is difficult to support equality between the sexes and also to forbid state intrusion into the interior life of the family. For the tradition of making the male sovereign within the family protected the family from extensive state intrusions at the expense of requiring the woman to submit to arbitrary authority, while the rectification of that evil inevitably draws the state into more and more details of child-rearing, marriage agreements, divorce, child support, and household financial planning. It is impossible to ratify heterosexuality as the true sexual identity without treating homosexuality as a sickness or a vice. And, as a final example, it is difficult to extend the state's involvement in the international economy while keeping the state fully accountable to its internal electorate. For intensification of international interdependencies compromises the terms of internal accountability.

In each of these cases institutional interdependencies and conceptual limitations require that one set of identity claims be adjusted, modified, or excluded in response to other sets. These are among the conditions that make the *politics* of identity inevitable: to establish an identity is to create social and conceptual space for it to be in ways that impinge on the spaces available to other possibilities. The appropriate response to this condition is not merely to reconsider the structure of some identities generally endorsed today, but to reconsider the *way* in which individuals and collectivities experience identities invested in them.

The position I advance involves me in selective conflict with both theories of liberal "neutralism" and radical ideals of collective identity.[1] The liberal neutralist recognizes the political volatility of competing claims to identity. Roughly, the neutralist would like to exclude such conflicts from public arenas. He would do so by claiming that while we lack the grounds to agree upon a common good, we can establish criteria of public dialogue or justice that are neutral between opposing conceptions of the good. Here is one presentation of this ideal:

> When you and I learn that we disagree about one or another dimension of the moral truth, we should not search for some common value that will trump this disagreement; nor should we seek to transcend it by talking about how some unearthly creature might resolve it. We should simply say nothing at all about this disagreement and put the moral ideals that divide us off the conversational agenda of the liberal state.[2]

But this places impossible limitations on public dialogue. It rules out most of the considerations that move people to present, defend, and reconfigure their identities in public space. It presupposes a minimal state that hardly touches the most intimate areas of life and identity. In more general terms, liberal neutralists give primacy to right and justice over the good by claiming that the former are indispensable to public policy and susceptible to consensus, while the latter is dispensable and unsusceptible to rational consensus. But the issue of identity persistently cuts across this divide. Any lived conception of personal identity projects standards of collective identity, and any lived conception of collective identity fixes a range of tolerances for personal identities. The issues of identity and the good thus cannot be excluded from public discourse. They inevitably seep back into the public arena in one way or another whenever attempts are made to exclude them by procedural means. The connections between personal and collective identity must be engaged overtly and politically if they are not to spawn a collective politics that unconsciously represses difference in the name of neutrality.

I am sympathetic, then, to an issue liberal neutralists have enunciated—the obstacles to achieving agreement upon a singular conception of identity or the good once the issue becomes an active part of public discourse—but I am wary of the way they seek to neutralize it. If such "agreements" are already sedimented in the life of every stable society, the pretense to neutrality functions to maintain established settlements below the threshold of public discourse. The issue must be politicized rather than neutralized, even though that response too contains its dangers.

These considerations might be advanced another step by considering a recent formulation by Habermas, as he continues his effort to sustain a politics of consensus transcending the limited consensus sought by liberal neutralists:

> A theory of society can perhaps provide a perspective, can offer—to put it cautiously—hopes and starting points for the conquest of unhappiness and misery which are generated by the structure of social life. But it can do nothing to overcome the fundamental perils of human existence—such as guilt, loneliness, sickness and death. You could say that social theory offers no consolation, has no bearing on the individual's need for salvation. Marxist hopes are of course directed towards a collective project, and hold out to the individual only the vague prospect that forms of life with greater solidarity will be able to eradicate, or at least diminish, that element of guilt, loneliness, fear of sickness and death, for which social repressions bear the responsibility. [3]

This enunciation is salutary in several respects. It separates neo-Marxism from the promise to resolve all agonies of existence through collective solidarity; it identifies a set of existential issues that people must grapple with somehow in any and every society; it promises only a common way of life that enables its members to come to terms with the issues of death, sickness, grief, suffering, loneliness, and guilt without the added burdens of severe material and social deprivation. But it fails to add that how people come to terms privately and publicly with existential issues bears a profound relation to how they engage the issue of identity, and that how they define the question of individual and associational identity bears a similarly close relation to the way collective identity is lived. Habermas is tempted by the wish to exclude existential issues from political theory, but, again, they seep back in. He appears to think that because no organization of public life can *resolve* or *eliminate* existential suffering, these issues can be excluded from public discourse.

There may be a subterranean affinity between collectivism of the left and liberal neutralism. In Chapter 1 I located these theories in a matrix with several others, where the categories across the horizontal axis were mastery and attunement and those along the vertical axis were the individual and the collectivity. And I suggested that proponents of each of these theories—as interpreted through a social ontology of dissonant holism—insist that the world is ultimately predisposed to us in one way or another. It must either contain a higher harmony and direction to which we can become more closely attuned or be susceptible to our best projects of mastery. Now we are in a position to identify another affinity binding these opponents together. While they disagree on whether the individual or the collectivity is the privileged locus of identity and on the ideal of identity endorsed, each player on this checkerboard endorses a theory of an unambiguous, intrinsic identity. Their common commitment to a strong theory of rationality (as opposed to one that emphasizes the indispensability *and* ambiguity of practices of rationality) reveals this affinity between them. Each can bracket these issues out of public debate only because each has already shuffled a lot of contestable responses into the "neutral" or "rational" background of discourse.

To treat identity, as I do, as a site at which entrenched dispositions encounter socially constituted definitions is not to insist that any such definition will fit every human being equally well or badly. Some possibilities of social definition are more suitable for certain bodies and certain individuals, particularly after each has had branded into it as "second nature" a stratum of dispositions, proclivities, and preliminary self-understandings. Some possibilities doubtless stretch the human as such beyond its effective range of variation, and some possibilities may fit us better than others— though "we" are almost always far too confident about "our" ability to identify which set fits "us" best, and though that confidence is commonly bolstered by treating the definitions of otherness through which identity is fixed as if they designated independent traits of the other unrelated to the maintenance of "our" identity. Such a thematization does suggest that the fit among entrenched contingencies in a self is always imperfect and generally filled with tensions, that the fit between contingencies and social definitions within a self is always imperfect, and that the relational character of identity always raises the issue of how the self-constitution of identity is established through the constitution of differences. Identity is a site of multiple disjunctions in need of politicization as well as unities that enable life. The task is to identify those patterns of insistence in a society to idealize its own formations and then to project counter-strategies by which to expose multiple points of discrepancy between institutional idealizations and that which they contain or subjugate.

It is perhaps at this juncture that the spirit of these reflections makes contact with the spirit of liberal neutralism. For neutralists want to immunize politics against the effects of strong, factional identities, and I aspire to politicize the connections between identity and politics so that a covert politics of existential resentment will not burrow too deeply into the operative politics of civic justice and the common good.

Identity, Life, and Mortality

One way to engage the "how" of identity—how it is constituted, lived, and experienced—is to explore the ways a culture defines the relation of life to death. We pursued this issue in one way at the beginning of this study. Augustine has another take on it. Perhaps it can be pursued in yet another way, by examining a contending perspective that brings out latent commonalities in the plurality of contemporary orientations in this domain. One thing that many secularists and theists concur upon today, for instance, is that the taking of one's own life is always or almost always a mistake, sickness, crime, or evil to be resisted. Nietzsche thinks that all of these orientations contain a pool of existential resentment that infiltrates the relations of identity to difference.

Zarathustra, in "On Free Death," says: "Many die too late, and a few die too soon. The doctrine still sounds strange: 'Die at the right time.'"[4] In *Twilight of the Idols*, Nietzsche announces the same theme: "To die proudly when it is no longer possible to live proudly. Death of one's own free choice, death at the proper time, with a clear head and joyfulness, consummated in the midst of children and witnesses; so that an actual leavetaking is possible while *he who is leaving is still there*. From love of *life* one ought to desire to die freely, consciously, not accidentally, not suddenly overtaken. . . ."[5] This commendation to die in the right way, amid friends and relatives who take leave of you while you are still there, is not entirely without precedent in western culture.[6] But the emphasis on the nobility of choosing the time of one's own death is distinctive.

The idea might be that by refiguring your own relation to death you are more likely to live without being overtaken by resentment against finitude, to live without projecting a fundamental unfairness into being and then resenting "it" for being unfair. In striving to fend off existential resentment by cultivating the power to die proudly (if the unlikely opportunity to do so should present itself), you may be more likely to cultivate an identity that can sustain itself without seeking to conquer, convert, marginalize, despise, or love to the point of suffocation every identity that differs from it. You may be more likely to see that part of the demand for a true identity for oneself and others flows from the demand to attain a self-reassurance deep enough to fend off the vicissitudes of life. You may become less likely to demand that wherever evil exists a responsible agent equal to its gravity must be identifiable. You may become less punitive in the name of love and humility, more prepared to constitute adversaries worthy of agonistic respect.

In *The Will to Power*, note 916, Nietzsche lists six practices, each of which has "been ruined by the church's misuse of it." The first five are asceticism, fasting, the monastery, feasts, and the courage to endure one's own nature. This is the sixth: "*death.*—one must convert the stupid physiological fact into a moral necessity. So to live that one can also will to die at the right time."[7]

To live so that one can die a timely death is to drain existential resentment from life. It is to draw out the poison of resentment by *living as if* there were no agent or principle to whom the unfairness of mortality can be attributed, thus no object to serve as the target of resentment for this stupid fact, and thereby no ontological basis for the recurrent temptation to compensate for the loss of a clear agent of responsibility through the generalization of resentment against alter-identities. To prepare to die at the right time is to express "love of life."

To *say* there is no unfairness here is one thing, but to prepare oneself to live that judgment is another, involving a different relation to the stupid physiological fact. To drain resentment from life *in this way* is to combat the fundamental sense of existential unfairness from which the production of scapegoats flows. The sense of unfairness begins to float unless this new disposition is cultivated. It might emerge as a doctrine of original sin (where "you yourself are responsible" for the fact of mortality) or emerge more indirectly in the general dogmatism of identity. This unstated resentment selects new agents responsible for new evils when the primary agent is taken away because the initial disposition to locate responsibility for the necessity of death is too deeply inscribed to drift away of its own accord. Its signs are everywhere. That is the claim.

To convert the physiological fact of death, when the time is right, into a moral choice is simultaneously to modify one's relationship toward one's own identity and to take a crucial step toward combating the second problem of evil. It is a crucial, though insufficient, step. There probably is no fully sufficient step. That, any-way, is how I interpret Nietzsche's commendation. It is at the level of the slippery experience of existential injustice—rather than at the level of the social distribution of burdens and possibilities–that it seems to me to deserve a close hearing.

The tenacity and universality of this struggle with finitude might provide a common point of departure through which agonis-tic respect can be cultivated between contending identities. It is not that each of us implicitly strives for the same identity or that reason reveals one true set of identities that can be housed together harmo-niously in the same society. It is that the very contingency of identity and the universality of the struggle with mortality can sometimes solicit in the self a fugitive experience of identification with life that stretches below and above any particular identity. It can invoke an agonistic respect for difference through the self-experience of a life not exhausted by the identity that endows it with definition, predictability, and standing in its society—a re-spectful strife with the other achieved through intensified experi-ence of loose strands and unpursued possibilities in oneself that exceed the terms of one's official identity. These things too die with the end of life, and they signify that life is not exhausted by the identity branded into it.

One is implicated ethically with others, first, through sharing an identity with some of them, second, through the stirrings of unpur-sued possibilities in oneself that exceed one's identity, and third, through engagement with pressures to resent obdurate features of the human condition. Reflection on these connections can also encourage one to reflect on how life overflows the boundaries of identity. You could not be what you are unless some possibilities of life had been forgone ("to do is to forgo"). And you now depend upon the difference of the other for your identity. Recognition of these conditions of strife and interdependence, especially when such recognition contains an element of mutuality, can flow into an ethic in which adversaries are respected and maintained in a mode of agonistic mutuality, an ethic in which alter-identities foster ago-nistic respect for the differences that constitute them, an ethic of care for life. Of course, as stated, this ethic remains out of touch with limitations persistently structured into political life. But this abstract statement may still be worth making, since it combats at *their* highest levels of articulation regulative principles that govern the idealism of the normal individual and the harmonious commu-nity.

The capacity for ethicality exceeds the bounds of identity, once the ethical bond is seen to encompass the agonism of difference. Ethicality flows into agonistic appreciation of difference. When this bond through differentiation is acknowledged, the moral demand for an all-embracing identity grounding the truth of a fixed moral code loses some of the power it exercised over the self. This identification with humanity through the experience of difference and finitude may achieve its most influential presence in life, though, if death is taken as a theme of reflection and treated as one of the tests around which life is organized.

These intimations are neither certain nor necessary. They must ultimately be tested through experience. The responses they solicit must emerge—or n.ot—from the encounters they foment: the affirmation of life in its lightness and plurality; the affirmation of a Dionysian dimension enabling the self to bestow value upon the alter-identity it contests. These latter orientations, on my reading, seldom if ever *eliminate* dogmatic orientations to identity, difference, and otherness. The considerations designed to elicit them may even exacerbate the drive to strong, exclusive identities in some people and some circumstances. At best, though, they support new possibilities of strife among dispositions in the self and the polity, a strife that enables a peculiar respect for difference to compete on more even terms with attachment to personal and collective identities. It is this *possibility* that deserves attention, even if there are dangers in attending to it. The dangers are outweighed by the cruelty to difference operative in a culture that refuses to cultivate the possibility.

Of course, there is no necessity that things will flow in the desired direction. A discursive ethic of cultivation can tap into fugitive experiences arguably submerged by alternative accounts and then strive to draw its interpretation of them into the established terms of discourse. Because it appeals to partially shared experiences, it can hope to receive a hearing; because these are susceptible to multiple interpretations—some of which suggest revisions, adjustments, modifications in its initial perspective—it cannot assure that its own interpretation will withstand a variety of experiential, existential, and dialogic tests. Because it does not proceed from universal premises through argumentation to necessary conclusions, an interpretive ethic of discursive cultivation is highly unlikely to generate unavoidable implications. It folds a certain agonism into the center of ethical discourse. Can other orientations to ethics really vindicate a stronger claim to necessity for themselves? At what cost? But we shall follow further the course already charted without pursuing that detour this time around.

Cultivation of willingness to die a timely death simultaneously involves exploration of the attachment to existence already installed in life. The attachment to life flows deeper than the commands of identity and the phenomenology of decision. That is the key. Think, perhaps, of one who attempts suicide through an overdose of medication and then finds his body fighting and overturning this decision. Or one who recovers from a life-threatening accident. The attachment to life, flowing below and through the boundaries of will, consciousness, and identity, can become brilliant and luminous after such experiences.

"Only now are you going to greatness: Peak and abyss—they are joined together."[8] "Abyss" refers here specifically to the way in which the thought of eternal return of identity and difference implies the eternal return of resentment and revenge too. It refers at the same time to the way in which affirmation of life and acceptance of a timely death are bound together in strife and interdependence. Peak and abyss are contained in the same experience.

One would have to plumb the unfathomable depths of life before one could prepare oneself to choose to die at the right time. But the tenacity of life is exactly what pulls us to hold off death until it comes of its own accord. It impels us towards philosophies of permanence in god, nature, or reason. So it is insufficient to chant (with Zarathustra's dwarf) that "everybody lives; everybody dies." One reaches further: "as deeply as man sees into life, he also sees into suffering."[9]

This attachment to life, flowing over and through the "small chamber of consciousness," can impress itself through suffering and the capacity to bear it. Tolerance of acute suffering exposes the tenacity of life. The struggle to accept a timely death might expose the pervasiveness, *overflowing specific structures of identity and consciousness*, of the drive to life. This is a Nietzschean counterpoint to the Christian call to probe the attachment to its god through self-meditation and prayer.

How, though, does this relation become a live issue for those who have not attempted suicide, recovered from a devastating accident, or attended a loved one struggling with terminal illness? How, indeed, since even these experiences carry no inevitability that the issue will be joined.

There are several possibilities. Reflection on Greek tragedy may be one. At least Nietzsche thought so. For the tragic vision teaches some to affirm life even after they have experienced the tragic possibilities that form its core. Drawing upon the rich experience of ordinary life already available to most individuals may be another. Take memory, for instance.

One lives through events. Some become stuck in memory. Some memories are heavy and momentous. Others are light and touching. Here is one of the latter: Three friends in their twenties, urban dwellers, glide around a bend in a river in a northern state; two of them lift their paddles to propel the canoe forward, as they have during several hours of conversation and casual observation of the "scene." They halt in midair, observing a doe and a faun, up to their chests in the river, frozen in place as the canoe drifts by. The three amateur canoeists remain immobile for a few seconds, until the deer splash awkwardly out of the water and scamper off. Then they iterate and reiterate this little event to one another, reviewing it well beyond its importance to anything in particular. They laugh at this compulsion to celebrate it. And they laugh at how their laughter renews the celebration that occasions their laughter.

Later, the event becomes a memory, framed in a mental picture, a picture that returns of its own will occasionally on a winter evening, one that through its unwilled recurrences bonds together three people who no longer have much occasion to visit one another, one that recalls the particular time in which it is situated. It is a slight and slender memory. Nothing definite turns on it, as it floats in and floats out whenever it will.

Life is full of light memories sailing through the soul at odd moments. It contains heavy ones, too, and others of ambiguous weight. They accumulate and enrich it. Death, among other things, erases this fund of memory. The fund dies with you. And yet *it wants to continue.* Such memories choose one at least as much as one chooses them; they compromise the language of subjectivity through which primacy is bestowed upon the willing, choosing, knowing, remembering agent.

But how could I *choose* to die if these, too, have to go with me? What about a host of other attachments that, to some degree or other, define my being and flow beyond the grasp of my agency? "My longing for this laughter gnaws in me; how do I bear to go on living: and how could I die now?"[10]

"Have you," asks Zarathustra, "ever said Yes to a single joy? O my friends, then you said Yes to *all* woe. All things are entangled, ensnarled, enamored: if ever you wanted one thing twice, if ever you said, 'You please me, happiness! Abide, moment!' then you wanted all back. . . . For all joy wants—eternity."[11] Joy wants eternity. Perhaps this is overwrought and overstated. But it underlines connections between joy, memory, and the wish for their continuation. Acceptance of a timely death might mean that one accepts the ensnarlements and contingencies of life amid experience of its sweetness and tenacity. It might signify a victory of sorts over existential resentment. But these very reflections may also foment a burst of laughter over the self-indulgence accompanying them. In another of his moods Nietzsche ridicules those who spend much of their time pondering death. Such rumination contradicts the fervency of life. It is full of self-importance and secret pleading. It quickly becomes what it purports to oppose. These two moods, I think, counter and balance each other in the effort to probe the limits of identity for life.

Aren't the odds low that you will be in a position to act upon the disposition to die a timely death? Who is prepared to give an operational definition of "the right time," anyway?[12] And doesn't the very formulation of this issue threaten to backfire by fostering a "dread" of death that immobilizes and contradicts the spirit to be cultivated? Yes, on all counts. But still, these risks and ambiguities do not erase the point of the reflection. One prepares oneself to respect the diversity of life flowing over and through officially sanctioned identities. The issue of a timely death exposes a fervency for life, a fervency already flowing through one's daily thoughts, actions, routines, decisions, struggles, and successes, a fervency inscribed in the fibers of the body. One thus engages a fervency already there. Life exceeds identity.

Such a reflection might reduce existential pressure to vindicate life by some promise or assurance projected into divinity or the plasticity of nature. Life requires no external vindication. It *is* the fugitive experience standing at the end of the vindication line. One thus opens up the question of how much evil is done through a mode of life that strives to resolve the problem of evil by constructing a substantial, exclusive, deep identity. Identity is an indispensable dimension of life; yet it does not exhaust the tenacity and multifariousness of life.

This use and misuse of Nietzsche does not *settle* anything. At best, it unsettles things. The point is not to provide a single, exclusive interpretation of the relations between life, identity, and death, but to place another candidate onto the field of discussion, to introduce a more robust agonism into this territory, so as to challenge the hegemony of religious piety or of the secular demand for compensation. Judgment between these alternatives is confirmed or rebutted through one's experience of life, but this experience itself may become more reflective when engaged by an enlarged variety of interpretive possibilities.

Such a speculation should problematize itself and confess itself to be contestable to the core. But I would seek to apply this directive to alternative perspectives on life, identity, suicide, death, and salvation as well. No single set of conclusions should become, say, the object of legislation or fixed cultural expectation. That is why the bearers of aggressive conventionality in this domain must be challenged through reflectively articulated alternatives.

To prepare to "die proudly when it is no longer possible to live proudly" drains existential resentment from life. And confronting this dimension of finitude may pave the way to engage others such as the element of difference in identity, fatefulness in action, opacity in knowledge, and ambiguity in ethical ideals. The cumulative effect of these engagements can help to fend off cruelties to difference flowing through dogmatism in identity, innocence in action, the pursuit of transparency in knowledge, and the urge to moral simplification. "The doctrine still sounds strange: to die at the right time . . ." But perhaps its place in a political perspective has become intelligible enough.

Identity and Contingency

Must one *truly* have a *true* identity? If one comes to terms with the tenacity of life and the contingency of death, one may be in a better position to appreciate contingent elements in one's own identity, to live one's own identity in a somewhat different way.

Even a contingent identity is worth living. Even a life that ends in oblivion is sweet. Even suffering, up to some undefinable point, is worth the living that brings it. The store of resentment against the human condition, fueling efforts to locate and punish responsible agents for every evil, may be attenuated by this recognition.

Even a contingent identity is worth living. But another detour is needed prior to pursuing that trail.

Many contemporary theorists proceed as if identity were fractured today and we must find some way to solidify it. Society is treated as fragmented or alienated or shot through with anomie; individuality or selfishness is said to defeat the possibility of finding and pursuing a common good. Such theorists worry about relativism, atomism, egoism, nihilism, and estrangement. There are elements in these interpretations that make sense to me. That is, there is a crisis brewing in late modernity as peoples and states find historically institutionalized patterns of economic growth, mastery over the environment, and democratic sovereignty running up against the globalization of contingency, as they encounter new limitations placed on democratic sovereignty through the internationalization of economic and social relations, the fragility of international economic stability, the threat of nuclear war, and the declining ability of powerful states to ensure international political stability.

But at the most fundamental level these interpretations do not make sense to me. The standards of unity and harmony they presuppose seem closer to death than to life. The difficulty resides not primarily in a fragmentation of identity and the concomitant loss of a common identity. It resides, at one level, in a fixing and consolidation of a set of contending identities, each of which takes itself to be the true identity deserving hegemony. And it resides, at another level, in the universalization of the drive to affluence and mastery among states in the late-modern time. It resides, to overstate the case, in wrong ways of living identity, not in the absence of individual and common identities. It resides in the closure of identities in response to the fragility of things more than in a nihilism, anarchy, or relativism estranged from identity as such.

Instead of defining the most basic problem as one of general alienation or fragmentation and the most fundamental response as one of achieving a more harmonious collective identity, one may define the problem as an intensification and territorial extension of pressures for normalization that, ironically enough, then produce fracturing and fragmentation by defining an enlarged variety of types that do not or cannot conform to established standards of normality. Intensive pressure for unity, consensus, and normality manufactures new abnormalities, to which idealists of unity then respond by . . . demanding more unity.

The way to loosen the boundaries of that circle is to render prevailing standards of identity more alert to incorrigible elements of difference, incompleteness and contingency within them. What is needed is a robust problematization of established realisms and idealisms through a political orientation that expresses reverence for life, attends to the fragility of the earth as a re-source of human life, insists upon the ambiguity of identity, and struggles to draw political implications from this complex appropriate to contemporary circumstances. Identities, in the ordinary course of events, tend to congeal of their own accord into hard doctrines of truth and falsity, self and otherness, good and evil, rational and irrational, common sense and absurdity. Is it really necessary to seal them over a second time with transcendental proofs?

Anarchism is a real threat, for instance, in countries like Lebanon and Northern Ireland. But such anarchism reflects more a war between total and exclusive identities than an alienation from identity itself. Nor is relativism the consummate danger in the late-modern world, where every culture intersects with most others in economies of interdependence, exchange, and competition. Relativism is an invention of academics who yearn for a type of unity that probably never existed, who worry about an alienation from established culture that seldom finds sufficient opportunity to get off the ground, and who insist that ethical discourse cannot proceed unless it locates its authority in a transcendental command. The invention of relativism as a worry represents an attempt to save the idea of a true identity through negation—as if identity were something easily lost or misplaced. Perhaps it is timely to say: stop worrying about relativism, or at the very least, stop acting as if this worry were one everyone must attend to before striving to engage patterns of closure, insistence, and exclusion in contemporary patterns of identity.

What is it, then, to have a contingent identity, or better, an identity alert to elements of contingency in its relational constitution? I will not focus directly on the general level signified by the idea of the free, rational, responsible agent, partly because this site has been the object of attention in previous chapters and partly because these more general traits (and their contingencies) filter into particular features of the self. Think, rather, of specific "traits" and "dispositions" installed in a self—the sort of listing you might place in the personal column of an urban newspaper (were that compatible with your "traits"), consisting of statements that stand somewhere between your parents' characterization of you and the characterizations through which you wish to be recognized.

You are female, white, pretty, straight, young, ambitious, political, athletic, nonethnic, religious, adventurous, single, and disposed to remain so. You might have been male, gay, apolitical,
conventional, mildly retarded, agnostic, and family-centered had
things turned out differently, or hermaphroditic, fundamentalist,
chaste, crippled, and nationalistic.

Each of these socially mediated traits and dispositions is contingent, then, in one sense of that word. For given a different pool
of genes, time of birth, family setting, education, cultural lineup,
and so on, your set might have been different. The specific set that
helps to define you is contingent in another sense. Since the entire
complex is not the product of a single hand or design but formed
through a complex history of parental relations, historical events,
disparate experiences, and contingent biological endowments, it is
highly probable that a variety of tensions, disharmonies, and disjunctions reside within this complex of conjunctions. Some of the
elements mesh reasonably well, and others conflict. The self predisposed to both a highly conventional moral code and heterodox
sexuality, for instance, faces conflict across a set of constitutive
traits. Various resolutions, evasions, adjustments, and troubles are
possible here.

This set is contingent in a third sense. Some elements will be
crucial to the constitution of your identity, while others will be
more like dispensable attributes you can maintain or drop. Perhaps
your definition as female is fundamental to you, while being single
is not. The former enters into your identity, into the constitution of
your self, while the latter is a revocable status you accept and
endorse.

Which ones are which is not entirely, or even primarily, up to
you. Perhaps you would treat being female as a relatively unimportant cultural artifact imposed upon a diverse range of bodies sharing
at most a few general and flexible traits, while the culture in which
you live insists upon treating femaleness as one side of a natural
gender duality naturally lived one way rather than others. Every
attempt to express your conviction is met by insistent attributions
of the second standard. In this instance, your attempts to escape a
certain identification only succeed in getting you recognized as a
deviant member of the category you resist, and this definition
eventually enters somehow or other into what you actually become.
Only politics could save you now. This is a fourth dimension of

contingency in the constitution of identity, then: identity is a site of interdependence and strife between incipient formations/presentations of self and intersubjectively constituted modes of identification.

If you live in a time when homosexuality is treated as fundamentally constitutive of the self and *the* homosexual is defined as either sick or morally deficient, then your sexual identity will be impressed upon you through a set of contingent, institutionalized conventions. It is unlikely that you will escape fully the imprint of these conventions upon your soul, even as you strive to struggle against them. The cultural parameters within which your sexuality is defined and organized chose you before you affirmed or resisted them. This can be true of one's sexual orientation, one's gender identification, one's race, one's job, one's age, one's political perspective, one's orientation to conflict, one's religious convictions, and so on. There is a powerful element of contingency in the degree to which one's contingent dispositions are treated as part of one's identity and in the way those dispositions are constituted through socially established standards of normality, integrity, and self-awareness.

The language we have used so far to separate dispositions from their cultural identification can never be deployed so cleanly in life: identity involves naming cultural formations that have become naturalized and interiorized, and naturalized dispositions always contain a set of operational beliefs and judgments that help to constitute them. This slippery territory forms another site of conjunction and disjunction in the politics of identity, where cultural constitution and contingent dispositions inscribed into the body enter into relations of consonance and dissonance unsusceptible to independent specification through a culturally neutral vocabulary. It is a mistake to resolve the fugitive character of relations between "disposition" and "cultural determination" into a solution giving simple primacy to one dimension or the other. The experience of life, as Augustine well understood, reveals the grave difficulty that can accompany attempts to break a bad habit even after one has struggled to change the beliefs installed within it; it also exposes difficulties in shaking off a negative name even after one has struggled to reject the value it injects. The body forms an indispensable basis of discourse about identity and an insufficient and unreliable basis from which to draw culturally unmediated representations.

"Body," of course, is another term for "life," as that which exceeds the organization of a discourse nonetheless unable to proceed without it.

Finally, then, there is a dimension containing, shall we say, double contingency within it. Some of the contingent elements that enter into your identity are susceptible to reconstitution, and others remain highly resistant to it, even if you desire to transform them and even if there is cultural support for doing so. Let us call the latter branded or entrenched contingencies, to emphasize how they are both contingent formations and resistant to modification once consolidated. A branded contingency is a formation that has become instinctive, even though it may not be reducible to instinct as a biological drive. Indeed, the term "contingency" as used here in no way implies that a contingency is always something that can be changed through will or decision. There are obdurate contingencies, and it is a mistake to assume that the constructed character of a self-identity automatically implies its susceptibility to reconstruction.

"Heterosexuality" might be a contingency branded into you. That is, as a result of a history of complex interactions, difficult to trace, by the time you reached your teens in this culture, you were constituted as (say) a male drawn toward sex with women and away from sex with men. In this instance, you identify with the category culturally preselected for you. Things might have turned out differently: your affectional/sexual orientation might have been reversed; or you might have been attracted to both genders; or you might have been drawn to women sexually and resistant to affectional relations with them; or you might have experienced that split in relation to males; or you might have been drawn to modes of erotic/affectional relations that scramble in one of a myriad of possible ways the categories (hetero/homo/bi–male/female) through which such entrenchments are now culturally organized, interiorized, and naturalized.[13]

Anyway, once things turned out the particular way we have hypothesized, this particular "heterosexuality" became branded into you as part of your second nature. It may be a mistake to try to "explain" individual "cases" too deeply, for to do so is very probably to introject dominant cultural understandings more deeply into standards of individual identity.

Through a reflective genealogy you might begin to experience this formation as an entrenched contingency. It is now yours and it corresponds to currently dominant conventions, but it does not necessarily correspond to the nature of things for all that. Your sexual identity may receive its determinacy in part from a contingent aversion that you, as a male, feel toward sex with other males. But this orientation, when understood as a branded contingency (it is irrelevant here whether it contains ambivalence), may now be open to new possibilities of reflection. You are now in a position, first, to question the tendency to ethicize this disposition as if it flowed from a universally proper identity for males ("heterosexuality") and, second, to resist the conviction that you cannot really accept "homosexuality" in others unless you purge the aversion to sex with men in yourself.

Without a particular set of entrenched formations you could not have an identity, even though there is more to identity than this. But everything turns upon how these contingent formations are lived and how they relate to different formations in others. The demand to *ethicize* or universalize the entrenched contingencies on the grounds that they flow from a true identity is a recipe for repression of difference; by treating alternative types of sexuality as immoral, deviant, or sick, it calls upon you to purge any such dispositions lingering in yourself and to support the treatment or punishment of others who manifest them more robustly. This demand grounds your sexual ethic in the self-idealization of a contingent, relational identity that takes itself to be natural and independent.

The alternative demand to *purge* the entrenched contingency in yourself because it is unworthy of ethicization is a recipe for self-repression; it treats another contingent identity as the natural standard everyone must attain. It grounds its ethical idealism in the loathing of a self for what it is. When this track is pursued very far, others will eventually pay a price for the self-loathing you feel . . . for surely you will want to purge any signs of this tendency in them too.

What the demand to ethicize and the demand to purge this branded contingency share is an uncritical imperative of moral purity and an overly developed enthusiasm for normalization: one must either ethicize one's instincts or purge them because they are unworthy of ethicization. Both demands naturalize visceral formations by acting as if they must be either grounded in a universal self-identity or reformed until they are. Both express and engender a certain self-contempt, an inability to accept oneself unless one can either universalize one's contingent dispositions or eliminate them because they are not susceptible to universalization. Both orientations also express a strong disposition to punishment, a demand either to defeat the other in oneself and other selves or to love it until it replicates one's ideal self. Both project the egoism of identity into the idealism of morality. Self-loathing is another contingent disposition that can infiltrate identity; and reflection on the contingency of identity might increase the susceptibility of *this* contingency to tactics of self-modification.

To accept the contingency of identity is not to oppose every effort to work on the self. Far from it. Such acceptance requires considerable work on the self. Moreover, if you are drawn to sex with members of one gender but averse to affectional relations with them, the destructive effects such a combination has on you and others might encourage you to try to reconstitute elements in this combination, even while you do not hold yourself thoroughly responsible for the combination presently installed in you. (Unless, of course, you strive to politicize the connection between sexuality and love installed in this culture.) You might explore tactics by which to modify dispositions branded into the self.

But to acknowledge a variety of contingent elements in the formation of identity is to take a significant step toward increasing tolerance for a range of antinomies in oneself, countering the demand to treat close internal unity as the model toward which all selves naturally tend when they are in touch with themselves, shifting part of the primacy currently attached to the will when the question of self-modification arises.

To recall that an entrenched formation does not merely contain "blind" directionality, but expresses presumptive beliefs and judgments in action, is to come to terms with some of the most obdurate difficulties in negotiating relations between antagonistic formations (both within the self and between selves, but I will focus on the latter here). One response, suitable for some issues on certain occasions, is to strive to convert an antagonism of identity into an agonism of difference, in which each opposes the other (and the other's presumptive beliefs) while respecting the adversary at another level as one whose contingent orientations also rest on shaky epistemic grounds. An antagonism in which each aims initially at conquest or conversion of the other can now (given other supporting conditions) become an agonism in which each treats the other as crucial to itself in the strife and interdependence of identity\difference. A "pathos of distance" (to borrow a phrase from Nietzsche) begins to unfold whereby each maintains a certain respect for the adversary, partly because the relationship exposes contingency in the being of both.

Each cultivates an appreciation of contingency and disjunction in the experience of identity so that the agonism of difference will not always have to be rolled back into the strategies of conquest, conversion, community, or tolerance. These alternatives are not thereby eliminated from life, but another one is added to them in a way that enables people to expose cruelties in the first set concealed by the previous terms of comparison. Sometimes one shows respect for another by confronting him with alternative interpretations of himself, sometimes by just letting him be, sometimes by pursuing latent possibilities of commonality, sometimes by respecting her as the indispensable adversary whose contending identity gives defini-tion to contingencies in one's own way of being.

When confronted with the (inevitable) objection "You yourself accept a theory of true identity; you treat contingency as the truth of identity and the refusal of contingency as an evil to be exposed," the theorist of contingent identity might say: "Yes, of course, in some sense of the protean phrase 'true identity,' I do. I seek to install in the lived experience of identity an enhanced sense of its con-tingency and relationality. And I seek to promote in every reflection on identity a sense of its contestability as a theory. If you go this far with me in your conception of identity, we will have gone some distance toward politicizing an issue heretofore shuffled to the margins of legitimate political discourse through the ruse of self-referential delegitimization. We may have helped to shift an uneven battle between true and false identities into an agonism of differ-ence between identities and alter-identities whose constitutive rela-tions of interdependence and strife are infused with respect."

To endorse contingency in identity with its thematic of branded contingencies is to acknowledge tragic possibilities in the life of the individual. To take one instance, one might have violent, destruc-tive dispositions inscribed in oneself, dispositions neither chosen in the past nor susceptible to reconstitution now. Brutalization and deprivation can produce such results; most people of extremely violent disposition probably bear these latter experiences in their background. Here, others must strive to contain one, if one fails to try oneself or if one's best attempts are unsuccessful. Typically, it is unclear in such cases whether failure represents a refusal, an inability, or a complex unamenable to these fixed categorizations. But even here, the general understanding of contingency in identity opens up alternative possibilities for treating those condemned by such dangerous dispositions. Strategies of self-modification may be pursued, but they will not always succeed. Then, the need to take the minimum legal action needed to protect others from the danger of violence installed in such an individual can take precedence over the drive to punish him for an evil will or to "store" her out of view to protect the public from confronting living counter-examples to complacent ideals of self-identity. Under such conditions the case on behalf of lifting the circumstances of the individual's confinement from the realm of public denial and revenge might make itself felt more powerfully.

The one who construes her identity to be laced with contingencies, including branded contingencies, is in a better position to question and resist the drive to convert difference into otherness to be defeated, converted, or marginalized. One will surely end up ethicizing some of one's dispositions if care for the interdependence and strife of identity\difference has been cultivated; one may strive to reconstitute some; one may deploy techniques to conceal, sublimate, restrain, or revise others that do not synchronize with one's ideals and are unsusceptible to elimination. But one will do so less because one takes one's particular identity to be intrinsically true than because one's reflective experience of contingency and relationality in identity elicits a reverence for life responsive to the politics of difference. And this latter orientation may itself gradually slide into one's identity, a possibility that shows the elasticity of the idea of identity.

One may live one's own identity in a more ironic, humorous way, laughing occasionally at one's more ridiculous predispositions and laughing too at the predisposition to universalize an impulse simply because it is one's own. Laughing because one senses that the drive to moralize difference is invested with the wish to reassure oneself that one is what any normal being should be. Laughing at *us*, too, for the same reasons. Laughing in a way that disrupts this persistent link between ethical conviction and self-reassurance while affirming the indispensability of ethical judgment in life. Such laughter pays homage to fugitive elements in life that exceed the organization of identity, otherness, rationality, and autonomy. It has effects. "Learn to laugh at oneself as one must learn to laugh." Such laughter counters and subverts a Hobbesian sense of humor, where I show myself to be ahead and you to be behind—though the fact that Hobbes advances this definition reveals that his own sense of humor exceeds the definition he offers of it.

Genealogy and Ethicality

It is not so easy to broaden one's "reflective experience of contingency and relationality in identity." It involves considerably more than a decision or an acknowledgment. It is necessary to engage genealogical histories of the social construction of normality and abnormality. Genealogy is indispensable to what I will call "ethicality" in life, that is, to the cultivation of care for the strife and interdependence of identity\difference.

A genealogy exposes ways in which established debates over the treatment appropriate to abnormalities often sustain implicitly the sanctity of the normal, how they protect the normal from critical scrutiny through the very terms of contestation over sources and remedies of abnormality. "Is the defect a result of free choice or original sin? Is it immorality or sickness? Is it socially determined or psychologically caused? Is it rooted in genetics or grounded in culture? Is it susceptible to psychoanalysis or shock therapy? Is it dangerous or self-destructive? Is it susceptible to punishment or to therapy?" The primacy given to these questions subdues contests over the standards of normality they presuppose.

Counter-histories of normality are genealogical also in the way the strive to bracket established teleotranscendental assumptions. These assumptions are inscribed in global dualities of good/evil, normal/abnormal, and identity/otherness, as well as in secondary divisions on the negative side of these dualities: irresponsibility/ sickness, psychological defect/social anomie, genetic ground/cultural determination, and so on. We have encountered capsulized versions of such double analyses in previous discussions of madness, the normal individual, suicide, procrastination, the drive to salvation, homosexuality, evil, and responsibility. The general point is that critical genealogies are indispensable to cultivation of the experience of contingency in identity\difference.

Genealogy brackets teleotranscendental legitimations of established dualities in order to problematize established frames within which social and theoretical debates over these issues have been set. It strives to problematize the frame within which theoretical alternatives have been set rather than to provide an appraisal of one or two theories within the frame. The goal is problematization rather than simple elimination or replacement because the genealogical thinker too swims in the culture that establishes these settings and because one does not expect to locate a space wholly outside them. The goal is to problematize the present by recourse to the past without promising a perfect time in the past to return to.

From the vantage point of theories of deep identity, a genealogy might seem to be only destructive: it can only destroy established standards of evaluation without introducing new ethical directions. But from within a genealogical perspective, this judgment presupposes rather than shows that only a theory of deep identity can provide a source for ethics.

The genealogist sees her own enterprise differently. She replaces the vertical line that culminates in a transcendental command with one that cultivates a care for identity and difference already operative in life through accentuation of the experience of contingency. And whenever that tilling digs into barren soil, he tries again, without pretending he can devise a final *argument* that will command the seed to grow. The soil must be fertile for cultivation to succeed. The genealogist takes comfort in the knowledge that ethicality has retained a presence in previous cultures even when ontotheological strategies of transcendence have run into dead ends.

You can call *this* a teleological perspective, if you like, as long as you remember that in it "life" exceeds the terms of any particular identity, instrument of knowledge, or harmonious end, and that it would be unethical to forget this key point when affixing that label to the perspective in question.[14] You can even call it a new "essentialism," if you wish, one that construes its "ground" as contestable, fugitive, and ambiguous rather than fixed, solid, and harmonious.

A genealogy calls theories of intrinsic identity and otherness into question in order to tap agonistic care for difference from the experience of not being exhausted by the identities that fix a particular life. It is an ethic of cultivation, drawing upon the "rich ambiguity of existence" and powers of imagination derived from it.

The "nihilism" of genealogy may exist in the eye of the beholder—the beholder who castigates genealogy to protect the future possibility of a transcendental argument to secure morality as he defines it. When the debate is elevated to this "metaethical" level, it seems unlikely that it will ever be definitively resolved. But the genealogist does not need a definitive settlement here, being content to remind the transcendentalist that he seems to get along in daily life even though he has never yet delivered on the achievement he assumes to be necessary. It may even be that the genealogist is "parasitic" on modalities she opposes, while her opponents are too. But that irony will have to be set aside for now. It is not necessary, anyway, that the genealogical perspective become the view of everyone. It will suffice if it finds a robust, competitive presence in the life of the culture.

Nietzsche and Foucault are unsurpassed masters of genealogical analysis, though today a large cluster of scholars in a number of fields is beginning to practice it.

But if genealogical reflection involves multiple levels of analysis and depends upon access to critical histories of the present, once one has access to a few of these histories it is not all that difficult to launch pertinent investigations into one's own settled moral dispositions and to revise the shape of some of one's preliminary orientations. Most people have experienced gaps between the identity ascribed to them and subversive orientations to life that press upon them, between social standards of identity and that in themselves and their friends which neither fits those standards nor seems evil, between the standards of responsibility they accept for themselves and those they demand of others. Attention to these gaps can encourage the cultivation of genealogical history, and genealogical histories can accentuate the experience of contingency in identity. The two experiences foster each other. They can open the self to a more ironic posture toward itself, to a new sensibility to possibilities foreclosed by its history of self-formation.

Reflection on the contingencies of identity does not provide a key to the resolution of every ethical paradox and dilemma. Since no other ethical orientation has passed such a test, this perspective need not achieve such purity either. Indeed, the demand for ethical purity is itself susceptible to genealogical analysis. A genealogical analysis of established ethics only seeks to make a difference by plugging into established ethical proclivities and standards that always already permeate a way of life. It does not seek to construct a new ethic from scratch, nor does it find any other orientation to ethics actually proceeding in this way.

Reflection on the contingency of identity is likely to foment a tragic experience of life, or at least an intensified experience of the ambiguity in every worthy achievement. It is likely, even, to register strong teleological and transcendental theories as attempts to conceal the ambiguity of life. Perhaps every achievement also entails injury and sacrifice. Perhaps the claims of individuality and commonality inevitably collide at numerous points in any ordered way of life, even while it is impossible to function as humans outside some particular order of existence. Perhaps reflection on mortality for the sake of cultivating care for life also contains the possibility of deepening the strain of cruelty in some. Perhaps the drive to normality and consensus is an uneasy compound of pressures emanating from the inertia of language, the quest for self-reassurance, the human need for stability of expectation, the requirements of social coordination, the claims of justice, and the contingent boundaries of a particular order; and perhaps the elements in this compound that inflict injuries and sacrifices upon life are not neatly detachable from those that promote the good of all.

To ponder the indispensability and contingency of identity is not to eliminate the paradox of ethics, but neither is it to resign people and institutions to treating established settlements as if they already provided the optimum balance available to life. By (contestably) revealing what other perspectives conceal through their unconscious ontologizations of actuality, genealogy politicizes the established constitution of possibility and necessity. It incites some injured by established standards of normality while it also enables some beneficiaries of those standards to respond affirmatively to struggles to modify or loosen closures in the order. It challenges fixed limits of possibility by politicizing unthematized presumptions in actuality. It is thus predisposed to interrogate consensus where it becomes fixed and to question the terms of division where they become stabilized.

The "principle" from which these priorities proceed is care for identity and difference in their ambiguous relationships of interdependence and strife. In its generality this principle is necessarily vague, amenable to detailed specification only within concrete interpretations of particular situations and predicaments. It shares these traits with every other principle nominated in ethical life.

For now it may suffice to say that genealogy is an indispensable means to ethicality. But it is insufficient to sustain a theory of agonistic democracy.

The Pathos of Distance

A democrat who draws upon Nietzsche to think about contemporary issues of identity, ethics, and politics will soon be compelled to take several steps away from him. The question is whether it is possible to cut out central elements in his message without reducing the complex to a bloody mess.

One seeks to remain tied to Nietzsche's skeptical contestation of transcendental and teleological philosophies, indebted to his genealogies, touched by his reverence for life and the earth. But the position elaborated here stands in a relation of antagonistic indebtedness to the bearer of these gifts. The antagonism moves on three levels.

First, the stance pursued here distances itself from certain familiar readings of Nietzsche as the philosopher of identity through domination over others and as the philosopher who aspires to freedom through mastery over nature. Second, on my own reading, Nietzsche is not essentially a political thinker, but is primarily apolitical in his idealism. Third, contemporary followers of Nietzsche such as Foucault and Deleuze, who have politicized the spirit of Nietzsche's thought and thereby reconstituted some of its key dimensions, have not pursued this project far enough to sustain a political theory.

I will advance some ingredients in a post-Nietzschean political theory by working on the second and third points. Let me say something, though, about the first one, the reading of Nietzsche as the consummate philosopher of world mastery. While such a reading is possible, it is not *the* single or necessary reading to be drawn from a thinker as protean as Nietzsche. It tends to be given by those who endorse strong transcendental or teleological perspectives. They presume that any ethic of care and self-limitation must flow from a teleotranscendental perspective, and that since Nietzsche noisily repudiates such a perspective, the coiner of the phrase "will to power" must endorse a ruthless philosophy in which a few exercise mastery over other humans and nature. Many may find *this* Nietzsche reassuring as a negative counterpoint to their own thinking, implying that since this is where all followers of Nietzsche must end up, anyone of "good will" should buy into their perspective to avoid this result. Nietzsche thus becomes a foil used to cover a weak affirmative argument through negation of the opposing one. There is irony in this strategy, since it is the strategy Nietzsche exposes as a favorite tactic of *ressentiment*.

These theorists have failed to explore the possibility that Nietzsche combines a tragic conception of life with nontheistic reverence, and that together these provide a human basis for agonistic care and self-limitation.

If Nietzsche is to play the negative role for which he has been nominated, it must be shown not only that the mastery reading *can* be constructed out of Nietzsche's texts but also that no other possibilities more disturbing to the aura of necessity attaching to the teleotranscendental alternative can be distilled from them. And this task, in my view, has not been accomplished.

From another side, the most sustained reading of Nietzsche as a philosopher of "world dominion" is provided by Heidegger, who in his later work then quietly siphons another set of Nietzschean themes into a perspective that seems too passive and apolitical to speak affirmatively to the late-modern condition.[15]

The question I will focus on, then, is: What changes and alterations in *my* Nietzsche are needed to sustain an agonistic ideal of democratic politics?

What, first, are the considerations that support a politicization of Nietzschean themes today? One way to identify them is to reflect on images and metaphors that present one face when Nietzsche deploys them at the end of the nineteenth century and another when they are placed in the late twentieth century.

Zarathustra says: "The most concerned ask today, 'How is man to be preserved?' But Zarathustra is the first and only one to ask: 'How is man to be overcome?' "[16] The idea is to stop worrying about the preservation of man, to strive to create a few overmen. Leave to their own devices those who insist upon being consumed by resentment, so that a few can cultivate another type of humanity. The new type to be cultivated consists of a few free spirits who fend off the resentment against the human condition that wells up in everyone, a few who rise above the insistence that there be symmetry between evil and responsibility, who live above the demand that some guilty agent worthy of punishment be located every time they themselves suffer, who recognize that *existential* suffering is a precondition of wisdom.

But this typological differentiation between man and overman no longer makes much sense, if it ever did. For the overman—constituted as an independent, detached type—refers simultaneously to a spiritual disposition and to the residence of free spirits in a social space relatively insulated from reactive politics. The problem is that the disappearance of the relevant social preconditions confounds any division of humanity into two spiritual types. If there is anything in the type to be admired, the ideal must be dismantled as a distinct caste of solitary individuals and folded into the political fabric of late-modern society. The "overman" now falls apart as a set of distinctive dispositions concentrated in a particular caste or type, and its spiritual qualities migrate to a set of dispositions that may compete for presence in any self. The type now becomes (as it already was to a significant degree) a voice in the self contending with other voices, including those of *ressentiment*.

This model is implicitly suggested by Foucault when he eschews the term "overman" (as well as "will to power") and shifts the center of gravity of Nietzschean discourse from heroes and classical tragic figures to everyday misfits such as Alex/Alexina and Pierre Rivière. These textual moves are, I think, part of a strategy to fold Nietzschean agonism into the fabric of ordinary life by attending to the extraordinary character of the latter. I seek to pursue this same trail.

The Nietzschean conception of a few who overcome resentment above politics while the rest remain stuck in the muck of resentment in politics is not today viable on its own terms. Today circumstances require that many give the sign of the overman a presence in themselves and in the ethicopolitical orientations they project onto the life of the whole. But this break with the spirit of Nietzsche requires further elucidation.

The shift results partly from the late-modern possibility of human self-extinction. In this new world the failure to "preserve man" could also extinguish the human basis for the struggle Nietzsche named "overman." Preservation and overcoming are now drawn closer together, so that each becomes a term in the other: the latter cannot succeed unless it touches the former. But the entanglement of each with the other in sociopolitical relations means, when the logic of this entanglement is worked out, that the "overman" as a type cannot eliminate from its life some of the modalities definitive of the "human." If the overman was ever projected as a distinct type—and this is not certain—it now becomes refigured into a struggle within the self between the inclination to existential resentment and an affirmation of life that rises above this tendency.

But the collapse of two *types* called "man" and "overman" also results from disappearance of the social space in which this figure of solitude was supposed to reside. The overman, remember, rises above the reactive politics of society, both by cultivating certain dispositions while residing within society and by clearing a space on the edge of social life. In this marginal space projected by Nietzsche, one could not stifle the definitions others gave one, but one could avoid extensive implication in a dense web of relations that would render it necessary either to accept those identifications or to struggle against them politically. The Nietzschean overman, in its dominant presentation in *Thus Spoke Zarathustra*, lives a life of relative solitude—one that escapes, for instance, the hold of the state, that "superfluous new idol," that "coldest of cold monsters" that "tells lies in all the tongues of good and evil": "Only where the state ends, there begins the human being who is not superfluous: there begins the song of necessity, the unique and inimitable tune. . . . Where the state *ends*—look there my brother! Do you not see it, the rainbow and the bridges of the overman?"[17]

But this picture of a marginal space beyond the effective reach of the tentacles of the state no longer refers to any discernible place in the late-modern time. The avoidances it counsels are no longer available, if they ever were. The clean air it seeks is too polluted at low altitudes and too thin to breathe at the highest.

Exactly what late-modern life renders inescapable is the intensive entanglement of everyone with everyone else. No one is left alone anymore, though too many are compelled to fend for themselves as they respond to the violent impositions of state and society. The social fabric of interdependencies and conflicts is now too tightly woven; the gaps between the lines of regulation and surveillance have tightened up. This tightening of the social fabric cannot be measured by ascertaining whether more or fewer people now live on the wrong side of officially defined norms—a mistake critics of the theme of "disciplinary society" repeatedly make when they support the thesis they seek to refute by pointing to those who resist, evade, elude, and disrupt social practices of discipline and normalization. It can be measured by pointing to the enlarged network of intrusions and regulations the army of misfits face as the standards of normality are extended and intensified; it can be discerned in the resistances they require in order to sustain themselves amid these demands, and in the extension of disciplinary techniques to overcome those resistances. Those who want aggregate measures can count the number of people today whose primary job is to control, observe, confine, reform, discipline, treat, or correct other people (think of the police, military personnel, welfare agents, therapists, state security agents, private security agents, advertising firms, prison officials, parole boards, nursing home attendants, licensing agents, tax officials, and so on) and the various clients, patients, delinquents, misfits, troubled souls, losers, subversives, and evaders who provide the primary objects of these practices. And they can compare this index—after sorting out the complex dimensions that make every aggregate comparison extremely coarse—with its counterpart a hundred (or even fifty) years ago.

Perhaps we can today listen to enunciations by Nietzsche a hundred years ago with ears attuned to a century of social intensification:

> Do you have courage, O my brothers? Are you brave? Not courage before witnesses, but the courage of hermits and eagles, which is no longer watched even by a god.[18]

> Avoid all such unconditional people! They are a poor sick sort, a sort of mob: they look sourly at this life, they have the evil eye for this earth. Avoid all such unconditional people! They have heavy feet and sultry hearts: they do not know how to dance. How should the earth be light for them?[19]

One dimension in Zarathustra's message can still be heard by those with ears, but the metaphors of wildness, hermits, eagles, snakes, caves, silence, deep wells, high mountains, solitude, mob, flight, and earth that populate Nietzsche's invocations of the overman no longer do *double* duty today. The "hermit" has become an anonymous member of a regulated multitude who are homeless; the "eagle" has become a protected species; the "mob" has become a criminal network entangled with official intelligence agencies; the "deep well" accumulates pollutants from road maintenance, toxic wastes, and fertilizer runoffs; urban "caves" have become nightly residences for homeless outcasts who restlessly haunt the streets by day; the "earth" has become a deposit of finite resources for late-modern production. The Nietzschean metaphors now refer to a spiritual disposition disjoined from topographical space; they are drained of reference to identifiable sites between the lines of social organization. Even the metaphors have become infiltrated by the significations they would rise above.

These changes in the signifying power of Nietzsche's nineteenth-century metaphors point to the collapse of social space for the overman as an independent, solitary type. The *distinction between types* now gives way to *struggle within and between selves*. The elevation to a fictive space above the muck of reactive politics must be translated into political engagement with institutionalized practices. Put another way: the overman must either become a beautiful soul or be dismantled as an apolitical type; either Nietzschean critique of *ressentiment* becomes an anachronism or it is refigured into a political philosophy.

The first alternative in each of these disjunctions would exclude nontheistic reverence for life from active presence in the late-modern time. Better, then, to dismantle the typology of "man" and "overman," even if it liquidates the dream of an elevated being floating above the politics of resentment, even if it entangles one in the very reactions and relations one strives to loosen or refigure, even if it means that everything becomes even more ambiguous.

It is necessary to recontextualize yet further the Nietzschean thematic of discordance, with its impulse to struggle against existential resentment. I have introduced elsewhere a conception of democracy expressing a social ontology of "discordant concordances," and there is no need to rehearse that argument here.[20] But even though the apolitical Nietzsche was an adversary of democracy, a politicized left-Nietzscheanism unearths building stones in the democratic edifice all too easily buried under the rocks of identity, consensus, the common good, legitimacy, and justice also needed in its construction. The buried stones deserve a place, even if their asperity and irregularity of shape takes room away from other blocks in the structure, even if they make the entire construction less smooth, regular, even, and ratic.

In *Twilight of the Idols*, Nietzsche attacks "Christian and anarchist":

When the anarchist, as the mouthpiece of *declining* strata of society, demands with righteous indignation 'his rights', 'justice', 'equal rights', he is only acting under the influence of his want of culture, which prevents his understanding *why* he is really suffering—in *what respect* he is impoverished in life. A cause-creating drive is powerful within him: someone must be to blame for his feeling vile. . . . His 'righteous indignation' itself already does him good; every poor devil finds pleasure in scolding—it gives him a little of the intoxication of power.[21]

Nietzsche himself, of course, takes pleasure in scolding, though he picks distinctive targets. The *respect* in which the dissatisfied ones find life impoverished is the key:

Whether one attributes one's feeling vile to others or to *oneself*—the Socialist does the former, the Christian does the latter—makes no essential difference. What is common to both, and *unworthy* in both, is that someone has to be to *blame* for the fact that one suffers—in short that the sufferer prescribes for himself the honey of revenge as a medicine for his suffering.[22]

These, clearly enough, are antidemocratic sentiments. Nietzsche is ridiculing anyone who demands equal rights and justice as a medicine for existential suffering. He insists that these narcotics cover up more fundamental sources of suffering and forestall confrontation of them; he suggests that such refusals take a heavy cumulative toll on the life of oneself and others; and he implies that a collective identity formed through these dispositions intensifies this toll.

Any egalitarian or democrat or critical theorist is tempted to stop reading Nietzsche at this point. But this response, while readily permitted by the texts, remains too single-minded. It represses dimensions in those same formulations that speak critically to the democrat as a democrat. A more nuanced response is possible.

The perspective of the social critic opens one's eyes to structural injustices inflicted by the routine operation of established institutional arrangements. But the sociocritical perspective can also blind through its very power of illumination. Social critique must become more attentive to generic sources of suffering (arguably) rooted in the human condition itself if its institutional criticisms are to sink more deeply into the texture of public life.

Through its very powers of disclosure, sociocritique tends to conceal the strain of resentment against the human condition flowing underneath social critique and democratic idealism. It does so partly out of anxiety that a Nietzschean critique of existential resentment will foster resignation to social injustice.

Perhaps it is possible to devise an alternative analysis of resentment, responsibility, freedom, and suffering, one that folds social critique into a mode of sensibility it too often excludes, one that simultaneously refuses to reduce suffering to defects in the structure of society *and* opposes injustices in the distribution of burdens, dangers, and sacrifices imposed by the prevailing order of things.

So, let's relocate the critic temporarily, placing him in a hypothetical world. He now lives in a democracy in which each citizen has a hand in maintaining the accountability of the state; in which no member has, say, more than five or six times as much income as any other; in which, therefore, general laws tend to apply to everyone in a similar way; and in which if it is necessary to risk death to defend the country, everyone in the appropriate age and health category is equally susceptible to selection. This is a world in which everyone has effective standing as a citizen, partly because each has the effective opportunity, should it prove attractive or necessary, to participate in the common life of the society—a world in which the preconditions of agonistic democracy are effectively installed.

During his middle period, Nietzsche was not oblivious to the attractions of this hypothetical world. It might be pertinent to listen to a formulation of the "end and means of democracy" that resonates, despite its typical logic of exaggeration, with elements in the perspective advanced here:

> Democracy wants to create and guarantee as much *independence* as possible: independence of opinion, of mode of life and of employment. To that end it needs to deprive of the right to vote both those who possess no property and the genuinely rich: for these are the two impermissible classes of men at whose abolition it must work continually, since they continually call its task into question. It must likewise prevent everything that seems to have for its objective the organization of parties. For the three great enemies of independence . . . are the indigent, the rich and the parties.—I am speaking of democracy as something yet to come.[23]

In his later writings, however, Nietzsche generally expected that any practice of democracy would curtail independence and enhance existential resentment. Indeed, democratic idealism was likely to become the most efficient conduit of the latter. I agree that no democracy will terminate existential resentment. But *if* it unfolds through the right idealism, democratic politics can be a medium through which to expose and redress the politics of resentment.

Agonal democracy *enables* (but does not require) *anyone* to come to terms with the strife and interdependence of identity\difference, to ask whether the drive to punish difference is an expression of existential resentment and whether the overt feelings of indignation reflect a mix of injustices in the world and the demand that the world provide a meaning for existential suffering. When democratic politics is robust, when it operates to disturb the naturalization of settled conventions, when it exposes settled identities to some of the contestable contingencies that constitute them, then one is in a more favorable position to reconsider some of the demands built into those conventions and identities. One becomes more able to treat one's naturalized assumptions about identity and otherness as conventional categories of insistence.

Such a result is not necessary. Indeed, it is easy to identify pressures in and around the self that push in the opposite direction. These pressures will never be eliminated; nor would it be possible to *be* a social creature if they were. It is just that the *ambiguity* of democracy adds the possibility of engaging the contingency of existence to other pressures already extant, whereas other social forms either suppress this possibility altogether or exclude it from a robust role in political life. More than other social forms, democracy accentuates exposure to contingency and increases the likelihood that the affirmation of difference in identity will find expression in public life. This intensification of the experience of the constructed, relational character of identity\difference constitutes both a virtue and a danger of democracy.

The danger resides in the permanent possibility that the experience will propel a reactive politics of dogmatic identity through resentment. That is why democracy functions best in a world where the culture of genealogy has also gained a strong foothold. But the danger is certainly not unique to democracy. In the late-modern time, when politics regularly impels leaders to mobilize entire populations for collective projects of war, productivity, international hegemony, drug control, justice, or ecological recovery, all states contain this proclivity. Only democracy generates a counteracting tendency as well: the democratic contestation of settled identities and conventions can help to call forth a more robust affirmation of interdependence and strife in the politics of identity. Agonistic democracy, where each of these terms provides a necessary qualification to the other, furnishes the best political medium through which to incorporate strife into interdependence and care into strife. This virtue provides a powerful argument on behalf of democracy. It also provides considerations pertinent to the shape the *ideal* of democracy assumes in the late-modern age.

So, let's bypass my version of the Rousseauian paradox—namely, that democratic virtue presupposes a democratic way of life, while that way of life in turn presupposes the virtues it should precede. Let's pretend that this democracy and these virtues have already unfolded together to some degree. We have attained our hypothetical world where income inequality is reduced, and so on. And one of the justifications for this achievement is that it gives everyone the opportunity to participate in the common life and, in particular, to engage the mysteries of identity and difference through democratic agonism.

Some agents in this democracy—upon examination of their history and current projects—may come to suspect that the drives to master the world and to improve everyone according to an official model of development contain dangers. Some of these democrats may now listen to demands for greater community, more refined terms of membership, enhanced centrality of purpose, and even greater reduction of economic inequality with long ears, with ears attuned to a strain of resentment against the human condition flowing through overt appeals for social improvement—a strain more difficult to sort out under other conditions of existence. It is within a democratic setting that critical attention to this strain might aspire to make a political difference, and it is partly because of the ambiguity of democracy that a particular response is needed.

But what might be said? Consider a few passages in such a message:

Are you *still* whining about estrangement and a lack of unity? About the need for greater equality and consensus? Is it still necessary to find someone or something to blame for every evil you suffer? Have you ever seriously asked how much the erection of *every* ideal of identity has cost? How much reality has had to be misunderstood and slandered, how many lies had to be sanctified . . . ? Isn't the form your idealism takes now one of the evils to combat?

I know these charges against you echo those you level against others. I would hold you responsible for your orientation to identity and difference. At least I demand an enhanced *responsiveness* to contingency in these relationships. Hence, too, I must acknowledge that the appeal to responsibility cannot be eliminated, even by those who contest its hegemony and who expose instabilities in the historical legacy upon which it draws. That is the strain of injustice in *my* sense of justice. It cannot be expunged. Its *form* can be modified, though, and its *direction* can be shifted. It is possible, you know, to become a little more honest about what one is and a little more ironic about how one is constituted . . . A few others concur with me on these points.

Our claim in a nutshell: your consuming drive to the reassurance of identity stultifies the politics of difference in the name of morality. The medicine you prescribe for everyone offers you the sweet honey of revenge, but it relocates the existential suffering that occasions it . . .

Perhaps you can finally acknowledge that there is a small dose of *revenge* in every complaint, that one reproaches those who are different for one's own feeling of vileness, as if they had perpetrated an injustice or possessed an *impermissible* privilege. But complaining is not of any use: it comes from weakness. It quickly becomes poison in the system. It would refuse, if it could have its way, to allow anyone else to have what you lack or to be what you are not. So it encapsulates others in relentless evaluations of inferiority, degradation, sickness, need, or dysfunctionality.

Do you ever *revel* in differences that disclose unexplored possibilities in the self you have become? That reveal the life within you to exceed the identity you have assumed? The moral plea for yet greater equality, uniformity, normality, identity, productivity, and commonality contains a secret demand to eliminate contrasts that make one suffer by comparison. This is the fear that propels one type forward: that the robust expression of difference will melt down the solidity of its self-identity.

Grow up. But if you won't, we will not try to compel you—as long as you restrain, or we can deflect, your impulse to moral uniformity. Our objective: To resist prescribing the honey of revenge for the suffering that comes with life; To admit these secret recipes manufacture enemies who *deserve* to be conquered or converted, because their difference from us suffices to make them evil or sick. It is because we see our own shadows on the mirror into which you stare that we are able to expose these insidious games of moral sweetness.

At our best—we are not always at our best—we revel in the form we have acquired while giving thanks that it does not exhaust the life in us. Can you at least admit that this *standard* of "the best" diverges from those you propagate . . . ? Or must you insist that we have no ideals because we struggle against the type that moves you?

Your version of democracy is too insipid—and too dependent. Here everyone helps everyone else; here everyone is an invalid and everyone a nurse. You call *this* compassion and *that* virtue. You seek a kind of stationary level of humankind. You *still* think humankind can find its best meaning as a machine in the service of the economy or the community—as a tremendous clockwork, composed of ever more subtly "adapted" gears . . . As if increasing the *expenditure* of everybody must necessarily increase the *welfare* of everybody.

Can you acknowledge, to take one instance, the extent to which a particular form of life—say, a highly refined, interdependent, productive society—manufactures criminals out of many whose instincts cut against its grain? Or does that place too much strain on those reassuring ideals of responsibility, identity, punishment, and rehabilitation?

For one criminal type is a strong human being under unfavorable conditions, a strong human made sick. What he lacks is the wilderness . . . His *virtues* have been excommunicated by society. Because he has never harvested anything from his instincts but danger, persecution, disaster, his feelings too turn against these instincts. In this society he degenerates into a criminal, though he might have been a warrior, a hunter, a frontiersman, an explorer, or a conquerer in other times and places. And *you* would have admired him in *those* times and places!

Many humans *embody* a mismatch between what they are and what their society demands. Perhaps a *democratic* theory of criminality and punishment must acknowledge somehow the contribution each social form makes to the production of *its* misfits, even when it reaches its highest level of attainment . . .—especially when it does so. Can you at least perceive an element of the tragic in this condition, and, perhaps, try to think in new ways about definitions of crime and criminality? And about the variety of misfits a society produces and condemns through its successes and failures?

Late-modern democracy invariably entangles everyone with everyone else. No solitary life is available here. But that is exactly why the protean idea of freedom must find its presence *within* this setting—one that connects freedom with the tension of distance, with the *pathos of distance*, with the creative tension of contrary perspectives belonging to each other in interdependence and contestation.

For what does freedom mean? That one has the *will* to self-responsibility. That one preserves distances that divide us. That one lives so that one can also will to die at the right time.

That one respects adversaries, not by reducing them to the same but by engaging, resisting, and challenging them. That one sometimes selects as a friend one whom one respects foremost as adversary. That one infuses interdependence with strife and strife with respect. That one stretches beyond oneself through one's encounters, drawing life from the resonances of absence, difference, and possibility they evoke in the self. That one refuses to fix the protean idea of freedom once and for all by hooking it to a singular model of identity.

How, then, is freedom to be measured? By the resistance that has to be overcome, by the effort it costs to stay *aloft* while confronting the contingencies of life.[24]

This, then, is not exactly my Nietzsche, but the strain of Nietzscheanism in me and the I that taps into Nietzscheanism.

Such a harangue would be inappropriate in a world lacking the preconditions hypothesized above. It could too readily be received as yet another attack on those already excluded from democratic politics. In the actual world, then, these themes are to be given a modulated expression, one that takes pains to counter misuses some would make of them as they allow a laudatory concern for social justice to screen out the elemental issue of existential resentment.

No political thematization of Nietzschean sentiments can dispense with selecting a context for its presentation. The point, then, is not to offer the true account of the true Nietzsche hiding behind a series of masks, but to construct a post-Nietzscheanism one is willing to endorse and enact.

CHAPTER SEVEN

The Politics of
Territorial Democracy

Personal and Collective Identity

The channels that connect personal identity to collective identity in late-modern states are multiple and deep.

First, personal and collective identity are connected through the channel of freedom. If I wish to identify myself as a free agent, there must be some coherence between the social roles I am called upon to play and the purposes I adopt upon reflection. If *we* wish to see ourselves as free, free as a people, we must believe that state institutions of electoral accountability carry with them sufficient efficacy to promote the collective ends we most prize. One connection between these two levels is this: if I find certain institutionalized roles in which I am implicated repressive or unduly restrictive, and if I am unable to escape them or to alter the rules that govern them, my freedom is still potentially intact if *we* could reconstitute them collectively should others come to concur in my assessment (or me in theirs). Thus one's self-identification as a free individual is bound up with a common belief in the capacity of the state to promote publicly defined purposes. Correspondingly, one's self-identification as a citizen in a democracy, where one's choices and judgments matter in the public realm, informs the orientation one takes to a variety of other social roles such as those of spouse, lover, student, worker, taxpayer, and consumer.[1] One is likely to be more independent, more assertive about one's rights, more disposed to respond politically to grievances or injustices in these domains if one has interiorized the definition of oneself as a citizen in a democratic state.

These relations between personal and collective identity in a democracy provide one basis of that honorable and dangerous bond of identification between the individual and the state. When circumstances are favorable, the relation is one of patriotism chastened by skepticism of state authority; when they are unfavorable, the relation degenerates into either disaffection with the state or a nationalism in which the tribulations of the time are attributed to an evil "other" who must be neutralized.

Ironically, then, serious threats to freedom grow out of these intersections between individual and collective freedom. These threats become most severe when the state suppresses claims to self-identity that might jeopardize its own claim to be an effective vehicle of freedom, and when large segments of the populace vindicate this response out of a wish to see the state as an effective instrument of collective freedom.[2]

This artery linking personal identity to collective identity through the medium of the state is surrounded by the flesh and bone of social commonality. In sharing a culture, a set of institutionalized roles, and a language, we share, albeit variably and imperfectly, a set of preliminary understandings, proclivities, and repugnancies that infiltrate the structure of perception, judgment, and decision. My identity is fixed within this setting, drawing some elements from it and reacting negatively to others. Who knows enough about these processes of selective osmosis to explain, let alone predict, any particular structure of self emerging out of them? But still, my identity is never neatly separable from the identifications and negations that constitute our way of life. The particular identity invested in each of us is essentially implicated in the common setting in which it arises, and the state constantly draws upon these investments in its definitions and resolutions of public issues.

This suggests another line of linkages between the structure of collective identity and that of personal identity. If you are marginalized, stigmatized, vilified, or excluded by public identifications inscribed upon you, and if these identifications are somehow fundamental to the integrity of collective identity, the politics of identity places you in double jeopardy. First, the collective identifications constitute you in ways that you would resist or oppose and that impinge upon your freedom in significant ways. Second, your public engagement in pressing for shifts in these terms of identification is severely cramped by the categorizations presumptively applied to you. A "welfare mother" who complains about the education of her children, her conditions of living, or policies that infringe upon her affectional relations is impaired in representing herself as long as that identification retains its hegemony. A "criminal-prisoner" who seeks to politicize his formative circumstances or the counterproductive effects of imprisonment faces even more severe disabilities. Here the politics of collective identity sustains the negative definitions it bestows by insisting that the categories up for political contestation be applied to those contesting them.

Democracy, if organized correctly and lived in the spirit summarized in the preceding chapter, both expresses and unsettles these connections between personal and collective identity. The experience of democracy and the experience of contingency in identity can sustain each other, especially when the first is supported by an intellectual culture of genealogy. Democratic turbulence disturbs established commonalities: it shows them to be complex contrivances; it brings out elements of contestability within them; it exposes possibilities suppressed and actualities enabled by contestable settlements. By fostering the experience of contingency and relationality in identity, democracy disturbs the closure of self-identity and, sometimes, provides a medium for modifying the terms of collective identity. This combination increases the chance—when this destabilization is part of struggle against existential resentment—that a larger variety of identities will be allowed to contend with one another on democratic terms. It increases pressure to revise the contours of the social form so that its institutional tolerances for democratic agonism can expand.

Certainly, other tendencies within democracy point in other directions—the normalizing pressures in it without which it could not be. But let us not allow the dangers in this ambiguity to deflect too much attention from its virtues.

The specter facing democracy today is that formal procedures of democratic accountability might become vehicles for systemic closure as the public identity faces a series of circumstantial threats to its integrity. The globalization of contingency, discussed in Chapter 1, creates a series of such pressures for closure in democratic politics today. It puts the squeeze on the territorial ideal of democracy; it intensifies pressures to preserve the appearance of internal democracy by denying the significance of global issues that escape the terms of accountability in the territorial state. The globalization of contingency provides the background from which the following assessment of identity and democracy proceeds.

Identity and the State

The functionality of collective identity. Self-reassurance through collective identity. Habituation to collective identity. Resentment and violence in collective identity. What is the "collective identity" of the late-modern state, and how does it function? I take the United States as my model, partly because I know it best and partly because it amplifies tendencies in other states of its type. We begin with a summary more or less uncritical of that identity. Several ingredients can be discerned.

First, there is the treatment of the state as the ultimate agency of self-conscious political action. Other institutions and affiliations, such as family, corporations, crime rings, religious entities, regional groupings, racial divisions, gender identifications, and ethnic affiliations, provide other sites of identification and produce aggregate social effects through their actions and transactions. But the state is the official center of self-conscious collective action. It is the institution of last recourse and highest appeal, the one that symbolizes what *we* are, for better or worse, and the one that enacts what we seek to be through its institutions of accountability and effectivity. It is the sovereign place within which the highest internal laws and policies are enacted and from which strategies toward external states and nonstate peoples proceed. It is the site of the most fundamental division between inside and outside, us and them, domestic and foreign, the sphere of citizen entitlements and that of strategic responses. It is the center surrounded by a periphery and the community surrounded by danger. For if the state does not serve as a center of self-conscious collective action in pursuit of common purposes, then nothing does.

Second, the legitimacy of the state, as the sovereign center of collective action, is most assured when the state appears to be accountable to a democratic electorate that can replace its officials and revise its priorities through competitive elections. In the late-modern time the ideal of democracy sets the terms for state legitimacy. From another angle, the democratic ideal itself has been colonized by the state. Both perspectives are central to established idealizations of democracy, even though the second is so universally accepted that it seldom becomes a topic of elucidation: the state receives its highest contemporary legitimation when it presents a democratic appearance; democracy receives its highest contemporary idealization through the medium of the state.

Third, the centrality of the state is conditioned by a set of constitutional forms prescribing relations between it and its citizens. The relation between constitutional prescription and state power is not, however, a one-way street. For "reason of state," in the state's sovereign relations with other states, also helps to define internal constitutional restrictions. This becomes apparent in appeals to the national interest or national security, the immunization of state officials from ordinary procedures of law and penalty, and the routine classification of state documents otherwise susceptible to publicity and accountability. Most appeals to reason of state are accepted as legitimate by most people most of the time because of a perception that security from external threat is essential to internal democracy, because state security is perceived to be in perpetual peril, and because outside the territory of the state the cherished life of democracy can find no institutional foothold. International "realism" and domestic "idealism" converge toward this effect.

Fourth, in the late-modern state the military dimension of life becomes pervasive and ubiquitous. Since the state is the preeminent provider of security against foreign attack and since its security is in perpetual jeopardy, it is in a continual state of military preparedness. This self-definition enters into the perception of constitutionality delineated above. It enters, as well, into most facets of civilian life—particularly welfare, the instrumentalities of social discipline, the modes and rationale of state surveillance, the terms of scholarly research and student scholarships, and the structure of the corporate economy. It enters into the identity of the state as the central bearer of the power and sovereignty of a people. The national security state registers itself as the ultimate agent of power, security, and freedom.

Fifth, and as a product of the first four, the governing regime in the state is set up to be a central target of collective resentment when its actions challenge or demean crucial dimensions of the collective identity. It is also the preeminent recipient of national loyalty when internal or external threats to collective identity emerge. Either way, the state is a pivotal object of collective sentiments. Its international status and domestic standing invade the emotional life of its members, preparing them to project intense loyalties, resentments, or ambivalences upon it at the drop of a hat (or an issue, bomb, public event, scandal, crisis).

Sixth, among the primary ends to be pursued through economic institutions and the state is the pursuit of private affluence through the expansion of productivity and science, access to raw materials inside and outside the nation, control over foreign markets, the production of roles and identities congruent with the ends of productivity, the protection of worldwide systems of transportation, exchange, and communication, domestic and foreign surveillance, military action against foreign peoples, and so on. The internationalization of the corporate economy flows from the pursuit of productivity and affluence, and the intensification of ambiguity between the state and the corporate economy is one of its effects. For the state is expected simultaneously to serve the corporate system, to regulate it, and to maintain the performance of the economy—and it is to do all this while remaining accountable to an electorate that also participates in this economy. The internationalization of the corporate economy both aggravates demands upon the sovereign state to serve and regulate the domestic economy and compromises the state's ability to do so. The sovereignty of the state, deeply etched in a collective identity that construes the state as the highest instrument of collective freedom, depends upon the state's ability to juggle these pressures.

Seventh, the experience of freedom is implicated in the generation of private affluence, and affluence is bound up with the civilization of productivity, from its organization of work and education, through its interpretation of psychological syndromes that foster or impede productivity, to its consolidation of state policies to protect markets, guide investment, and procure jobs. The state and the economy are dual vehicles of this ideal of freedom: the threads of affluence, productivity, state accountability, and military prowess are bound together through a complex series of knots. An ideal of freedom, as the attainment of autonomy through education, affluence, and electoral representation, circulates throughout this network, so that whenever one of these strands is pulled in the wrong direction, the experience of freedom sustained by the others becomes more tangled too.

Eighth, a persistent effect of this civilization is the creation of a diverse population shuffled to the margins of freedom, dignity, social participation, and affluence as these are defined and valued within the culture. This constellation of losers and misfits provides a living contrast through which generally admired conventions of identity and responsibility are tested, validated, and vindicated. The state, as a pivotal embodiment of collective identity and the final agent of electoral accountability, must find ways to elevate, depoliticize, stigmatize, or conceal this heterogeneous cast of the unemployed, the working poor, drug users, illegal aliens, and assorted dropouts if it is to sustain the role invested in it.

Ninth, a further subordinate end is to maintain total institutions for a subclass of criminals, the terminally ill, the immobile aged, and the hopelessly insane—to house and guard beings who cannot sustain themselves or who constitute a danger to the populace. This subclass plays its own ambiguous role in the collective identity, sometimes being hidden behind the cover of institutions and sometimes encouraging others living close to the margin themselves to compare their own situation with that of those unwilling or unable to measure up to minimal standards of normal participation in the culture.

The Politics of Negation

The elements that form the ends, priorities, and identifications of the civilization of productivity have never fit neatly together. They have never formed a smooth, harmonious pattern of mutually sustaining parts. Rather, they are best represented as a constellation of conjunctions and disjunctions joined by links of interdependence and disrupted by obstructions, frictions, and contingencies built into these interdependencies. A collective identity is a set of interlocking elements in strife and tension, a set periodically scrambled, reorganized, blocked, and gridlocked by contingencies from within and without. But it tends to represent itself to itself as a relatively harmonious set of parts that function smoothly together unless irresponsible, evil, sick, or naive forces—inside or outside its boundaries—disrupt this harmony.

A collective identity recapitulates the contingent, conflicted character of personal identity; it also *inflates* tendencies in the latter to dogmatize its configuration when confronted by disruptive contingencies. This collective politics of transcendental egoism flows from the role of the state as the sovereign institution of final accountability: legitimate bearers of personal and associational identity can appeal to a more inclusive center of action and accountability to respond to the grievances and aspirations they project; but the sovereign center of collective identity has no higher center of accountability to which it can appeal. So, in the territorial state, the politics of collective identity tends to organize the idealisms and egoisms of its legitimate members into a collective egoism. And the politics of collective egoism becomes most intense whenever the state is faced with internal or external affronts to its self-assurance.

These considerations suggest that it is insufficient to hold up a mirror in which the collective identity of the late-modern state can see itself reflected. A critical appraisal is needed as well. For in the late-modern time, the identity of the civilization of democratic productivity has become brittle and insistent as it responds to an unruly world setting, to a variety of internal constituencies who have lost faith in their eventual inclusion, and even to the gap between the projections of the future it must advance to legitimize its disciplines and the probable future increasingly discernible to many of its contemporary beneficiaries.[3]

This last development points to a thread that runs through the entire complex. Viewed from inside the collective identity, the emergence of religious fundamentalism, hedonism, and a drug culture, the expansion of litigiousness, the concentration of affluent youth on careerism, tax revolts and tax stringency, extensive public corruption, the extension of disciplinary controls over corporate workers, and the toughening of prison sentences doubtless appear to be disparate phenomena reflecting, variously, modes of deviance, patterns of self-indulgence, and breakdowns in social discipline. Viewed from another angle, these same phenomena signify diverse responses to a general set of pressures and perceptions—responses to disciplinary pressures of the present linked to perceptions of a bleak future among a growing number of constituencies and officials. For all these developments exemplify a logic of political contraction—contraction by the state from the effort to draw excluded constituencies into the circle of freedom, by careerists from emotional involvement in the future of the whole, by fundamentalists from confidence in the officially charted future course, by hedonists from self-discipline for the sake of future attainments dependent upon institutional support to immediate pleasures more susceptible to self-control, by users of hard drugs from hope in the future to a struggle to get through one day at a time.

Such *signs* of retreat from contemporary disciplines and future promises are discernible everywhere to those who are not so attached to the collective identity that they treat these developments as independent causes disrupting an otherwise intact circle of meanings. But the terms of democratic accountability prevent electoral constituencies, campaign organizations, and state officials from representing these developments in this way. A critical account of the contemporary identity must come to terms both with these signs and with pressures within that identity to convert them into catalysts for more belligerent identification. In the contemporary setting, the central configurations of collective identity remain intact, the disciplines required to maintain them have become more harsh, extensive, and exclusionary, and signs of cracks in that identity are converted into new energies for its political maintenance.

In several domains, the state no longer emerges as a consummate agent of *efficacy*, even though it expands as a pivotal agent of *power*.[4] A crack in the very unity of "power" has opened up. We have entered a world in which state power is simultaneously magnified and increasingly disconnected from the ends that justify its magnification. As obstacles to its efficacy multiply, the state increasingly sustains collective identity through theatrical displays of punishment and revenge against those elements that threaten to signify its inefficacy. It launches dramatized crusades against the internal other (low-level criminals, drug users, disloyalists, racial minorities, and the underclass), the external other (foreign enemies and terrorists), and the interior other (those strains of abnormality, subversion, and perversity that may reside within anyone).

The state becomes, first, the screen upon which much of the resentment against the adverse effects of the civilization of productivity and private affluence is projected; second, the vehicle through which rhetorical reassurances about the glory and durability of that civilization are transmitted back to the populace; and third, the instrument of campaigns against those elements most disturbing to the collective identity. In the first instance, the welfare apparatus of the state is singled out for criticism and reformation. In the second, the presidency is organized into a medium of rhetorical diversion and reassurance. In the third, the state disciplinary-police-punitive apparatus is marshaled to constitute and stigmatize constituencies whose terms of existence might otherwise provide signs of defeat, injury, and sacrifice engendered by the civilization of productivity itself.

By "state" I mean the political dimension of the entire order—

individuals as citizens and taxpayers, electoral campaigns and processes, public officials, lawmaking institutions, executive and enforcement agencies, rhetorical modes of consolidation and division, and so on. The primary targets of state negation are most functional if (a) they can be constituted as evils responsible for threats to the common identity, (b) their visibility might otherwise signify defects and failings in the established identity, (c) they are strategically weak enough to be subjected to punitive measures, and (d) they are resilient enough to renew their status as sources of evil in the face of such measures. The state today is a ministry for collective salvation through a politics of generalized resentment. This ministry proceeds by making "foreign" a variety of "external" and "internal" developments that would otherwise constitute signs of disruption within the collective identity. Consider examples of each type.

The power of definition, as Hobbes knew, is a highly strategic power invested in the state. The contemporary distillation of "terrorism" from the international sea of war, violence, surveillance, oppression, and torture provides a paradigmatic example. The moral isolation of nonstate violence from other modalities of violence produces multiple effects: it invests nonstate violence with unique causality and danger; it implicitly endows state violence with special sanctity; it conceals holes and cracks in the international economy of states that might otherwise be disclosed through the response of nonstate peoples; it deflects attention from deficiencies in state efficacy with respect to the environment, inequality, and coexistence with third-world peoples.

Terrorism, as the other constituted by the state system, allows the state and the interstate system to protect the logic of sovereignty in the international sphere while veiling their inability to modify systemic conditions that generate violence by nonstate agents; it also provides domestic constituencies with agents of evil to explain the vague experience of danger, frustration, and ineffectiveness in taming global contingency. There are, certainly, groups and effects to which the term terrorism refers: innocent human lives are lost through these acts. But the number of innocent lives lost through state-sponsored wars and nonwar military adventures is huge by comparison. The production of "terrorism" protects the identity of particular states and the state system as a whole more than it reflects an ethical imperative to apply general principles to distinctive instances of violence.

Domestic constituencies excluded from the culture of productivity and private affluence provide internal counterparts. To the degree that this heterogeneous constellation of misfits and outcasts is fashioned into an object of political disposability—that is, into a welfare class—the theatricality of state power is magnified and its inefficacy remains deniable.[5]

The consolidation of this constellation into a pliable and disposable mass provides the state with a stage upon which to display its power and conceal its inefficacy. The very constitution of this internal object of externality enables the state to present itself as an institution of democratic accountability, since electoral constituencies are able to choose in each election between punishing welfare freeloaders again and reforming state programs of economic support for the deserving poor one more time. Because the newly elected regime can replace the alternative that has most recently failed, the electorate is able to convince itself that "welfare failure" is the effect of the last option pursued rather than of the set of options legitimately available to the state. The electorate focuses on how the renewal of each program gives it a choice rather than on how this cycle of alternatives helps to create and maintain an identifiable object of political disposability by means of which the terms of accountability to the effective electorate can be organized. The welfare class thus becomes a permanent demonstration project in the theatricality of power. It becomes a dispensable subject of political representation and an indispensable object of political disposability.

This ambiguous status, magnified immensely through the racial casting of its members, endows the welfare class with a pivotal role in electoral politics. Each campaign organization has an implicit incentive to maintain it as an object of state action and an explicit incentive to propose a new program to deal with it. The effective electorate participates in this perpetual game. For the electorate can construe state power as *potentially* commensurate with state efficacy as long as it can blame each blatant failure in welfare policy on the unwillingness of the outgoing administration to enact the program of the incoming one. It thus can always identify the state (which includes itself in its political capacity) as a potential agent of collective freedom and accountability within the existing order of things.[6]

The political constitution of the welfare class also, of course, allows those living on the edge of uncertainty and insecurity to solidify their own identities, by drawing stark contrasts between the vices of the losers and the virtues of marginal nonlosers and by constituting the losers as targets against which the accumulated resentments of marginal standing can be relieved.

The "failure of welfarism" is actually the success of welfarism as a political project in the construction and disposition of otherness. It is a "failure" that resists deconstitution from its present mode as long as it sustains the identity of the state as an agent of power, fosters the appearance of state accountability to the effective electorate, and provides an outlet for generalized resentment.

In the case of both terrorism and welfarism, actions taken by the state demonstrate its punitive and disciplinary power, conceal its deficits in efficacy, and translate defects in the established identity into evils against which the collective identity can be reinstated.

Noncapitalist military powers such as the Soviet Union and China play a somewhat different role. They are not vulnerable enough to serve as direct objects of attack, but they are well located to support western self-definition through contrast and negation. They provide western states with a state-centered enemy through which to vindicate militarism and national chauvinism while deflating internal critique by construing it as fraternization with the enemy or a recapitulation of totalitarian idealism.

Some noncapitalist states may be undergoing internal reconstitution even as these words are being written. The possibilities and dangers in those developments remain highly uncertain. But the possible devaluation of such states as objects of collective negation will also propel the production of new objects to replace them. Japan, Latin American regimes, drug dealers and users, illegal aliens, environmentalists who threaten the progress of productivity, and so on will be wheeled into place to fill the gap. The collective identity of the civilization of productivity will not reduce its demand for external targets until its internal dogmatism undergoes modification. The success of regimes in Eastern Europe and the Soviet Union in recasting themselves might provide a catalyst for such a modification. But the removal of a specific enemy will not suffice by itself.

The state deploys this diverse set of objects to organize discourse. A circle of representations is formed here: the state receives a fund of generalized resentment from those whose identity is jeopardized by the play of difference, contingency, and danger; it constructs objects of resentment to protect the identities it represents; and it then receives a refined supply of electoral resentments aimed at the objects it has constituted. Electoral politics contains powerful pressures to become a closed circuit for the dogmatism of identity through the translation of difference into threat and threat into energy for the dogmatization of identity.

In Chapter 2 we saw how the sixteenth-century Spanish "conquest of America" vindicated itself through its opposition to the Aztec culture of sacrifice—and how it failed to recognize its own strategies as modalities of sacrifice. We have also seen how the anti-Semite sacrifices the Jew to a fictive ideal of national unity. Is the late-modern time also infiltrated by a culture of sacrifice concealed in the terms of its self-vindication? When the issue is posed in these terms, a second question becomes pertinent: Is this fugitive and endless quest for surety of identity really worth the sacrifices it entails? Perhaps the sacrifice of this surety is the debt identity owes to life.

Democracy and Sovereignty

This circle of self-reinforcing significations, while impressive in its powers of seduction, is never entirely closed. It does not exhaust life. The objects it constitutes and the audience to which it plays are also active centers of energy, resistances, and subjectivity implicated in other circles of self-presentation and reception. The official circle of significations is constantly exceeded, subverted, obstructed, and confounded both by actors who resist roles for which they have been cast and by audiences imperfectly colonized by the circle of significations within which the prevailing politics of identity moves.

Imagine a two-dimensional film, rolling at slow speed with the sound switched off. Only one strain of political life is framed by it, one usually blotted out and reduced to noise by the conventional flow of political self-presentations. Then the film speeds up; 3-D glasses add a dimension of depth; a sound track switches on with its foreground speeches, conversational contexts, and background noises. The first image settles back into the flow of the frames. But it retains a presence that was unevident to some before its recent isolation. And voices that may before have been inaudible are now heard differently by a perceptive ear. Since the audience for the silent, two-dimensional film also played parts within it, the later multimedia version may even stimulate new voices in some actors as the film continues on a sound/imagery track without a hand in charge of its projection. Every presentation, after all, films the film that preceded it. Things are filmy all the way down. That is the figure through which I would like the foregoing presentation of the politics of public identity to be received. But what else might be said? Can the interpretation of identity governing this study support corollary critical responses at the level of public identity? I suspect it can, but here I offer only preliminary and fragmentary anticipations of this faith.

If, as I have argued, democracy is the key practice to be nourished and protected, then modifications in other aspects of the collective identity become crucial. For continuation along the established historical trajectory threatens to seal up those closures in collective identity least congruent with democratic life.

A *democracy* infused with a spirit of agonism is one in which divergent orientations to the mysteries of existence find overt expression in public life. Spaces for difference to be are established through the play of political contestation. Distance becomes politicized in a world where other, topographical sources of distance have closed up. The terms of contestation enlarge opportunities for participants to engage the relational and contingent character of the identities that constitute them, and this effect in turn establishes one of the preconditions for respectful strife between parties who reciprocally acknowledge the contestable character of the faiths that orient them and give them definition in relation to one another.

But for a politics of democratic agonism to flourish, what I have called the politics of generalized resentment must be subdued. Only when both of the hands holding our necks in the grip of resentment are loosened can the politics of agonal democracy be enhanced. Today existential resentments and resentments against injustice in the social distribution of opportunities, resources, sacrifices, and burdens combine to tighten the grip of dogmatism upon the life of identity.

One compelling attraction of democracy is that it enables anyone to engage fundamental riddles of existence through participation in a public politics that periodically disturbs and denaturalizes elements governing the cultural unconscious. But these same characteristics can intensify the reactive demand to redogmatize conventional identities if a large minority of the society is already suffering under severe burdens of material deprivation and effective exclusion from the good life offered to a majority. General access to economic, educational, and cultural opportunities seems to be one of the preconditions of more widespread engagement with the contingency of identity, a precondition whose significance becomes apparent when one considers the class distribution of tendencies toward fundamentalism in its numerous modern forms. Agonal democracy therefore presupposes a reduction in established economic inequalities, and this objective in turn requires a mobilization of public energies to promote it.

I will not pursue this last thesis further (while granting it needs much further argument). Rather, I will consider its implications for the relation between democracy and hegemony within the conception of democracy endorsed here. According to some theorizations, the very juxtaposition of the terms "democracy" and "hegemony" represents a category mistake.[7] For democracy means government by public will, and hegemony means the predominance of some wills over others in public life. This sense of disjunction between the vision of democracy and the practice of hegemony flows from several directions. Some theorists who endorse political minimalism in the interests of protecting private sanctuaries for freedom discourage any attempt to build a hegemonic political bloc on the grounds that the effort to do so will compromise the plurality, diversity, flexibility, and slack already thought to exist in the order. Others emphasize the need for concerted action by the state (though not in support of egalitarian aims), but they seek to find ways to insulate political elites from effective accountability to the electorate in order to secure more rational and consistent management of public life. These theorists may be pleased when an election campaign focuses on "symbolic" issues, because such diversionary tactics provide the desired insulation for state officials. Still others, who emphasize the importance of democratic political action in support of general social objectives, tend to gesture toward a time when a rational consensus will convince everyone of the desirability of the direction they already endorse. These minimalists, elite separatists, and consensualists may be able to avoid reflection on the relation between democracy and hegemony. But the conception of democracy advanced here must come to grips with the unavoidable connection between democratic politics and the formation of hegemonic coalitions. If the very fundaments of a way of life are contestable, then any political coalition with sufficient public presence to give some semblance of direction to public policy is likely to face resistance and opposition from other elements who feel assaulted by some of the priorities of that coalition. What I will call a relation of democratic hegemony obtains when the perspective of an identifiable constellation attains predominance in several areas of public debate, resisting factions remain effective in publicly articulating the terms of their opposition and compelling compromises on some of these fronts, and the news media, judiciary, and electoral system function to keep the terms of contestation among coalitions reasonably open and to protect elemental rights to life, a significant degree of personal self-governance, freedom of expression, and full citizenship in a representative government.

These latter rights are "elemental" not in the sense that they flow from a transcendental command or a necessary consensus, but in that they are fundamental to a perspective that cultivates care for the diversity of life as life expresses itself through those ambiguous· relations of identity and difference. If others support these rights out of different considerations, agonistic liberals will try to convince them that their own arguments are driven more fundamentally by the care they have cultivated and the interpretation of danger and possibility within which that care finds expression than by any iron-clad logic separable from either; but we will also join them politically whenever they support these rights in a viable way. The areas of disagreement between *us* are likely to revolve, first, around the restrictive conditions they are pressed to place around the category "person" or "agent" in order to generate the arguments they require to vindicate rights—often placing too many implicit limits on the sorts of people and the varieties of life for which the language of rights is pertinent—and, second, around the restrictive visions of politics they endorse in responding to the relations of identity and difference in contemporary life.

Anyway, from the standpoint endorsed here, there can easily be hegemony without democracy, but seldom democracy without the political hegemony of some perspectives over others. In the United States, for instance, neoconservatism retained hegemony through the 1970s and 1980s. Its combination of social conservatism, national chauvinism, state subsidy of corporate priorities, and state retreat from economic policies designed to reduce inequality is organized around particular conceptions of freedom and identity. As long as these latter orientations—rehearsed from a critical perspective in the second section of this chapter—retain hegemony, the politics of identity and difference will be fueled by the energies of *ressentiment* and the dogmatization of identity. It would take a pluralistic counter-movement to counter the hegemony of neoconservatism—making ample room within its compass for those who seek to combat existential resentment, create greater space for diversity in identity, reduce economic inequality, and adjust economic priorities in the interest of curtailing ecological devastation. Neoconservative hegemony thus can be *resisted* by a variety of tactics; but it can be overcome only if it is countered by an opposing coalition establishing a degree of hegemony through alternative articulations of identity, interests, freedom, equality, and the human relation to the earth.

An alternative hegemonic coalition of the sort envisioned would not express a unified consensus either within its own frame or for the entire society. Rather, it would consist of a variety of constituencies drawn together in varying proportions by considerations of interest, identity, and ethical concern and moved to varying degrees by new interpretations of danger and possibility. Agonistic liberalism could aspire to form an arc within this rainbow, but it could not expect to dominate the entire spectrum or to paint a neutral hue upon which the others *must* inscribe their identities, interests, and concerns. The attraction of other colors is too powerful within everyone and too predominant within some to anticipate either result. The cultivation of agonistic respect, indeed, presupposes the inevitability of such a plurality within any coalition that is both hegemonic and democratic.

This study has confined itself to the politics of identity and difference. But to illustrate its linkages to another set of issues, let me outline just one ingredient in an economic project elaborated somewhat more fully elsewhere. Today, economic growth has become a system imperative rather than a freely chosen end of democratic politics; it is an imperative that fuels generalized resentment and fouls the earth-shelter even while it receives generalized support. Perhaps only shifts in established forms of consumption, shifts that enable more people to make ends meet without the misleading promise of perpetual growth in household earning power, could loosen those imperatives sufficiently to allow electoral support for a second spiral of modifications in the political economy of expansion, inequality, and environmental degradation. A variety of possibilities are available here. The forms of health care, housing transportation, and higher education supported by the state infrastructure of consumption (insurance laws, fee systems, road systems, mortgage subsidies, gasoline taxes, state revenues, and so on) now approximate the status of exclusive goods: if restricted to the affluent, they create hardship for many who pay taxes to sustain them but cannot afford to use them; if extended to lower-income groups, they increase social expenses borne by the state, fuel inflationary pressures, intensify damage to the natural environment, and fuel the next round of electoral pressures for economic growth along the same lines. Other possible modes of consumption in these areas are much more inclusive in form. They can be expanded to broader sectors of the society while relieving pressure on low- and middle-income budgets, thereby reducing economic inequality, relaxing electoral pressures for economic growth on the same old terms, curtailing some forms of environmental degradation, and allowing a broader segment of the populace to participate in democratic politics.[8] A modicum of success on this front is a precondition for a degree of success on any other.

But such economic modifications, while crucial, are certainly not sufficient, nor are these modifications likely to emerge from internal political pressures alone. Central to the project of retheorizing democracy to fit the circumstances of late-modern life is the task of rethinking the contemporary relation between sovereignty and democracy. Perhaps today the state, as the legitimate center of sovereignty, citizen loyalty, and political dissent, must give more ground to other modes of political identification. Earlier chapters in this study have emphasized ways in which the domestic politics of identity and difference exceeds state-sponsored activity while remaining within the confines of the territorial state. But this same logic operates on the external boundaries of the territorial state as well. Perhaps today the state must be thought and lived as one site of membership, allegiance, obligation, and political mobilization on a globe that presents other viable possibilities of identification, inside and outside state boundaries.

If democracy is not to become a political ghetto confined to the territorial state, the contemporary globalization of capital, labor, and contingency must be shadowed by a corollary globalization of *politics*. In such a globalization of politics, the political energies and loyalties of many activists will not be confined to the state in which they reside and (if lucky) vote. These loyalties will also be bestowed, strange as this may sound on first hearing, upon the late-modern *time* as such.

Late modernity is a systemic time without a corresponding political place. It faces distinctive dangers and possibilities, as well as issues of legitimacy and political responsiveness. These, too, must become catalysts for creative political engagement, for engagements that challenge and supplement state-centered modalities of political action. Loyalty to the normal individual, to the state, and to the established interstate system must be compelled to contend with loyalty to this distinctive time.

What does it mean to say that late modernity is a time without a corresponding political place? Well, the priorities of mastery and attunement that compete generally and unevenly for hegemony within this time, the effects of that competition on the globalization of contingency, the gap between the universalist pretensions of modern ideals and nagging doubts that the most distinctive achievements of modernity can ever be universalized to the entire world— these and other developments provoke questions about the legitimacy of the time as a time. Does the contemporary world order embody a self-destructive trajectory? Does the earth flow over with resources sufficient to the worldwide demands imposed upon it, or do limitations here demand reconfiguration of the ideals of production and consumption governing this time? Can existing standards of universality really be universalized in this system of conflictual interdependencies? Is a coordinating center as broad in scope as the globe a condition of democratic achievement, or another threat to its existence?

These questions, perhaps distinctive as political questions internal to a time as such,[9] call the sufficiency of sovereignty into doubt. The reach and effects of global processes exceed the reach of sovereign states, and state-centered definitions of these matters may exclude exactly those issues and possible responses that would significantly compromise the claims of sovereignty.[10] The state as a sovereign entity is unlikely to generate internal recognition of the need to compromise its sovereign status.

But to articulate such questions and issues is not to locate a corresponding political *site* where these issues could be posed and disposed politically, a site where the level of democratic accountability would be commensurate with the scope of those issues distinctive of the late-modern time. Perhaps the demand that democratization only be institutionalized in a territorial space itself poses one of the limits to creative thought in this domain.

Some of the pressure for closure in collective identity today may flow from anxiety that any conceivable response to this asymmetry between global time and political place would itself undermine the future of democratic politics. Even idealists of democracy lapse into an uneasy silence about this issue. Perhaps this silence is revealing. This is the double bind of late-modern democracy: its present terms of territorial organization constrict its effective accountability, while any electoral campaign within this territory that acknowledged the import of this limitation would meet with a predictable rebuff at the polls. Who wants to elect representatives who concede the inefficacy of the unit they represent? or who call upon the state to revise priorities that currently provide a stable base of identity and unification for a majority coalition within it? or who compromise the principle of sovereignty through which the sense of the self-sufficiency of established institutions of accountability is secured? One source of the politics of negation and exclusion that puts the squeeze on late-modern democracy, then, is the territorial basis of contemporary democratic ideals. The restriction of democratic idealism to territorial democracy helps to perpetuate results democratic idealists oppose.

Defined *within* the terms of sovereignty, the alternatives are these: either democracy remains confined to the territorial state and becomes increasingly a conduit for converting global pressures into disciplines and burdens for its most vulnerable elements, or the terms of sovereignty itself are extended to supranational institutions that progressively widen the gap between the scope of democracy and the source of policies governing people. Either way, the asymmetry between the late-modern time as an indispensable object of political reflection and the sovereign state as the exclusive site of democracy places the established terms of democratic accountability under tremendous stress.

In contemporary academic discourse, democratic "political theorists" and "international relations theorists" generally have little to say to each other. It might be (and has been) said that intrastate political theory, with its debates over "domestic" issues such as legitimacy, rights, identity, justice, individuality, belonging, community, and accountability, helps to constitute the terms of interstate theory, with its focus on "foreign" issues of security, preparedness, alliances, violence, war, and subversion. "Realist" interstate theory is the negation of "idealist" political theory, though each disciplinary domain contains a minority voice that echoes the majority voice of the other.[11] I am suggesting that the very terms of democratic idealism, both in the academy and in the territorial state more generally, nourish this discursive division of labor, allowing the effects of changes in the late-modern time to slip through the cracks of democratic theory. But the time requires that this academic division of labor be rescrambled.

Democratic politics must either extend into global issues or deteriorate into institutionalized nostalgia for a past when people believed that the most fundamental issues of life were resolvable within the confines of the territorial state. The contemporary need, perhaps, is to supplement and challenge *structures of territorial democracy* with a politics of *nonterritorial democratization of global issues*.

I have not yet explored this nonterritory with the attentiveness needed. But one implication seems clear. What the time demands, today and tomorrow, is the formation by nonstate activists of regional combinations organized across and against state boundaries, focusing upon particular global problems and the practices through which specific states and constellations of states produce and perpetuate them. Such nonstate formations would disturb the normal operation of state-centered politics, exposing how these structures themselves depoliticize troubles and dangers that must be overtly defined as issues today. The members of these nonstate constellations would compromise loyalty to their own states, to the standards of citizenship within their states, to a local ideal of community, and even to timeless ideals as such. Each and all of these familiar loyalties would be compromised by loyalty to a time without a corresponding place of political organization. The aspiration would be to represent, through extrastate-generated organization, publicity, exposés, and articulation of alternative possibilities, ways in which particular states and state alliances jeopardize the resourcefulness of the earth, compromise the rights of those repressed within states or living outside the protection of any state, impose codes of security classification and secrecy that undermine democratic publicity, inflame the possibilities of war through arms exports or expansionary demands, and pursue economic priorities that impede the prospects for long-term coexistence of a plurality of peoples on a crowded planet. The longer-term goal would be to foster reconsideration of some of the most pervasive spatiotemporal presumptions that legitimize these practices.

Nonterritorial democratization ventilates global issues through creative interventions by nonstate actors. Effective ventilation could even reinvigorate the internal democracy of territorial states, crystallizing such issues in a way that allowed citizens to place them on the agenda of the territorial state, energizing citizens who come to discern more closely the relations of dependence between vigorous territorial democracy and nonterritorial democratization. Nonterritorial democratization might disrupt state-centered definitions of political responsibility, public identity, normality, system imperatives, disposability, danger, and possibility, spawning internal/external pressures to reconstitute readings of those negative significations that sustain collective identity today.

The project of nonterritorial democratization necessarily exudes an air of unreality, especially when it is assessed through institutionalized practices of territorial democracy that may have sufficed for a time already left behind. It lacks, and will continue to lack according to the most optimistic projections, a stable set of electoral procedures through which accountability could be organized. Perhaps disparate and discrete phenomena such as Amnesty International, Greenpeace, the consolidation of international corporations, divestment movements aimed at global corporations doing business with states that trample on human rights, the series of movements to assist "boat people," Palestinians, and others residing outside the protection of territorial states, and nonstate movements like the "nuclear freeze" to foster arms reduction between states might provide reflection in this area with more specific exemplifications from which to proceed.

But, it must be conceded, the aura of unreality cannot be lifted entirely by such explorations or by a more effective activism in this nonterritory. For nonterritorial democratization differs from its territorial sibling: it is perpetually in the process of becoming and never secure in the terms of its accountability because it lacks a territorial base through which these terms could be solidified.

This is only part of the picture, though. For territorial democracy exudes its own aura of unreality in the late-modern time. Today, the territorial state stands to the globe as the city has to the state since at least the 1950s. This enlarged gap between the institutional scope of representation and the pressures to which representative institutions must respond cannot be dismissed. The traditional ideal of democracy has always sought to close that gap through expansion of the formal terms of accountability. But that no longer remains a viable means of extending democratization. Perhaps the basic issue today, then, is which unreality to attack and which to succumb to—the unreality of territorial democracy or the unreality of nonterritorial democratization. Or perhaps it is best to conclude that neither of these modalities of democratic life can thrive in this time unless it enters into an active relation with the other.

Those who find democracy to be the most enduring and compelling component in late-modern identity may be drawn to supplement and challenge territorial democracy through nonterritorial democratization. For today democracy is the living ideal through which the territorial state receives its highest legitimation. But to confine the ethos of democracy to the state today is to convert the state into the penitentiary of democracy.

The Ground of the Perhaps

These responses, certainly, are insufficient to the issues defined. I am not in charge of all the intersections in this text. But the operative faith governing it is that the terms of contemporary debate can be broadened and enlivened by the introduction of a perspective organized around nontheistic reverence for being, the presence of difference in identity, the problematic terms of relation between personal and collective identity, the cultivation of agonistic care for strife and interdependence in identity\difference, democracy and genealogy as ways to foster the experience of contingency, political attentiveness to the globalization of contingency, and the activation of nonterritorial democratization to supplement and invigorate territorial democracy in the late-modern time. All these elements provide some degree of support for one another within the same perspective, though there are doubtless tensions and intersections between them yet to be explored.

No interpretation of the contemporary condition escapes the territory of the unthought. To construct a political interpretation is also to project into it a contestable set of presumptions. But some perspectives may be more alert than others to the ambiguous status of the presumptions from which they proceed, and, especially, to the case for devising strategies of reflection to subject these predispositions to self-problematization.

The reading I have presented is certainly infiltrated by such presumptions. Its accounts of identity, reverence, agonistic democracy, life, contingency, and difference bristle with them. I do not know how to prove or disprove these projections. But I do believe that no interpretation of actuality dispenses with some such set and that any set of projections can articulate and defend itself only in competition with other alternatives. Nor do I say that "everything is discourse" or that "there is nothing outside the text," *if* those protean slogans are taken to deny that theories and discursively mediated practices recurrently encounter resistances, voices, surprises, contingencies, events, and discrepancies that open them to contestation, throw them into disarray, or incite defensive pressures to place them on ice. Though there is no neutral method or procedure of falsification or universal protocol of rationality sufficient to resolve disputes between opposing interpretations, each interpretation is susceptible to unexpected movement, disruption, and destabilization in the signs it reads. This is particularly so in political life, where what presents itself as a sign within the zone of one account often also reflects the life of an "other" motivated to confound the play of significations within which the alter-identity would enclose it. There is more to life than can be incorporated into the frame of any single interpretation, but that does not make interpretation a dispensable dimension of life.

I wish to assert at once, then, the indispensability of interpretation in life, the unavoidable infiltration of interpretation by contestable elements, the radical insufficiency of "neutral" tests to adjudicate between interpretations, and the persistent play of disturbances within and between interpretations capable of confounding the self-confidence of those carried by them. Much of contemporary academic discourse can be read as a series of attempts to disarm the politics of interpretation by denying one or more of these conditions. But an excellent case can be made for embracing all of them together. That's life.

If the actual field of contending political interpretations is always less extensive than the terrain of possible readings, perhaps a renewed awareness of this condition can foster a paradoxical sensitivity to the presence of the unthought in thought, encouraging more of us to push against pressures to treat constructed compounds of identity and difference as if they provided the natural ground of existence or, at least, inciting us periodically to probe the density of those clouds of identity upon which we float. Can such considerations support an agonism infused with respect? Perhaps, though there is no assurance that they must.

Maybe my insistent valorization of "perhaps" itself underplays the ambiguity of the enterprise it depicts, silently folding a temporal qualification into its confession of the excess of being over interpretation and life over identity. For this word loudly proclaims a lack of certainty now and quietly suggests improved prospects for it tomorrow. Perhaps some such ambiguity is ineliminable from life. At any rate, this text, like the others to which it is most indebted, testifies to the indispensability of interpretation and to the ambiguity of its ground.

Notes

Introduction: The Problem of Evil

1. Augustine, *Concerning the City of God against the Pagans*, trans. Henry Bettenson (Harmondsworth: Penguin, 1985), bk. 11, chap. 13, 446.
2. Ibid., bk. 12, chap. 5, 477.
3. Ibid.
4. Ibid., chap. 6, 479.
5. Ibid., chap. 9, 482.
6. George Steiner, *The Death of Tragedy* (Oxford: Oxford University Press, 1980), 6.
7. This book was in production when Charles Taylor's *Sources of the Self: The Making of the Modern Identity* (Cambridge: Harvard University Press, 1989) appeared. Its earlier appearance (or the later appearance of mine) would have abetted a sharper crystallization of certain issues—with respect, for instance, to the "sources" of ethics (or morality, as he calls it). Taylor, in his new book, admirably delineates a variety of "moral sources" that have been cultivated in the history of the west. These sources are not reducible to transcendental commands; they reside in a more intimate relation to the self and the culture from which they emanate, as well as to fugitive experiences that are susceptible to reflective articulation but not to forthright representation as independent objects. "Articulation" of these sources empowers one morally: "Moral sources empower. To come closer to them, to have a clearer view of them, to come to grasp what they involve, is for those who recognize them to be moved to love or respect them, and through this love/respect to be better enabled to live up to them. And articulation can bring them closer. That is why words can empower; why words can at times have tremendous moral force" (p. 96). Taylor then strives—though with qualifications and an enlarged sense of the diversity of moral sources operative in modern life—to fold the moral sources he admires most into a social ontology that is more teleological than the one endorsed in this study. This effort may lead him to underestimate the extent to

[223]

which he is in alliance with post-Nietzschean thought along one dimension even though he remains very much at odds with it along another. To put the point briefly: he shares a conception of ethical discourse with certain post-Nietzscheans (one that opposes, in my language, a variety of "command theories" while endorsing "an ethic of cultivation"), while the interpretive framework through which his articulations proceed is at odds with those operative in these other texts. It makes as much preliminary sense to treat "life" and "*différance*" as fugitive ethical sources to be cultivated in relation to the prevailing terms of cultural organization as it does to treat "God" or "the embodied self." But while Taylor sometimes treats Nietzsche as one who is engaged in an ethical enterprise, he consistently denies that standing to Foucault and Derrida. Anyway, after reading this new book I find myself attracted to its discussion of moral sources and at odds with the interpretive framework it privileges. On this latter score too, though, it seems to me that Taylor has now become more attentive to the fundamentally contestable character of his most fundamental presumptions. When his positions on civic liberalism and responsible agency are considered briefly later in this book, the discussions refer to his previous writings in those domains.

8. *I Pierre Rivière, Having Slaughtered My Mother, My Sister and My Brother*, ed. Michel Foucault, trans. Frank Jellinek (Lincoln: University of Nebraska Press, 1975).

9. Jacques Derrida, *Margins of Philosophy*, trans. Alan Bass (Chicago: University of Chicago Press, 1982), 11.

1. Freedom and Resentment

1. This compensatory code of reassurance is located less in the assertions and arguments of contemporary texts than in the rhetorical structure of those texts. The theories swim in a rhetorical sea that provides ontological reassurance. Several examples are examined in chapters 5, 6, 8, and 10 of my *Politics and Ambiguity* (Madison: University of Wisconsin Press, 1987). Michael Shapiro in *The Politics of Representation* (Madison: University of Wisconsin Press, 1988) insightfully explores how several political texts insinuate fundamental conclusions into their rhetorical and narrative structures, so that the "findings" of evidence are prefigured by the discursive modalities in which the evidence is enclosed.

2. Milan Kundera, *The Unbearable Lightness of Being*, trans. Michael Henry Heim (New York: Harper and Row, 1984), 222.

3. Ibid., 8.

4. Martin Heidegger, "The Age of the World Picture," in *The Question concerning Technology*, trans. William Lovitt (New York: Harper and Row, 1977), 115–54. "The essence of the modern age can be seen in the fact that man frees himself to himself. But this correct characterization remains, nonetheless, superficial. . . . Certainly the modern age has, as a consequence of the liberation of man, introduced subjectivism and individualism. But it remains just as certain that no age has produced a comparable objectivism and that in no

age before this has the non-individual, in the form of the collective, come to acceptance as having worth. Essential here is the necessary interplay between subjectivism and objectivism. It is precisely this reciprocal conditioning of the one by the other that points back to events more profound" (ibid., 127–28).

5. I will take rational choice theorists, most American political economists, and theorists such as John Rawls and Ronald Dworkin to exemplify the first view. Geofg Lukács and Jürgen Habermas can be seen as exemplars of the second. And Charles Taylor, Michael Sandel, and Alasdair MacIntyre can be seen to represent the third. Their differences are clear enough; it is the affinities between them that interest me here. One way of putting it is that each invokes a social ontology that is, from the vantage point I am defending, insufficiently attentive to the ambiguities residing in the highest possibilities it recognizes.

6. This means that one of the possible slots—the individualist who also seeks attunement to a higher direction in the world—is not filled in. Perhaps William James and Ralph Waldo Emerson represent that position in American thought, though I have studied neither enough to be confident of this.

7. Martin Heidegger, "The Question concerning Technology," in *The Question concerning Technology*, 25. In the preceding sentence Heidegger says, "All revealing belongs within a harboring and a concealing." As I read Heidegger, the idea here is to respond to the mystery of Being by striving in thinking to let difference be, to let it be insofar as it can be in the Being-being relation available to thinkers at a given time. Heidegger is often read as if he fit into one of the "attunement" positions identified above. I do not read him this way, but if that reading prevails he will stand inside the frame of late-modern discourse I have delineated rather than on its edge. I am interested in that intersection of thought—inhabited by Nietzsche, Heidegger (as I read him), and Foucault—where the most thoughtful thinking about the circumstances of late modernity and the affinities among opposing thinkers thinking within the frame of modernity can occur. A thoughtful reading of Heidegger is offered by Reiner Schürmann, *Heidegger on Being and Acting: From Principles to Anarchy*, trans. Christine-Marie Gros (Bloomington: Indiana University Press, 1987). "The difference between the 'original' and the 'originary' then tells us something about presencing as such as opposed to its predominant modes in the West; namely, that it is without principle, an-archic. . . . But as long as one seeks to revert to the initial question of Western philosophy without also subverting the focal points into which that question has been crystallized, it will remain unintelligible why Heidegger can claim: 'finding the way into the truth of being' presupposes that we renounce 'instituting rules' " (ibid., 149).

8. When I endorse a *social* ontology of discordant concordances to emphasize the incorrigible character of contingency and resistances in human affairs, I am not saying that I *know* the *world itself* is a *chaos* that we cannot know. First, this social ontology is a contestable projection that competes with other projections in political interpretation that often remain implicit. Second, it does not speak of the world itself separate from our engagements but of human organization of the internal and external world; it is an essentially relational perspective. Third, it does not say that the world is chaos, but that every organization

of the self and the world meets with resistances as well as with variable degrees of receptivity and organizability. The point is not to fall into one of the tacit perspectives that postulate either the world's predisposition to some mode of mastery (capitalist or socialist) or some inner harmony in being available to those who will listen for it attentively. Much of modern political thought, in leaning over backwards to avoid the second, premodern projection, falls over unthoughtfully into the first. To try to think late-modern politics without invoking a social ontology would be, I think, to increase the extent to which one's thinking is governed unconsciously by one of the two dominant currents of our age. These currents cannot be avoided altogether, but some thinkers might develop strategies to contest their hegemony.

9. Michel Foucault presses the issue of "the hermaphrodite" into the issue of freedom with the publication of *Herculin Barbin: Being the Recently Discovered Memoirs of a Nineteenth-Century French Hermaphrodite*, trans. Richard McDougall (New York: Pantheon, 1980). I explore the issues posed by Alex/Alexina, the author of this memoir, in "Where the Word Breaks Off," chap. 10 of *Politics and Ambiguity*. More recently Judith Butler has subjected Foucault's account of Alex/Alexina to critical scrutiny in *Gender Trouble* (New York: Routledge, 1990).

10. While striving to support crucial aspects of the ideals enunciated in (with Michael Best) *The Politicized Economy* (Lexington, Mass.: Heath, 1976; 2d ed., 1982) and *Appearance and Reality in Politics* (Cambridge: Cambridge University Press, 1981), I now think those books ignored the issue posed here.

11. This chapter was first written in 1985 and presented at Princeton University to the Department of Political Science in the spring of 1986. At that time I became aware that Richard Rorty was writing a series of essays organized around the idea of contingency. These are now collected in his *Contingency, Irony and Solidarity* (Cambridge: Cambridge University Press, 1989). After a brief correspondence, it became clear to both of us that we clothed rather different political visions in the language of contingency. From my perspective, Rorty falls within the "mastery" perspective briefly adumbrated here, compensating the loss of a *telos* in nature with the implicit presumption of its pliability. And he straddles the individualist/collectivist divide, celebrating irony and creativity in the private sphere and a non-ironic version of liberalism in the public. It is notable to me that the issue of the resentment of contingency gets little play in his recent work and that there is no exploration of possible connections between the globalization of contingency and the role played by the project of world mastery in modern politics. For a review of his position that brings out some of the differences, see my contribution to "Review Symposium on Richard Rorty," in *History of the Human Sciences* (February, 1990), 101–22.

2. Global Political Discourse

1. Tzvetan Todorov, *The Conquest of America: The Question of the Other*, trans. Richard Howard (New York: Harper and Row, 1985).

2. My focus, in this chapter, is on the role the politics of identity and difference plays in shaping and delimiting international relations theory. I agree, of course, with the elementary point that greed, interest, strategic considerations, geographical location, fortuity, and so on all enter crucially into international relations. But these elements are also defined and interpreted in relation to the identities of those who examine them. It is the latter dimension that is both overtly neglected and covertly a source of commonality among the contending traditions of realism, neorealism, and idealism in international relations theory. The lack of attention in these texts to narrative, rhetorical, and intertextual issues signifies a literalist view of language (whether it is explicitly endorsed or not) and the assumption of the rational basis of established identities.

3. Todorov, *The Conquest of America*, 249.

4. The background to this elaboration of identity is developed in my *Politics and Ambiguity* (Madison: University of Wisconsin Press, 1987), especially chaps. 1, 7, 9, and 10.

5. Quoted from Nietzsche's *Nachlass* in Martin Heidegger, *Nietzsche*, vol. 2: *The Eternal Recurrence of the Same*, trans. David Farrell Krell (San Francisco: Harper and Row, 1984), 129. The interpretation that follows is mine.

6. Kenneth Waltz, "Laws and Theories," in *Neorealism and Its Critics*, ed. Robert O. Keohane (New York: Columbia University Press, 1986), 21.

7. Friedrich Nietzsche, *Beyond Good and Evil*, trans. Marianne Cowan (Chicago: Gateway, 1955), 8.

8. Ibid., 8–9.

9. The essay by Derrida that is perhaps most pertinent in this regard is "White Mythologies," in Jacques Derrida, *Margins of Philosophy*, trans. Alan Bass (Chicago: University of Chicago Press, 1982), 207–72. Here Derrida examines the "white" metaphors of light, illumination, "glimmers," "reflect," and so on, which tend to be literalized by those who adopt a spectatorial model of knowledge.

10. Jacques Derrida, "Différance," in ibid., 11, 20.

11. Kenneth Waltz, "Reflections on *Theory of International Politics*: A Response to My Critics," in *Neorealism and Its Critics*, ed. Keohane, 338.

12. Robert O. Keohane, "International Relations Theory: Contributions of a Feminist Standpoint," *Millennium* (Summer 1989), 245, 247.

13. Ibid., 249.

14. Ibid., 249–50.

15. Ibid., 249. In a recent essay Kathy Ferguson articulates beautifully the attractions of the perspective Keohane opposes for feminist theory. After reviewing two models of feminism, briefly describable here under the labels "standpoint" and "maternal" feminism, she considers how one type of "post-conventional" feminism proceeds. "But post-conventional could also indicate a deconstruction of the conventional through articulation of its constituted, hence political character. This meaning suggests an ethics not of transcending the conventional but . . . of struggling against the exclusionary pull of any entrenched identity in the name of that which is left out." Kathy Ferguson, "Knowledge, Politics and Persons in Feminist Theory," *Political Theory* (May

1989), 312. None of the statements cited by Keohane quite captures this central concern of "post-modern" thinkers. Moreover, it is difficult to find feminist texts that correspond to the stereotype of "postmodern feminism" articulated in Keohane's essay. Two recent examples surely contravene his account, but just as surely they fit into a "postmodern" or "poststructuralist" categorization if *any* texts do: Joan Wallach Scott, *Gender and the Politics of History* (New York: Columbia University Press, 1988), and Anne Norton, *Reflections on Political Identity* (Baltimore: Johns Hopkins University Press, 1988). Other texts deviate significantly both from the definition of "postmodernism" in Keohane's essay and from the conception of epistemology that governs his elaboration of types of feminism. Jean Bethke Elshtain, *Women and War* (New York: Basic Books, 1987), and Wendy Brown, *Manhood and Politics* (Totowa, N.J.: Rowman and Littlefield, 1988), can serve as excellent exemplifications of the limitations of this classification scheme.

16. The second saying is drawn from Heidegger, in an examination of a poem by Stefan George. It reads: "So I renounce and sadly see, where the word breaks off no thing may be." I discuss this saying, and the understanding of language it promotes, in "Where the Word Breaks Off," chap. 10 of *Politics and Ambiguity*.

17. Keohane, in the process of forging this "alliance" between two kinds of feminism and "neoliberal institutionalism," points to a "prescriptive" ideal: "Suppose planet earth were the primary affiliation rather than the separate nation state?" (Keohane, "International Relations Theory," 251). Here he opens the door to the sort of debate postmodernists seek when they try to explain why realists and neorealists are driven to question the sovereignty of the state (if and when they do) only by contrasting it with an ideal of global sovereignty. Both ideals operate within the problematic of sovereignty.

18. Michael Shapiro, "Representing World Politics: The Sport/War Intertext," in *International/Intertextual Relations*, ed. James Der Derian and Michael Shapiro (Lexington, Mass.: Heath, 1989), 71.

19. Richard Ashley, "Living on Border Lines: Man, Poststructuralism, and War," in ibid., 278, 284.

20. Ibid., 262.

21. The modernist insistence upon translating the code of paradox into the logic of integration is discernible in numerous texts, most notably in the following critiques of Foucault or Derrida: Jürgen Habermas, *The Philosophical Discourse of Modernity*, trans. Frederick Lawrence (Cambridge: MIT Press, 1987); Nancy Fraser, "The French Derrideans: Politicizing Deconstruction or Deconstructing Politics?" *New German Critique* (Fall 1984); Charles Taylor, "Foucault on Freedom and Truth," *Political Theory* (May 1984). Recent replies to these demands include Thomas Keenan, "The 'Paradox' of Knowledge and Power," ibid. (February 1987); Thomas Dumm, "The Politics of Post-Modern Aesthetics: Habermas contra Foucault," ibid. (May 1988). I have engaged Taylor's version of this demand in "Taylor, Foucault and Otherness," ibid. (August 1985), and in chap. 10 of *Politics and Ambiguity*. Taylor has pushed debate on this issue to a new plateau in "Overcoming Epistemology," in *After*

Philosophy, ed. K. Baynes, J. Bohman, and T. McCarthy (Cambridge: MIT Press, 1987).

22. Michel Foucault, *The Archaeology of Knowledge*, trans. A. M. Sheridan Smith (New York: Pantheon, 1972), 205 (emphasis added).

23. Ibid., 210.

24. I have reviewed some Foucaultian techniques of self-problematization in chap. 10 of *Politics and Ambiguity*.

3. Liberalism and Difference

1. I treat this social ontology as a "projection," but not as one for which no *comparative* defense can be given. Perhaps the best defense is one that proceeds at the level of a critical history of both lived ontologies and formally developed ones. Hans Blumenberg, *The Legitimacy of the Modern Age*, trans. Robert M. Wallace (Cambridge: MIT Press, 1983), is exemplary here. Blumenberg traces the history of teleological/transcendental philosophies, the internal difficulties they have encountered, and the obstacles a new version of such a philosophy will have to overcome. Michel Foucault's *The Order of Things* (London: Tavistock, 1970), provides an exemplary account as well, reaching its peak in the account of "Man and His Doubles," which indicates how the modern *episteme* presupposes assumptions about finitude that are incapable of grounding themselves. My own effort at this level is *Political Theory and Modernity* (Oxford: Blackwell, 1988).

2. Thomas Hobbes, *Leviathan*, ed. Michael Oakeshott (New York: Collier, 1962), pt. 1, chap. 8, 61.

3. Ibid., 63.

4. Thomas Hobbes, *Man and Citizen*, ed. Bernard Gert (New York: Doubleday, 1972), chap. 9, 141. Another version of this law, now the fifth law of nature, appears in *Leviathan*, pt. 1, chap. 15, 119. Once human beings have *become* self-interested beings with a moral face, *then* Hobbes strives to create some room for them to exercise individual freedom within an absolutist order. But it is the first step that needs more attention in readings of Hobbes, partly through attention to his discussion of madness. Hobbes, on my reading, treats the self-interested self as a construction valued to a considerable degree because it is a solid bulwark of order. The individual is not prior to order or consistently a limit to it: it is partly an effect of order and a bearer of it. When these themes are developed, contemporary individualism might be seen to be closer than is usually thought to those who give primacy to order.

5. Bosket is quoted in an op-ed piece, "Bosket's Law: Trouble Sets You Free," *New York Times*, 21 April 1989.

6. Martin Heidegger, *Identity and Difference*, trans. Joan Stambaugh (New York: Harper and Row, 1969), 32.

7. John Rawls, "Justice as Fairness: Political Not Metaphysical," *Philosophy and Public Affairs* (Summer 1985), 1. I participate in the ontotheological tradition in one way but not in two others, for the present study invokes a social ontology as it engages alternative theories. But, first, it problematizes its

own projections at this level, and second, it refuses to endorse either the perspective that treats being as if it were designed *for us* in some fundamental way or the perspective that treats the world as if it were a standing reserve thoroughly susceptible to mastery *by us*. It refuses the transcendental reassurances most commonly associated with ontotheology.

8. Ibid., 4.

9. Michael Shapiro examines the rhetorical strategies of some contemporaries in a way that is relevant to this issue. See "Politicizing Ulysses: Rationalistic, Critical and Genealogical Commentaries," *Political Theory* (February 1989), 9–31, and *The Politics of Representation* (Madison: University of Wisconsin Press, 1988), especially chap. 1.

10. George Kateb, "Democratic Individuality and the Claims of Politics," *Political Theory* (August 1984), 335.

11. Ibid., 343.

12. *New York Times*, 30 August 1988, 30.

13. This portion of the argument is developed more extensively in my *Politics and Ambiguity* (Madison: University of Wisconsin Press, 1987), especially chaps. 2 and 5.

14. The sources of closure and naturalization in identity are multiple and overdetermined as Nietzsche represents them. That is why it is so difficult and important to confront and contest those pressures. Nietzsche's treatment of language as a dense medium that condenses and consolidates values of the herd; of the limited capacity for consciousness and the extensive demands for social regularization that combine to drive many commonalities to the level of the tacit, the implicit, the unconscious, and the habitual; of the disturbance sown when a lived identity is exposed as conventional or artificial; of the limited capacity of each social order to tolerate diversity of identities—all of these themes must be considered when evaluating the quest to open up themes and norms that have become closed. For Nietzsche insists, first, that the sources of closure are powerful and, second, that no closed set of commonalities reflects a higher direction in being.

15. Friedrich Nietzsche, *On the Genealogy of Morals*, trans. Walter Kaufmann and R. J. Hollingdale (New York: Random House, 1967), 127.

16. Friedrich Nietzsche, *Beyond Good and Evil*, trans. Marianne Cowan (Chicago: Gateway, 1955), 70–71.

17. George Kateb's essay "Thinking about Human Extinction," *Raritan* (Fall 1986), 1–29, brings out this dimension of Nietzsche superbly. Nietzsche's version of individuality is superbly elaborated in Werner Hamacher, "Disgregation of the Will: Nietzsche on the Individual and Individuality," in *Friedrich Nietzsche*, ed. Harold Bloom (New York: Chelsea House, 1987), 162–212.

18. Kateb, "Democratic Individuality and the Claims of Politics," 355.

19. Ibid., 356.

20. Charles Taylor, "Connolly, Foucault and Truth," *Political Theory* (August 1985), 385. A more extensive comparison of Taylor and Foucault within the territory of language can be found in my "Where the Word Breaks Off," chap. 10 of *Politics and Ambiguity*. Taylor's book *Sources of the Self* (Cambridge:

Harvard University Press, 1989) appeared while the present book was in press. While harmonious community still seems to me to remain constant as his regulative ideal, the possibility of achieving a coherent unity in modern life that does not repress something essential and admirable is actively doubted in the new book. My discussion here is insufficient to that text. But the attribution of Augustinianism to Taylor's conceptions of identity and responsibility, pursued further in Chapter 4 below, hits the mark of this new book.

21. *The Confessions of St. Augustine*, trans. John K. Ryan (New York: Doubleday, 1960), 43.

22. Taylor, "Connolly, Foucault and Truth," 385.

23. Nietzsche does not always or consistently prove to be apolitical. But the presentation of the overman in *Thus Spoke Zarathustra*, trans. Walter Kaufmann (New York: Penguin, 1978), seems to me highly apolitical. Any other references to the overman, especially in the unpublished texts, might be referred to this foundational text for clarification and contextualization.

4. Responsibility for Evil

1. A.W.H. Adkins, *From the Many to the One* (Ithaca: Cornell University Press, 1970), 21, 25.

2. See Chapter 1 above.

3. Quoted in René Girard, *The Scapegoat*, trans. Yvonne Freccero (Baltimore: Johns Hopkins University Press, 1986), 2. Girard argues that the Gospels provide the first and definitive formulations that reveal the logic of persecution (including scapegoating) and express a doctrine that transcends it. In "The Christianity of René Girard and the Nature of Religion," in *Violence and Truth*, ed. Paul Drummond (Stanford: Stanford University Press, 1988), 160–79, Lucien Scubla contests this reading of the Gospels. He examines the attitudes of Jesus, and finds a more ambiguous orientation. He also contends that ritual is a means by which previous violence can be softened and refigured rather than simply carried forward.

4. Jean-Paul Sartre, *Anti-Semite and Jew*, trans. George Becker (New York: Schocken, 1948). Page references to this work are given in parentheses in the text.

5. Michel Foucault, *Discipline and Punish*, trans. Alan Sheridan (New York: Pantheon, 1977), pt. 3, chap. 3, "Panopticism."

6. Charles Taylor, "Responsibility for Self," in *The Identities of Persons*, ed. Amélie O. Rorty (Berkeley and Los Angeles: University of California Press, 1976), 291. Subsequent page references to this essay are given in parentheses in the text.

7. Excellent accounts of Augustine's struggles with Manichean and Pelagian accounts of will and evil are provided in E. R. Evans, *Augustine on Evil* (Cambridge: Cambridge University Press, 1982), and Peter Brown, *Augustine of Hippo* (Berkeley and Los Angeles: University of California Press, 1969). The first concentrates on the arguments Augustine develops in support of his own position. The second considers both the arguments and the institutional means by which the opponents were combated through judgments of heresy.

8. Michel Foucault, *Language, Counter-Memory, Practice*, ed. D. F. Bouchard (Oxford: Blackwell, 1977), 230.

9. Friedrich Nietzsche, *On the Genealogy of Morals*, trans. Walter Kaufmann and R. J. Hollingdale (New York: Random House, 1967), 94.

10. I have not offered, in this book, an "analysis" of responsibility. I would endorse much of what Stuart Hampshire says about it in *Thought and Action* (New York: Viking Press, 1959) and *Freedom of the Individual* (Princeton: Princeton University Press, 1975). Hampshire contends that more about the self than "we" (contemporary thinkers in the analytic tradition) had previously recognized is contingent and that more of it is also probably outside the purview of consciousness. In one formulation he says, "More of human conduct than we had thought and aspects of it that we had not expected, may be outside the possible control of practical action; less of human conduct than we had thought may flow from an unalterable natural endowment" (*Thought and Action*, 254). Hampshire, while endorsing a "kind of materialism," also acknowledges that neither he nor his opponents (dualists and idealists) have a set of concepts that integrate "mental" concepts with contemporary "physical" concepts of biology and physics. His materialism is, to a considerable degree, an expression of faith and a promissory note. Contemporaries, he suggests, constantly invoke a set of concepts in one context (ethical judgment or biological explanation) that they cannot coherently redeem in others. They can neither eliminate one set nor integrate both, in the current state of knowledge. Here is space, then, for contestability in discourse among contending theories, each of which contains elements of dissonance and mystery. Here, too, is a place where every theory runs into problems of coherence. See Hampshire's chapter "A Kind of Materialism" in *Freedom of Mind* (Princeton: Princeton University Press, 1971), 210–31.

11. I have not, in this chapter, considered the assumption of responsibility for oneself as opposed to the attribution of responsibility to others. Nietzsche, whose formulation quoted at the beginning of this section launched my own thoughts, often held that the "overman" accepts full responsibility for the full compass of its acts. In Chapter 6 below I argue that a Nietzschean conception of the overman is no longer tenable, and I would argue as well that the Nietzschean heroic assumption of self-responsibility is too demanding in a world where the full "compass" of one's actions extends far indeed. But the issue of the assumption of self-responsibility does deserve further treatment. It is bound up closely with the issue of existential resentment and the question whether that resentment can be transcended or can only be combated. Clearly, I am dubious both about the prospects for simple transcendence and about the dangers of pursuing such a heroic goal.

5. A Letter to Augustine

1. *The Confessions of St. Augustine*, trans. John K. Ryan (New York: Doubleday, 1960), bk. 1, chap. 2, 44. Subsequent references to this work (abbreviated *Conf.*) are given in parentheses in the text.

2. Augustine, *Concerning the City of God against the Pagans*, trans. Henry Bettenson (Harmondsworth: Penguin, 1984), bk. 4, chap. 1, 135. Subsequent references to this work (abbreviated *CG*) are given in parentheses in the text.

3. Peter Brown, *Augustine of Hippo* (Berkeley and Los Angeles: University of California Press, 1969).

4. I have profited from reading Brown, *Augustine of Hippo*; Elaine Pagels, *Adam, Eve, and the Serpent* (New York: Random House, 1988); Hans Blumenberg, *The Legitimacy of the Modern Age*, trans. Robert M. Wallace (Cambridge: MIT Press, 1983), pt. 2; and Sheldon Wolin, *Politics and Vision* (Boston: Little, Brown, 1960), chap. 4. Brown offers a careful account of your life, your conversion, your debates with opponents, and your mature philosophy. Pagels provides an account of your view of women as well as a summary of debates with the Manicheans and Pelagians. Blumenberg places you in the context of defending an unstable god who becomes open to displacement and to secular "reoccupation." Wolin thoughtfully explores the political context and implications of your theology.

5. Friedrich Nietzsche, *Thus Spoke Zarathustra*, trans. Walter Kaufmann (New York: Penguin, 1978), 100.

6. *St. Augustine: Select Letters*, trans. James Houston Baxter (Cambridge: Harvard University Press, 1930), epistle 191, 337–39.

7. *New York Times*, 12 April 1983.

8. Robert Austen Markus, *Saeculum: History and Society in the Theology of St. Augustine* (Cambridge: Cambridge University Press, 1970). This is a sympathetic book, written by one who examines your theology to ascertain how diversity and pluralism might unfold out of it. But it does not explore the centrality of the problem of evil in your thought and the ways in which your definition of and responses to that problem severely limit the pluralism you can sanction. I contend that something has to give on this first issue before the second possibility, which is surely there, can be opened up very far.

9. David Tracy, *Plurality and Ambiguity: Hermeneutics, Religion, Hope* (New York: Harper and Row, 1987), chap. 5.

10. Ibid., 110.

11. Friedrich Nietzsche, *Beyond Good and Evil*, trans. Marianne Cowan (Chicago: Gateway, 1955), 60 (emphasis added).

6. Democracy and Distance

1. One paradigmatic expression of liberal neutralism occurs in Ronald Dworkin, "Liberalism," in *Public and Private Morality*, ed. Stuart Hampshire (Cambridge: Cambridge University Press, 1978). Neutralism "supposes that political decisions must be, so far as possible, independent of any particular conception of the good life, or what gives value to life. Since the citizens of a society differ in their conceptions, the government does not treat them as equals if it prefers one conception to another" (ibid., 127). But the issue of what "gives value to life" is a fundamental one, and the response given to it infiltrates everything else in a theory and a way of life. I presented an early critique of

this version of neutralism in "The Public Interest and the Common Good," chap. 5 of *Appearance and Reality in Politics* (Cambridge: Cambridge University Press, 1981). The present analysis still concurs with that critique, though it would have to ambiguate more actively the conception of the common good advanced there.

2. Bruce Ackerman, paper presented at the Georgetown University Conference on Liberalism and the Good, 1–3 November 1988; published as "Why Dialogue?" *Journal of Philosophy* (January 1989), 16.

3. Jürgen Habermas, "Ideologies and Society in the Postwar World," in *Habermas and Solidarity*, ed. Peter Dews (London: Verso, 1986), 53–54.

4. Friedrich Nietzsche, *Thus Spoke Zarathustra*, trans. Walter Kaufmann (New York: Penguin, 1978), 71.

5. Friedrich Nietzsche, *Twilight of the Idols*, trans. R. J. Hollingdale (New York: Penguin, 1968), 88.

6. See, for instance, Philippe Ariès, *Western Attitudes toward Death*, trans. Patricia Ranum (Baltimore: Johns Hopkins University Press, 1974).

7. Friedrich Nietzsche, *The Will to Power*, trans. Walter Kaufmann and R. J. Hollingdale (New York: Random House, 1967), 484.

8. Nietzsche, *Thus Spoke Zarathustra*, 152.

9. Ibid., 157.

10. Ibid., 160.

11. Ibid., 323.

12. Nothing said or implied here should be taken to mean that some individual or public authority should decide this issue for another or create a context in which the "decision" is already preempted. Either response would defeat the point of self-engagement with this issue. Moreover, the current paucity of dialogue on this question does create just such a preemptive context.

13. The richness of these possibilities is suggested by two recent books that begin from different starting points but converge significantly in their appreciation of the multiple possibilities of sensual life: Joan Cocks, *The Oppositional Imagination: Feminism, Critique and Political Theory* (New York: Routledge, 1989), especially pt. 2; and Judith Butler, *Gender Trouble* (New York: Routledge, 1990). These books appeared too late to be considered in this study, but each pursues a conception of identity and gender that intersects with the position I endorse.

14. "Teleology" is another elastic term in theoretical discourse. Thus, since every political theory supports some purposes over others, every theory is teleological in this broadest sense of the term. But theories diverge in the degree to which they regard nature, history, the human body, language, or the form of a community either as containing an immanent purpose to which the rest of life can become attuned or as corresponding itself to a harmonious direction in being. Strong theories of teleology give hegemony to one of these sites of purpose and then claim that, rightly ordered, the other sites can harmonize with this purpose and with one another. These are theories of harmonious realization. The more sites a theory drains of *telos* in this strong sense, the more areas of indifference or resistance it encounters to the highest

purposes it recognizes, hence the more attuned it becomes to paradox and ambiguity. Such a theory is more likely to celebrate the ambiguity of politics as one of *its* highest ends or purposes.

15. See especially Martin Heidegger, *Nietzsche*, vol. 4: *Nihilism*, trans. Frank A. Capuzzi (San Francisco: Harper and Row, 1962).

16. Nietzsche, *Thus Spoke Zarathustra*, 287.

17. Ibid., "On the New Idol," 48–51.

18. Ibid., "On the Higher Man," 288.

19. Ibid., 293–94.

20. The presentation here builds upon themes in my "Democracy and Normalization," chap. 1 of *Politics and Ambiguity* (Madison: University of Wisconsin Press, 1987).

21. Nietzsche, *Twilight of the Idols*, 86.

22. Ibid., 86–87.

23. Friedrich Nietzsche, *Human, All Too Human*, trans. R. J. Hollingdale (Cambridge: Cambridge University Press, 1986), 383.

24. The fragments, sentences, and paragraphs from Nietzsche inserted into this text are drawn from *On the Genealogy of Morals*, trans. Walter Kaufmann and R. J. Hollingdale (New York: Random House, 1967), 95; *The Will to Power*, note 866, 463; and *Twilight of the Idols*, 88–102.

7. The Politics of Territorial Democracy

1. The ways in which citizenship helps to foster independence and individuality in other domains of life are persuasively developed by George Kateb in "The Moral Distinctiveness of Representative Democracy," *Ethics* (April 1981), 357–74. I pursue some of these themes through exploration of the ambiguity of democracy in "Democracy and Normalization," chap. 1 of *Politics and Ambiguity* (Madison: University of Wisconsin Press, 1987), 3–16.

2. This thesis is developed in my *Appearance and Reality in Politics* (Cambridge: Cambridge University Press, 1981), chap. 6. That chapter, while prefiguring a couple of the themes developed here, anchored them in a theory that squeezed too much ambiguity out of its ideals of subjectivity, responsibility, and the common good. Some arguments offered there in defense of those positions are the sort that I have in this study criticized others for advancing. Why criticize yourself when there are others around who continue to share the defects in question?

3. This theme, too, is more extensively developed in *Appearance and Reality in Politics*, chaps. 3–6.

4. Jane Bennett, in "Deceptive Comfort: The Power of Kafka's Stories," *Political Theory*, in press, explores compulsions within "conceptual analysis" to retain this unity between power and efficacy somewhere in the conception defended, and assesses critically the costs such compulsions impose.

5. Sheldon Wolin, in "Democracy and the Welfare State: The Political and Theoretical Connections between *Staatsräson* and *Wohlfahrtsstaatsräson*,"

Political Theory (November 1987), explores the functional relation between a fluid welfare populace and a welfare state that needs to demonstrate its powers of disposition. I explore the dual accountability of the welfare state and ways in which its constitution of the welfare class protects collective identity in *Politics and Ambiguity*, chaps. 4 and 6.

6. Karl Marx, in "Critical Notes on the Article 'The King of Prussia and Social Reform,'" repr. in *The Writings of the Young Marx*, ed. L. D. Easton and K. H. Guddat (New York: Anchor, 1967), presented a consummate analysis of a similar relationship between the state and "pauperism" in 1844. The fact that it still speaks to contemporary politics may tell us something.

7. Ernesto Laclau and Chantal Mouffe, in *Hegemony and Socialist Strategy: Towards a Radical Democratic Politics* (London: Verso, 1985), do an excellent job of recrafting the concept of hegemony through a reconstitution of Marxist theory. They dismantle two versions of "essentialism" in Marxism, that of a human essence suppressed by alienation and that of a mode of production providing a direction to history. In the process they elaborate a concept of hegemony consonant with democratic politics. They too emphasize the ways in which the construction of identity is political and relational. I generally endorse their critique of Marxism, follow them part of the way in their theorization of the relation between democracy and hegemony, and endorse as well the commitment to the "egalitarian imaginary" that permeates their text. A hegemonic bloc in a democratic society, then, is a persistent constellation that attains a fair degree of predominance in defining the fundamental alternatives and priorities of the day. It consists, to varying degrees, of elements whose predefined interests or principles are represented by hegemonic definitions and elements whose identities are in part reconstituted by them. A politics of democratic hegemony affects the way identities are experienced as well as the types of identity constituted. The stance of Laclau and Mouffe is distinctive, but not utterly alien to previous traditions of democratic theory in the United States. It can be viewed as a radicalization of themes elaborated effectively and persuasively by E. E. Schattschneider in *The Semi-sovereign People* (New York: Holt and Rinehart, 1960).

8. See Michael Best and William Connolly, *The Politicized Economy* (Lexington, Mass.: Heath, 1976; 2d ed., 1982), for a detailed account of exclusive and inclusive goods, with numerous exemplifications of each. This theme is brought into the fold of a theory of democracy on the way to the one elaborated here in my *Politics and Ambiguity*, chaps. 2, 3, and 4.

9. In *The Legitimacy of the Modern Age*, trans. Robert M. Wallace (Cambridge: MIT Press, 1983), Hans Blumenberg claims that "the modern age" was the first to assess its own legitimacy as an age while it was still intact. This may be an exaggeration, but Blumenberg deploys it to advance a fascinating defense of the legitimacy of the modern age against those who think that modernity depends upon premodern elements its defenders cannot acknowledge.

10. I first pursued the theme of this discrepancy between site and time in *Political Theory and Modernity* (Oxford: Blackwell, 1988). Since then conversations with David Campbell, James Der Derian, and Rob Walker have aided my

thinking considerably. For textual references see David Campbell, "Social Movements and Global Processes," in David Campbell et al., *The Discourse of International Relations*, forthcoming; James Der Derian, *On Diplomacy: A Genealogy of Western Estrangement* (Oxford: Blackwell, 1987); and R.B.J. Walker, *One World, Many Worlds: Struggles for a Just World Peace* (London: Lynne Rienner, 1988).

11. Martin Wight, "Why Is There No International Theory?" in *Diplomatic Investigations*, ed. H. Butterfield and M. Wight (London: Allen and Unwin, 1966), 17–34, provides the classic analysis of this division and its rationale, but does not criticize it.

Index

William E. Connolly teaches political theory at The Johns Hopkins University, where he is professor and chair in the political science department. In 1999 he received the Benjamin Lippincott Award for *The Terms of Political Discourse,* an honor given biennially for "a work of exceptional quality . . . still considered significant after a time span of at least fifteen years." His most recent publications are *The Ethos of Pluralization, Why I Am Not a Secularist,* and *Neuropolitics: Thinking, Culture, Speed,* all published by the University of Minnesota Press.